Mastering Android Development with Kotlin

Deep dive into the world of Android to create robust applications with Kotlin

Miloš Vasić

BIRMINGHAM - MUMBAI

Mastering Android Development with Kotlin

First published: November 2017

Production reference: 1061117

Published by Packt Publishing Ltd.
Livery Place
35 Livery Street
Birmingham
B3 2PB, UK.

ISBN 978-1-78847-369-9

www.packtpub.com

Credits

Author
Miloš Vasić

Reviewer
Vanja Petkovic

Commissioning Editor
Richa Tripathi

Acquisition Editor
Sandeep Mishra

Content Development Editor
Akshada Iyer

Technical Editor
Supriya Thabe

Copy Editor
Zainab Bootwala

Project Coordinator
Prajakta Naik

Proofreader
Safis Editing

Indexer
Francy Puthiry

Graphics
Jason Monteiro

Production Coordinator
Arvindkumar Gupta

About the Author

Miloš Vasić is a software engineer, author, and open source enthusiast. He holds a bachelor's degree in the programming of computer graphics and a master's degree in the field of Android programming; both degrees were gained at Singidunum University. He published his first book, *Fundamental Kotlin*, in October 2016, thus achieving his dream of becoming an author. He's currently employed at the Robert Bosch company, where he's working on SDKs for the auto-industry. When he is not working on new books, Miloš works on his open source projects.

Acknowledgments

This book has been a long and fun journey that I would not have manage to accomplish without help. So I think it's only polite to give gratitude.

First of all, I would like to thank my girlfriend and personal assistant, Maja. She was the one who supported me and helped me while writing my first book *Fundamental Kotlin* and continued to do so with this one. She improved this book greatly by helping me write coherent text that is understandable even for those who are not experienced in programming.

Next I would like to thank my editor at Packt Akshada. She was the best editor I could ask for and she helped me immensely with excellent advices and endless patience. The whole team at Packt that stands behind was book was incredibly supportive and helpful.

Big thanks also to my friends who tolerated me and constantly filled me up with large amounts of coffee. Especially to my friend Vanja Petkovic. He was the technical editor for this book and it wouldn't be the same without him.

And last but not least I would like to thank to my family for supporting me in my dream of becoming software engineer. They were with me and they were patient during all my phases! But, the most important of all, they believed in me!

None of this would be possible if there weren't people who read my first book. I am forever grateful for their support. See you in my next book!

Best wishes,

Miloš

About the Reviewer

Vanja Petkovic studied math and computer science at Belgrade University, Serbia. There, he also obtained his MSc in computer science. He has been working as a software engineer for more than 13 years. Currently, he lives in Switzerland and works for Leica Geosystems in the 3D scanning department. He has specialized in software development for mobile devices and backend services. He started with software development for Palm OS, through Windows Mobile OS and Blackberry OS to Android OS and iOS today. His preferred weapons for developing backend services are Java and Spring.

www.PacktPub.com

For support files and downloads related to your book, please visit www.PacktPub.com.

Did you know that Packt offers eBook versions of every book published, with PDF and ePub files available? You can upgrade to the eBook version at www.PacktPub.com and as a print book customer, you are entitled to a discount on the eBook copy. Get in touch with us at service@packtpub.com for more details.

At www.PacktPub.com, you can also read a collection of free technical articles, sign up for a range of free newsletters and receive exclusive discounts and offers on Packt books and eBooks.

https://www.packtpub.com/mapt

Get the most in-demand software skills with Mapt. Mapt gives you full access to all Packt books and video courses, as well as industry-leading tools to help you plan your personal development and advance your career.

Why subscribe?

- Fully searchable across every book published by Packt
- Copy and paste, print, and bookmark content
- On demand and accessible via a web browser

Customer Feedback

Thanks for purchasing this Packt book. At Packt, quality is at the heart of our editorial process. To help us improve, please leave us an honest review on this book's Amazon page at `https://www.amazon.com/dp/1788473698`.

If you'd like to join our team of regular reviewers, you can e-mail us at `customerreviews@packtpub.com`. We award our regular reviewers with free eBooks and videos in exchange for their valuable feedback. Help us be relentless in improving our products!

Table of Contents

Preface

Android is the most popular platform for mobile devices. Every year, there are more and more developers getting involved in Android development. The Android Framework makes it possible to develop applications for mobile phones, tablets, televisions, and much more! So far, all development has been done in Java. Recently, Google announced Kotlin as the second language developers can use. Because of this, and with Kotlin's ever-growing popularity, we decided to introduce you to Android using Kotlin as its primary development programming language.

With Kotlin, you can do everything you can do with Java, but with more joy and fun! We will show you how to play with Android and Kotlin, and how to create amazing things! Thanks to Kotlin, it's certain that the Android platform will evolve even more. In the near future, it's not impossible that Kotlin will become the primary development language for the platform. Take your seat and get ready for a great journey!

What this book covers

Chapter 1, *Starting with Android*, teaches you how to start Android development with Kotlin and how to set up your working environment.

Chapter 2, *Building and Running*, shows you how to build and run your project. It will demonstrate how to log and debug the application.

Chapter 3, *Screens*, starts with the UI. In this chapter, we will create the first screens for our application.

Chapter 4, *Connecting Screen Flow*, explains how to connect the screen flow and define basic user interaction with the UI.

Chapter 5, *Look and Feel*, covers the theming of the UI. We will introduce you to the basic concepts of theming in Android.

Chapter 6, *Permissions*, explains that in order to take advantage of certain system functionalities, it's necessary to get proper system permissions, which are discussed in this chapter.

Chapter 7, *Working with Databases*, shows you how to use SQLite as storage for your application. You will create a database to store and share data.

`Chapter` 8, *Android Preferences*, states that not all data should be stored in the database; some information can be stored in shared preferences. We will explain why and how.

`Chapter` 9, *Concurrency in Android*, explains that if you are familiar with concurrency in programming, then you will know that, in software, many things happen simultaneously. Android is not an exception!

`Chapter` 10, *Android Services*, presents Android services and how to use them.

`Chapter` 11, *Messaging*, says that in Android, your application can listen for various events. How to do this will be answered in this chapter.

`Chapter` 12, *Backend and API*, connects to the remote backend instance to obtain the data.

`Chapter` 13, *Tuning Up for High Performance*, is the perfect chapter to give you answers when you are not sure if your application is fast enough.

`Chapter` 14, *Testing*, mentions that before we release anything, we must test it. Here, we will explain how to write tests for your application.

`Chapter` 15, *Migration to Kotlin*, guides you if you plan to migrate the existing Java code base into Kotlin.

`Chapter` 16, *Deploying Your Application*, guides you through the deployment process. We will release everything we develop during this book.

What you need for this book

For this book, a modern computer running Microsoft Windows, Linux, or macOS is required. You will need Java JDK, the Git version-control system, and Android Studio installed.

To run all code examples and the code you write, you will need an Android phone running Android with OS version >= 5.

Who this book is for

The book is aimed at developers who want to build amazing Android applications in an easy and effective way. Basic knowledge of Kotlin is assumed, having no familiarity with Android development.

Conventions

In this book, you will find a number of text styles that distinguish between different kinds of information. Here are some examples of these styles and an explanation of their meaning.

Code words in text, database table names, folder names, filenames, file extensions, pathnames, dummy URLs, and user input are shown as follows: "We will add proper log messages for each lifecycle event of the `Application` class and the screen (activity) we created."

A block of code is set as follows:

```
override fun onCreate(savedInstanceState: Bundle?) {
  super.onCreate(savedInstanceState)
  setContentView(R.layout.activity_main)
  Log.v(tag, "[ ON CREATE 1 ]")
}
```

Any command-line input or output is written as follows. The input command might be broken into several lines to aid readability, but needs to be entered as one continuous line in the prompt:

```
sudo apt-get install libc6:i386 libncurse
libstdc++6:i386 lib32z1 libbz2-1.0:i386
```

New terms and **important words** are shown in bold. Words that you see on the screen, for example, in menus or dialog boxes, appear in the text like this: " Select **Tools** | **Android** | **AVDManager** or click on the AVDManager icon in the toolbar."

Warnings or important notes appear like this.

Tips and tricks appear like this.

Reader feedback

Feedback from our readers is always welcome. Let us know what you think about this book--what you liked or disliked. Reader feedback is important for us as it helps us develop titles that you will really get the most out of.

To send us general feedback, simply e-mail `feedback@packtpub.com`, and mention the book's title in the subject of your message.

If there is a topic that you have expertise in and you are interested in either writing or contributing to a book, see our author guide at `www.packtpub.com/authors`.

Customer support

Now that you are the proud owner of a Packt book, we have a number of things to help you to get the most from your purchase.

Downloading the example code

You can download the example code files for this book from your account at `http://www.packtpub.com`. If you purchased this book elsewhere, you can visit `http://www.packtpub.com/support` and register to have the files e-mailed directly to you.

You can download the code files by following these steps:

1. Log in or register to our website using your e-mail address and password.
2. Hover the mouse pointer on the **SUPPORT** tab at the top.
3. Click on **Code Downloads & Errata**.
4. Enter the name of the book in the **Search** box.
5. Select the book for which you're looking to download the code files.
6. Choose from the drop-down menu where you purchased this book from.
7. Click on **Code Download**.

Once the file is downloaded, please make sure that you unzip or extract the folder using the latest version of:

- WinRAR / 7-Zip for Windows
- Zipeg / iZip / UnRarX for Mac
- 7-Zip / PeaZip for Linux

The code bundle for the book is also hosted on GitHub at `https://github.com/PacktPublishing/-Mastering-Android-Development-with-Kotlin/branches/all`. We also have other code bundles from our rich catalog of books and videos available at `https://github.com/PacktPublishing/`. Check them out!

Downloading the color images of this book

We also provide you with a PDF file that has color images of the screenshots/diagrams used in this book. The color images will help you better understand the changes in the output. You can download this file from `https://www.packtpub.com/sites/default/files/ downloads/MasteringAndroidDevelopmentwithKotlin_ColorImages.pdf`.

Errata

Although we have taken every care to ensure the accuracy of our content, mistakes do happen. If you find a mistake in one of our books--maybe a mistake in the text or the code-- we would be grateful if you could report this to us. By doing so, you can save other readers from frustration and help us improve subsequent versions of this book. If you find any errata, please report them by visiting `http://www.packtpub.com/submit-errata`, selecting your book, clicking on the **Errata Submission Form** link, and entering the details of your errata. Once your errata are verified, your submission will be accepted and the errata will be uploaded to our website or added to any list of existing errata under the Errata section of that title.

To view the previously submitted errata, go to `https://www.packtpub.com/books/ content/support` and enter the name of the book in the search field. The required information will appear under the **Errata</span> section.**

Piracy

Piracy of copyrighted material on the Internet is an ongoing problem across all media. At Packt, we take the protection of our copyright and licenses very seriously. If you come across any illegal copies of our works in any form on the Internet, please provide us with the location address or website name immediately so that we can pursue a remedy.

Please contact us at `copyright@packtpub.com` with a link to the suspected pirated material.

We appreciate your help in protecting our authors and our ability to bring you valuable content.

Questions

If you have a problem with any aspect of this book, you can contact us at `questions@packtpub.com`, and we will do our best to address the problem.

1
Starting with Android

Kotlin has been officially announced by Google as a first-class programming language for Android. Find out why Kotlin is the best tool available for you as a newcomer and why senior Android developers first adopted Kotlin.

In this chapter, you will learn how to set up a working environment. You will install and run Android Studio and set up Android SDK and Kotlin. Here, you will also be introduced to some important and useful tools such as **Android Debug Bridge (adb)**.

Since you don't have your project yet, you will set it up. You will initialize a Git repository to track changes in your code and create an empty project. You will enable it to support Kotlin and add support for additional libraries that we will use.

After we have initialized the repository and project, we will go through the project structure and explain each file the IDE has generated. Finally, you will create your first screen and take a look at it.

This chapter will cover the following points:

- Setting up an environment for the development of Git and Gradle basics
- Working with Android Manifest
- Android emulator
- Android tools

Why Kotlin?

Before we start our journey, we will answer the question from the chapter title--Why Kotlin? Kotlin is a new programming language developed by JetBrains, the company that developed IntelliJ IDEA. Kotlin is concise and understandable, and it compiles everything to bytecode just like Java. It can also compile to JavaScript or native!

Kotlin comes from professionals of the industry and solves problems programmers are facing every day. It is easy to start and adopt! IntelliJ comes with a Java to Kotlin converter tool. You can convert Java code file by file and everything will still work flawlessly.

It is interoperable and can use any existing Java Framework or library. The interoperability is impeccable and does not require wrappers or adapter layers. Kotlin supports build systems such as Gradle, Maven, Kobalt, Ant, and Griffon with external support.

The most important thing about Kotlin, for us, is that it works perfectly with Android.

Some of the most impressive Kotlin features are as follows:

- Null safety
- Exceptions are unchecked
- Type inference works everywhere
- One-liner functions take one line
- Generated getters and setter out of the box
- We can define functions outside of classes
- Data classes
- Functional programming support
- Extension functions
- Kotlin uses Markdown instead of HTML for API documents! The Dokka tool, a Javadoc alternative, can read Kotlin and Java source code and generate combined docs
- Kotlin has a better generics support than Java
- Reliable and performant concurrent programming
- String patterns
- Named method arguments

Kotlin for Android - it's official

On May 17th 2017, Google announced that it's making Kotlin, a statically typed programming language for the Java Virtual Machine, a first-class language to write Android apps.

The next version of Android Studio (3.0, current one is 2.3.3) will support Kotlin out of the box. Google will put its effort in the future of Kotlin.

 It is important to note that this is only an additional language, not a replacement for existing Java and C++ support (for now).

Downloading and configuring Android Studio

To develop our application, we will need some tools. First of all, we will need an IDE. For that purpose, we will use Android Studio. Android Studio provides the fastest tools to build apps on every type of Android device.

Android Studio offers professional code editing, debugging, and performance tooling. It's a flexible build system that allows you to focus on building a top quality application.

Setting up Android Studio takes just a few clicks. Before we go any further, you need to download the following version for your operating system:

```
https://developer.android.com/studio/index.html
```

Here are the instructions for macOS, Linux, and Windows:

macOS:
To install it on macOS, follow these steps:

1. Launch the Android Studio `DMG` file.
2. Drag and drop Android Studio into the `Applications` folder.
3. Launch Android Studio.
4. Select whether you want to import previous Android Studio settings.
5. Click on **OK**.
6. Follow the instructions until Android Studio is ready for use.

Linux:

To install it on Linux, follow these steps:

1. Unpack the archive you downloaded to an appropriate location for your applications.
2. Navigate to `bin/directory/`.
3. Execute `/studio.sh`.
4. Select whether you want to import previous Android Studio settings or not.
5. Click on **OK**.
6. Follow the instructions until Android Studio is ready for use.
7. Optionally, select **Tools | Create Desktop Entry** from the menu bar.

> If you are running a 64-bit version of Ubuntu, you need to install some 32-bit libraries with the following command:
>
>
>
> ```
> sudo apt-get install libc6:i386 libncurses5:i386
> libstdc++6:i386 lib32z1 libbz2-1.0:i386
> ```
>
> In case you are running a 64-bit Fedora, the command is follows:
> ```
> sudo yum install zlib.i686 ncurses-libs.i686 bzip2-
> libs.i686
> ```

Windows:

To install it on Windows, follow these steps:

1. Execute the `.exe` file you downloaded.
2. Follow the instructions until Android Studio is ready for use.

Setting up Android emulators

Android SDK comes with **emulators** capable of running applications we develop. We will need it for our project! The purpose of an emulator is to simulate a device and displays all its activity windowed on your computer. What can we do with it? We can prototype, develop, and test--all this without a hardware device. You can emulate phones, tablets, wearables, and TV devices. You can create your own device definitions, or you can use predefined emulators.

The good thing about emulators is that they are fast. In many situations, it will take less time to run an application on an emulator instance than on a real hardware device.

Working with the emulators is just as easy with a real hardware device. For gestures, you use your mouse, and for input, your keyboard.

Emulators can do anything a real phone does! You can easily send incoming phone calls and text messages! You can specify the location of the device, send fingerprint scans, adjust network speed and status, or even simulate battery properties. Emulators can have a virtual SD card and internal data storage, both of them you can use to send real files to that space.

Android Virtual Device (AVD) configuration is used to define an emulator. Each AVD instance works as a completely independent device! For the purpose of creating and management of AVDs, we use the AVD Manager. An AVD definition holds a hardware profile, system image, storage area, skin, and other important properties.

Let's play with it! To run the AVD Manager, do one of the following:

Select **Tools** | **Android** | **AVDManager** or click on the **AVDManager** icon in the toolbar:

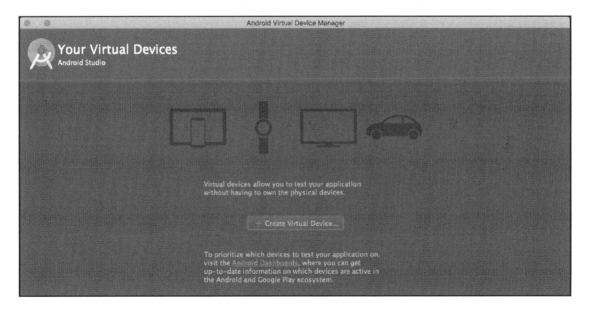

It displays all AVDs you've already defined. As you can see, we don't have any yet!

What can we do here? We can do the following:

- Create a new AVD
- Edit an existing AVD
- Delete the existing AVD
- Create hardware profiles
- Edit an existing hardware profile
- Delete an existing hardware profile
- Import/export definitions
- Start or stop the AVD
- Clear data and reset the AVD
- Access the AVD `.ini` and `.img` files on the filesystem
- View the AVD configuration details

To obtain the AVD instance, you can either create a new AVD from the beginning or duplicate an existing AVD and modify it by need.

Creating a new AVD instance

From the **Your Virtual Devices** of the AVD Manager, click on **Create Virtual Device** (you can do the same as you run your app from within Android Studio by clicking on the **Run** icon, and then, in the **Select Deployment Target** dialog, choose **Create New Emulator**). Please refer to the following screenshot:

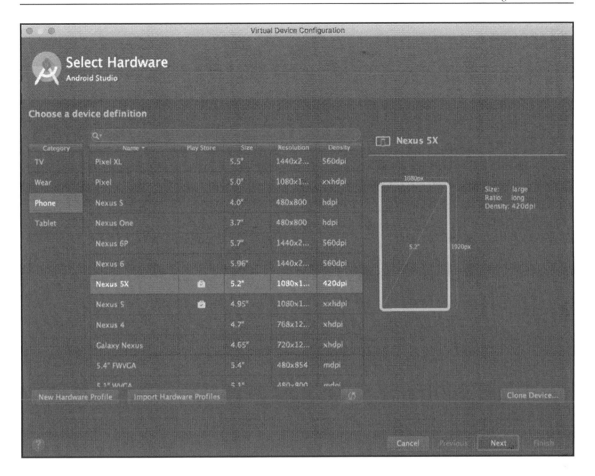

Select a hardware profile and then click on **Next**, as shown in the previous screenshot.

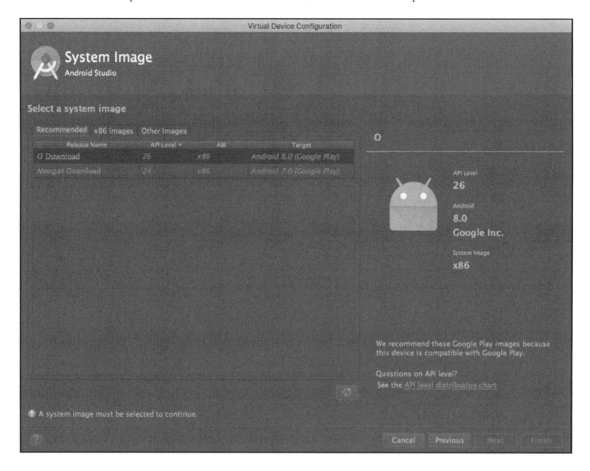

If you notice the **Download** link next to the system image, you have to click on it. The download process starts, as you can see in the following screenshot:

We must note that the API level of the target device is very important! Your application can't run on a system image whose API level is less than the one required by your application. That attribute is specified in your Gradle configuration. We will deal with Gradle in detail later.

Finally, **Verify Configuration** appears:

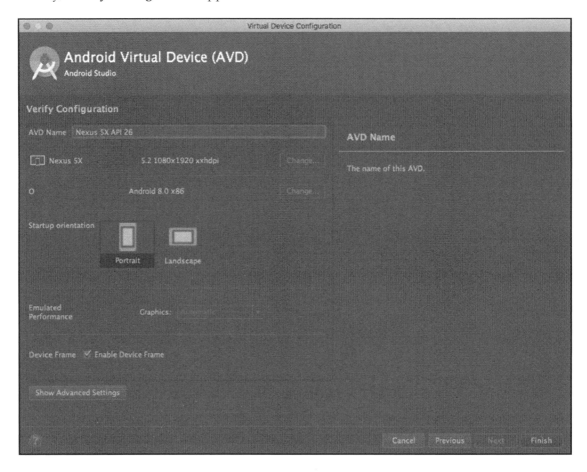

Change the AVD properties if needed and then click on **Finish** to complete the wizard. The newly created AVD appears in the **Your Virtual Devices** list or the **Select Deployment Target** dialog, depending on where you accessed the wizard from.

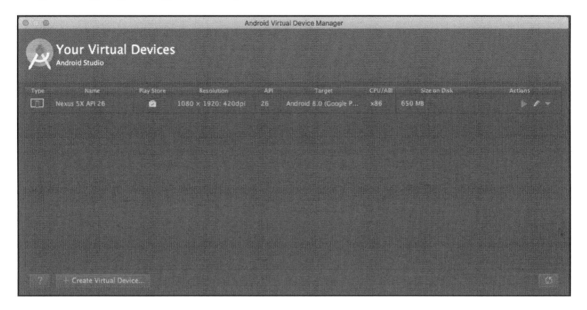

If you need to create a copy of the existing AVD, follow these instructions:

1. Open AVD Manager, right-click on the AVD instance, and select **Duplicate**.
2. Follow the wizard, and, after you modified what you needed, click on **Finish**.
3. A new modified version appears in our AVD list.

We will demonstrate dealing with hardware profiles by creating a new one from scratch. To create a new hardware profile, follow these instructions. In **Select Hardware**, click on **New Hardware Profile**. Please refer to the following screenshot:

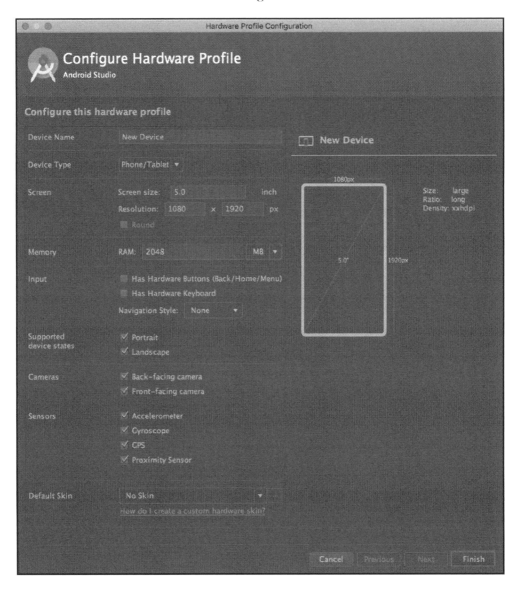

Configure Hardware Profile appears. Adjust the **hardware profile** properties as needed. Click on **Finish**. Your newly created **hardware profile** appears.

Duplicating an existing AVD and modifying it by need

If you need a **hardware profile** based on an existing one, follow these instructions:

1. Select an existing **hardware profile** and click on **Clone Device**.
2. Update the **hardware profile** properties by your needs. To complete the wizard, click on **Finish**.
3. Your profile appears in the **hardware profile** list.

Let's go back to the AVD list. Here, you can perform the following operations on any existing AVD:

- Edit it by clicking on **Edit**
- Delete by right-clicking and choosing **Delete**
- Access the `.ini` and `.img` files on the disk by right-clicking on an AVD instance and choosing **Show on Disk**
- To view the AVD configuration details, right-click on an AVD instance and choose **View Details**

Since we covered this, let's go back to the **hardware profile** list. Here, we can do the following:

- Edit a hardware profile by selecting it and choosing **Edit Device**
- Delete a hardware profile by right-clicking on it and choosing **Delete**

You can't edit or delete the predefined hardware profiles!

Then, we can run or stop an emulator or clear its data as follows:

- To run an emulator that uses an AVD, double-click on the AVD or just choose **Launch**
- To stop it, right-click on it and choose **Stop**
- To clear the data for an emulator, and return it to the same state as when it was first defined, right-click on an AVD and choose **Wipe Data**

We will continue our emulators' journey with the explanation of command-line features that you can use with *–.

To start an emulator, use the emulator command. We will show you some basic command-line syntax to start a virtual device from a terminal:

```
emulator –avd avd_name [ {-option [value]} ... ]
```

Another command-line syntax is as follows:

```
emulator @avd_name [ {-option [value]} ... ]
```

Let's take a look at the following example:

```
$ /Users/vasic/Library/Android/sdk/tools/emulator –avd Nexus_5X_API_23 –
netdelay none –netspeed full
```

You can specify startup options when you start the emulator; later, you can't set these options.

If you need a list of available AVDs, use this command:

```
emulator –list-avds
```

The result is a list of AVD names from the Android home directory. You can override the default home directory by setting the ANDROID_SDK_HOME environment variable.

Stopping an emulator is simple--just close its window.

It is important to note that we can run AVDs from Android Studio UI as well!

Android Debug Bridge

To access devices, you will use the adb command executed from the terminal. We will take a look into the common cases.

Listing all devices:

```
adb devices
```

Console output:

```
List of devices attached
emulator-5554 attached
emulator-5555 attached
```

Obtaining shell access to device:

```
adb shell
```

Accessing a specific device instance:

```
adb -s emulator-5554 shell
```

Where -s represents device source.

Copying a file from and to a device:

```
adb pull /sdcard/images ~/images
adb push ~/images /sdcard/images
```

Uninstalling an application:

```
adb uninstall <package.name>
```

One of the greatest features of adb is that you can access it through telnet. Use telnet localhost 5554 to connect to your emulator device. Terminate your session using the quit or exit command.

Let's play with adb:

- Connect to device:

```
telnet localhost 5554
```

- Change the power level:

```
power status full
power status charging
```

- Or simulate a call:

```
gsm call 223344556677
```

- Send an SMS:

```
sms send 223344556677 Android rocks
```

- Set geolocation:

```
geo fix 22 22
```

With `adb`, you can also take a screenshot or record a video!

Other important tools

We will cover some other tools you will need in everyday Android development.

Let's start with the following:

- `adb dumpsys`: To get information about a system and running an application, use the `adb dumpsys` command. To get a memory status, execute the following command--`adb shell dumpsys meminfo <package.name>`.

Next important tool is as follows:

- `adb shell procrank`: The `adb shell procrank` lists all the applications for you in the order of their memory consumption. This command does not work on live devices; you connect only with emulators. For the same purpose, you can use--`adb shell dumpsys meminfo`.
- For battery consumption, you can use--`adb shell dumpsys batterystats--charged <package-name>`.
- Next important tool is **Systrace**. To analyze performance of your application by capturing and displaying execution times, you will use this command.

When you have problems with application glitches, Systrace tool comes as a powerful ally!

It does not work with Android SDK Tools less than 20! To use it, you must have Python installed and configured.

Let's try it!

To access it from UI, open Android Device Monitor in Android Studio and then choose
Monitor:

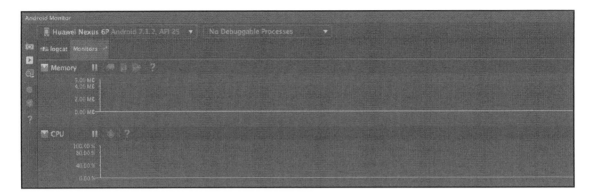

Sometimes, it can be easier to access it from the terminal (command line):

 The Systrace tool has different command-line options, depending on the
Android version running on your device.

Let's take a look at some examples:

General usage:

```
$ python systrace.py [options] [category1] [category2] ... [categoryN]
```

- Android 4.3 and up:

```
$ python systrace.py --time=15 -o my_trace_001.html
sched gfx  view wm
```

- Android 4.2 and lower options:

```
$ python systrace.py --set-tags gfx,view,wm
$ adb shell stop
$ adb shell start
$ python systrace.py --disk --time=15 -o my_trace_001.html
```

The last important tool we want to present is `sdkmanager`. It allows you to view, install,
update, and uninstall packages for the Android SDK. It is located in
`android_sdk/tools/bin/`.

Let's take a look at some common examples of use:

Listing installed and available packages:

```
sdkmanager --list [options]
```

- Installing packages:

```
sdkmanager packages [options]
```

You can send packages you got from `--list` command.

- Uninstalling:

```
sdkmanager --uninstall packages [options]
```

- Updating:

```
sdkmanager --update [options]
```

There are also some other tools you can use in Android, but we only showed the most important ones.

Initializing a Git repository

We have installed Android Studio and introduced ourselves to some important SDK tools. We also learned how to deal with emulated devices that will run our code. It is time to start working on our project. We will develop a small application for notes and todos. This is a tool that everybody needs. We will give it a name--`Journaler` and it will be an application capable of creating notes and todos with reminders that will be synced to our backend.

First step in development is initializing a Git repository. Git will be our code versioning system. It is up to you to decide if you will use GitHub, BitBucket, or something else for a remote Git instance. Create your remote repository and keep its URL ready, along with your credentials. So, let's start!

Go into the directory containing the project:

```
Execute: git init .
```

The console output will be something like this:

```
Initialized empty Git repository in <directory_you_choose/.git>
```

We initialized the repo.

Let's add the first file--`vi notes.txt`.

Populate `notes.txt` with some content and save it.

Execute `git add .` to add all of the relevant files.

- Then: `git commit -m "Journaler: First commit"`

The console output will be something like this:

```
[master (root-commit) 5e98ea4]  Journaler: First commit
1 file changed, 1 insertion(+)
create mode 100644 notes.txt
```

As you remember, you prepared your remote Git repository `url` with credentials. Copy `url` into a clipboard. Now, execute the following:

```
git remote add origin <repository_url>
```

This sets the new remote.

- Then: `git remote -v`

This verifies the new remote URL.

- Finally, push everything we have to remote: `git push -u origin master`

If you are asked for credentials, enter it and confirm by pressing *Enter*.

Creating an Android project

We initialized our code repository. It is time to create a project. Start Android Studio and choose the following:

Start a new Android Studio Project or **File** | **New** | **New Project**.

Create **New Project** and a window appears.

Fill the application information:

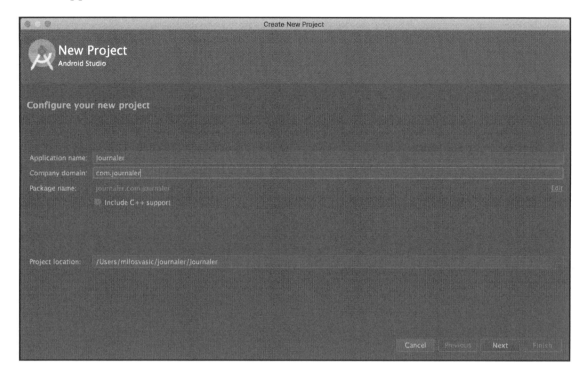

Then, click on **Next**.

Check the **Phone and Tablet** option, and then choose **Android 5.0** as the minimum Android version as follows:

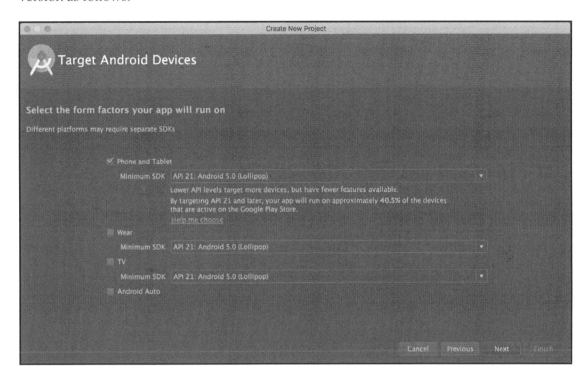

Click on **Next** again.

Choose **Add No Activity** and click on **Finish**, as follows:

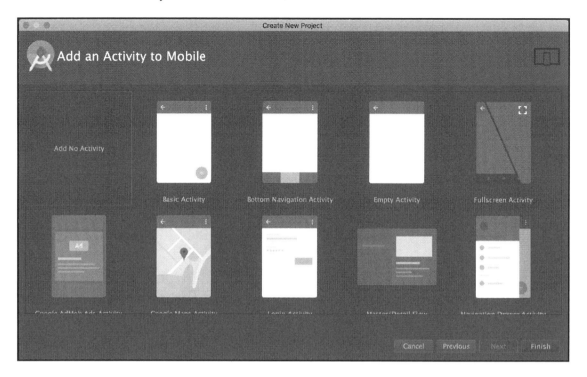

Wait until your project is created.

You will notice a message about **Unregistered VCS root detected**. Click on **add root** or go to **Preferences** | **Version Control** | , and then select our Git repository from the list and the click on then + icon, as shown in the following screenshot:

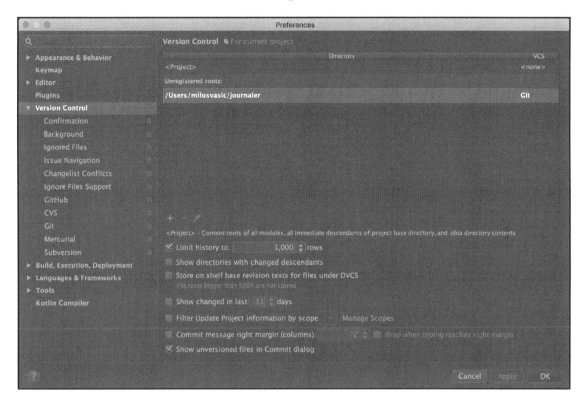

To confirm everything, click on **Apply** and **OK**.

Before committing and pushing, update your `.gitignore` files. The purpose of the `.gitignore` file is to allow you to ignore files, such as editor backup files, build products, or local configuration overrides that you never want to commit into a repository. Without matching the `.gitignore` rules, these files will appear in the `untracked files` section of the Git status output.

Open .gitignore located in your project root directory and edit it. To access it, expand Project by clicking on **Project** on the left side of Android Studio, and then, from the drop-down menu, choose **Project**, as shown in the following screenshot:

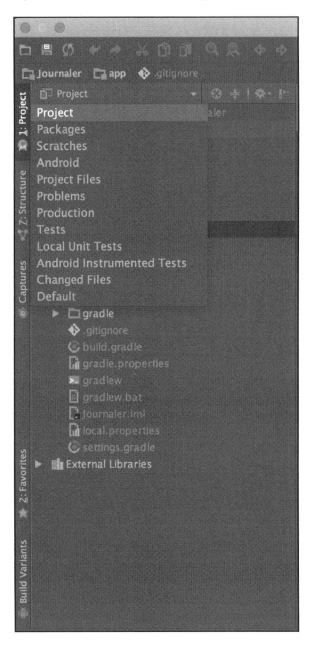

Let's add some lines:

```
.idea
.gradle
build/
gradle*
!gradle-plugins*
gradle-app.setting
!gradle-wrapper.jar
.gradletasknamecache
local.properties
gen
```

Then, edit `.gitignore`, which is located in the `app` module directory:

```
*.class
.mtj.tmp/
*.jar
*.war
*.ear
 hs_err_pid*
.idea/*
.DS_Store
.idea/shelf
/android.tests.dependencies
/confluence/target
/dependencies
/dist
/gh-pages
/ideaSDK
/android-studio/sdk
out
tmp
workspace.xml
*.versionsBackup
/idea/testData/debugger/tinyApp/classes*
/jps-plugin/testData/kannotator
ultimate/.DS_Store
ultimate/.idea/shelf
ultimate/dependencies
ultimate/ideaSDK
ultimate/out
ultimate/tmp
ultimate/workspace.xml
ultimate/*.versionsBackup
.idea/workspace.xml
.idea/tasks.xml
.idea/dataSources.ids
```

```
.idea/dataSources.xml
.idea/dataSources.local.xml
.idea/sqlDataSources.xml
.idea/dynamic.xml
.idea/uiDesigner.xml
.idea/gradle.xml
.idea/libraries
.idea/mongoSettings.xml
*.iws
/out/
.idea_modules/
atlassian-ide-plugin.xml
com_crashlytics_export_strings.xml
crashlytics.properties
crashlytics-build.properties
fabric.properties
target/
pom.xml.tag
pom.xml.releaseBackup
pom.xml.versionsBackup
pom.xml.next
release.properties
dependency-reduced-pom.xml
buildNumber.properties
.mvn/timing.properties
!/.mvn/wrapper/maven-wrapper.jar
samples/*
build/*
.gradle/*
!libs/*.jar
!Releases/*.jar
credentials*.gradle
gen
```

You can use this `.gitignore` configuration from the preceding. Now we can **commit and push** *cmd + 9* on macOS or *ctrl + 9* on Windows/Linux (shortcut for **View** | **Tool Windows** | **Version Control**). Expand unversioned files, select them, and right-click on **Add** to **VCS**.

Press *Cmd + K* (or *Ctrl + K* on Windows/Linux), check all files, enter **commit** message, and, from the **Commit** drop-down menu, choose **Commit and Push**. If you get **Line Separators Warning**, choose **Fix and Commit**. The **Push Commits** window will appear. Check **Push Tags** and choose **Current Branch**, and then **Push**.

Setting up Gradle

Gradle is a build system. You can build your Android application without one, but, in that case, you have to use several SDK tools by yourself. That is not simple! This is a part where you need a Gradle and Android Gradle plugin.

Gradle takes all the source files and processes them by tools we mentioned. Then, it packs everything into one compressed file with the `.apk` extension. APK can be uncompressed. If you rename it by changing its extension to `.zip`, you can extract the content.

Each build system uses its convention. The most important convention is about placing source code and assets in a proper directory with proper structure.

Gradle is a JVM-based build system, so that practically means that you can write your own script in Java, Groovy, Kotlin, and so on. Also, it's a plugin-based system and is easy to extend. One good example of it is Google's Android plugin. You probably noticed `build.gradle` files in your project. They are all written in Groovy, so any Groovy code you write will be executed. We will define our Gradle scripts to automate a building process. Let's set up our building! Open `settings.gradle` and take a look at it:

```
include ":App"
```

This directive tells Gradle that it will build a module named `App`. The `App` module is located in the `app` directory of our project.

Now open `build.gradle` from project `root` and add the following lines:

```
buildscript {
  repositories {
    jcenter()
    mavenCentral()
  }
  dependencies {
    classpath 'com.android.tools.build:gradle:2.3.3'
    classpath 'org.jetbrains.kotlin:kotlin-gradle-plugin:1.1.3'
  }
}
```

```
repositories {
  jcenter()
  mavenCentral()
}
```

We defined that our build script will resolve its dependencies from JCenter and Maven Central repositories. The same repositories will be used to resolve project dependencies. Main dependencies are added to target each module we will have:

- Android Gradle plugin
- Kotlin Gradle plugin

After you updated the main `build.gradle` configuration, open `build.gradle` located in the `App module` directory and add the following lines:

```
apply plugin: "com.android.application"
apply plugin: "kotlin-android"
apply plugin: "kotlin-android-extensions"
android {
  compileSdkVersion 26
  buildToolsVersion "25.0.3"
  defaultConfig {
    applicationId "com.journaler"
    minSdkVersion 19
    targetSdkVersion 26
    versionCode 1
    versionName "1.0"
    testInstrumentationRunner
    "android.support.test.runner.AndroidJUnitRunner"
  }
  buildTypes {
    release {
      minifyEnabled false
      proguardFiles getDefaultProguardFile('proguard-
      android.txt'), 'proguard-rules.pro'
    }
  }
  sourceSets {
    main.java.srcDirs += 'src/main/kotlin'
  }}
  repositories {
    jcenter()
    mavenCentral()
  }dependencies {
    compile "org.jetbrains.kotlin:kotlin-stdlib:1.1.3"
    compile 'com.android.support:design:26+'
    compile 'com.android.support:appcompat-v7:26+'}
```

The configurations we set enable Kotlin as a development language for our project and Gradle scripts as well. Then, it defines a minimal and target sdk version that an application requires. In our case, this is 19 as minimum and 26 as target. It is important to note that in the default configuration section, we set application ID and version parameters too. The dependencies section sets dependencies for Kotlin itself and some Android UI components that will be explained later.

Explaining directory structure

Android Studio contains everything you need to build an application. It contains source code and assets. All directories are created by the wizard we used to create our project. To see it, open the **Project** window on the left side of the IDE (click on **View** | **ToolWindows** | **Project**), as shown in the following screenshot:

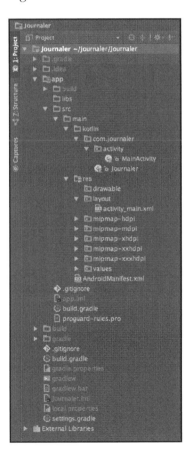

A project module represents a collection of source files, assets, and build settings that divide projects into discrete functionality parts. The minimal number of `modules` is one. There is no real limit on the maximal `modules` number your project can have. `Modules` can be built, tested, or debugged independently. As you saw, we defined the **Journaler** project with only one module named **app**.

To add a new module, following these steps:

Go to **File** | **New** | **New Module**.

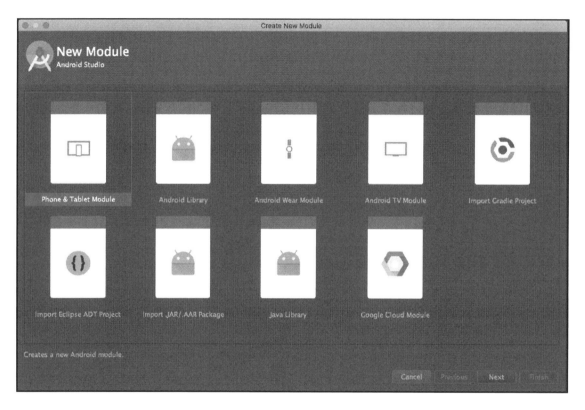

It's possible to create the following `modules`:

- Android Application Module represents a container for your application source code, resources, and settings. The default module name is **app**, like in our created example.
- **Phone & Tablet Module**.
- **Android Wear Module**.

- **Glass Module**.
- **Android TV module**.
- `Library` module represents a container for reusable code--a library. The module can be used as a dependency in other application modules or imported into other projects. When it's built, the module has an AAR extension--Android Archive instead of having an APK extension.

The **Create New Module** window offers the following options:

- **Android Library**: All types are supported in an Android project. The build result of this library is an **Android Archiver (AAR)**.
- **Java Library**: Only supports pure Java. The build result of this library is a **Java Archiver (JAR)**.
- **Google Cloud Module**: This defines a container for the Google Cloud backend code.

It is important to understand that Gradle refers to `modules` as individual projects. If your application code depends on the code for the Android library called **Logger** then in **build.config**, you use must include the following directive:

```
dependencies {
  compile project(':logger')
}
```

Let's navigate through the project structure. The default view Android Studio uses to display your project files is Android view. It doesn't represent the actual file hierarchy on disk. It hides certain files or directories that are not often used.

Android view presents the following:

- All the build-related configuration files
- All manifest files
- All other resource files in a single group

In each application, the module content is presented in these groups:

- Manifests and `AndroidManifest.xml` files.
- Java and Kotlin source code for application and tests.
- The `res` and Android UI resources.
- To see the real file structure of the project, choose **Project view**. To do this, click on **Android view** and, from the drop-down menu, choose **Project**.

By doing this, you will see a lot more files and directories. The most important of them are as follows:

- `module-name/`: This is the name of the module
- `build/`: This holds build outputs
- `libs/`: This holds private libraries
- `src/`: This holds all code and resource files for the module organized in the following subdirectories:
    - `main`: This holds the `main` source set files--source code and resources shared by all build variants (we will explain build variants later)
    - `AndroidManifest.xml`: This defines the nature of our application and each of its components
    - `java`: This holds the Java source code
    - `kotlin`: This holds the Kotlin source code
    - `jni`: This holds the native code using the **Java Native Interface (JNI)**
    - `gen`: This holds the Java files generated by Android Studio
    - `res`: This holds application resources, for example, **drawable** files, layout files, strings, and so on
    - `assets`: This holds files that should be compiled into an `.apk` file with no modification
    - `test`: This holds the test source code
    - `build.gradle`: This is the module level build configuration
    - `build.gradle`: This is the project level build configuration

Choose **File** | **Project Structure** to change settings for the project in the following screenshot:

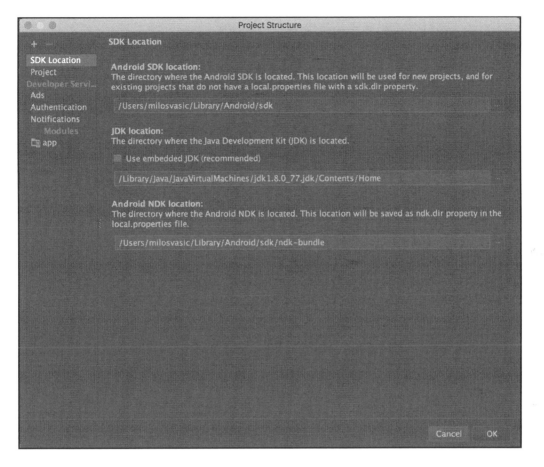

It contains the following sections:

- **SDK Location**: This sets the location of the JDK, Android SDK, and Android NDK that your project uses
- **Project**: This sets Gradle and Android Gradle plugin versions
- **Modules**: This edits module-specific build configurations

The **Modules** section is divided in the following tabs:

- **Properties**: This sets the versions of the SDK and build tools for module building
- **Signing**: This sets the certificate for APK signing
- **Flavors**: This defines flavors for the module
- **Build Types**: This defines build types for the module
- **Dependencies**: This sets dependencies needed by the module

Please refer to the following screenshot:

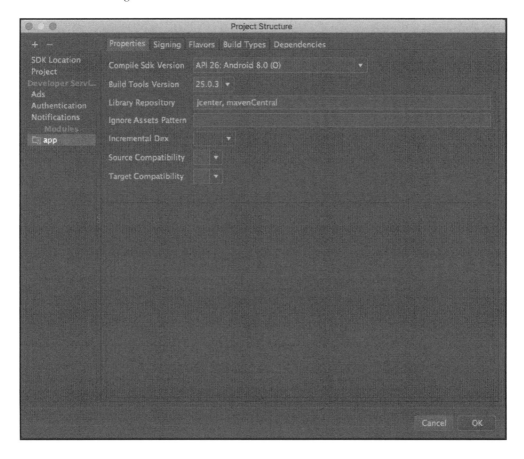

Defining build types and flavors

We are approaching an important phase of our project--defining build variants for our application. Build variant stands for a unique version of an Android application.

They are unique because they override some of the application attributes or resources.

Each build variant is configured per module level.

Let's extend our `build.gradle`! Put the following code in the `android` section of the `build.gradle` file:

```
android {
  ...
  buildTypes {
    debug {
      applicationIdSuffix ".dev"
    }
    staging {
      debuggable true
      applicationIdSuffix ".sta"
    }
    preproduction {
      applicationIdSuffix ".pre"
    }
      release {}
    }
  ...
}
```

We defined the following `buildTypes` for our application--`debug`, `release`, `staging`, and `preproduction`.

Product flavors are created in a similar way like `buildTypes`. You need to add them to `productFlavors` and configure the needed settings. The following code snippet demonstrates this:

```
android {
  ...
  defaultConfig {...}
  buildTypes {...}
  productFlavors {
    demo {
      applicationIdSuffix ".demo"
      versionNameSuffix "-demo"
    }
    complete {
```

```
          applicationIdSuffix ".complete"
          versionNameSuffix "-complete"
        }
        special {
          applicationIdSuffix ".special"
          versionNameSuffix "-special"
        }
      }
    }
```

After you create and configure your `productFlavors`, click on **Sync Now** in the notification bar.

You need to wait a while for the process to be done. Names for **Build Variants** are formed by the `<product-flavor><Build-Type>` convention. Here are some examples:

```
      demoDebug
      demoRelease
      completeDebug
      completeRelease
```

You can change the build variant to the one that you want to build and run. Go to **Build**, select **Build Variant**, and select `completeDebug` from the drop-down menu.

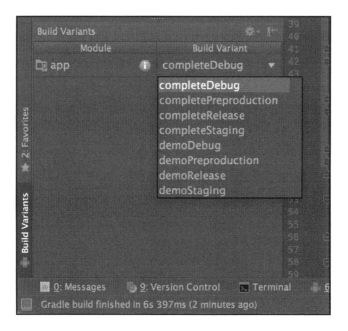

The `Main/source` set is shared between all build variants in your application. If you need to create a new source set, you can do that for certain build types, product flavors, and their combinations.

All source set files and directories must be organized in a specific way, similar to the `Main/Source` set. Kotlin class files that are specific to your *debug* build type must be located in `src/debug/kotlin/directory`.

In order to learn how to organize your files, open the terminal window (**View** | **ToolWindows** | **Terminal**) and execute the following command line:

```
./gradlew sourceSets
```

Take a look at the output carefully. The report is understandable and self-explanatory. Android Studio doesn't create the `sourceSets` directories. It's a work that has to be done by you.

If desired, you can change the location where Gradle is looking for a source set using the `sourceSets` block. Let's update our build configuration. We will update the following expected source code paths:

```
android {
  ...
  sourceSets {
   main {
   java.srcDirs = [
            'src/main/kotlin',
            'src/common/kotlin',
            'src/debug/kotlin',
            'src/release/kotlin',
            'src/staging/kotlin',
            'src/preproduction/kotlin',
            'src/debug/java',
            'src/release/java',
            'src/staging/java',
            'src/preproduction/java',
            'src/androidTest/java',
            'src/androidTest/kotlin'
    ]
    ...
  }
```

Code and resources that you want packaged only with certain configurations, you can store in the `sourceSets` directories. Here are given examples for build with the `demoDebug` build variant; this build variant is a product of a `demo` product flavor and `debug` build type. In Gradle, the following priority is given to them:

```
src/demoDebug/ (build variant source set)
src/debug/ (build type source set)
src/demo/ (product flavor source set)
src/main/ (main source set)
```

This is the priority order that Gradle uses during the build process and considers it when applying the following build rules:

- It compiles source code in the `java/` and `kotlin/` directories together
- It merges manifests together into a single manifest
- It merges files in the `values/` directories
- It merges resources in the `res/` and `asset/` directories

The lowest priority is given to resources and manifests included with library module dependencies.

Additional libraries

We configured our build types and flavors, now we will need some third-party libraries. We will use and add support for Retrofit, OkHttp, and Gson. This is an explanation for each of them:

- Retrofit is a type-safe HTTP client for Android and Java by Square, Inc. Retrofit is one of the most popular HTTP client library for Android as a result of its simplicity and its great performance compared to the others.
- `OkHttp` is an HTTP client that's efficient by default--HTTP/2 support allows all requests to the same host to share a socket.
- Gson is a Java library that can be used to convert Java objects into their JSON representation. It can also be used to convert a JSON string to an equivalent Java object. Gson can work with arbitrary Java objects including preexisting objects that you do not have a source code for.

There are a few open source projects that can convert Java objects to JSON. Later in this book, we will add Kotson to provide Gson bindings for Kotlin.

Let's extend `build.gradle` with dependencies for Retrofit and Gson:

```
dependencies {
  ...
  compile 'com.google.code.gson:gson:2.8.0'
  compile 'com.squareup.retrofit2:retrofit:2.2.0'
  compile 'com.squareup.retrofit2:converter-gson:2.0.2'
  compile 'com.squareup.okhttp3:okhttp:3.6.0'
  compile 'com.squareup.okhttp3:logging-interceptor:3.6.0'
  ...
}
```

After you updated your Gradle configuration, sync it again when asked!

Getting familiar with Android Manifest

Every application must have an `AndroidManifest.xml` file and the file must have exactly that name. Its location is in its `root` directory, and, in each module, it contains essential information about your application to the Android system. The `manifest` file is responsible for defining the following:

- Naming a package for the application
- Describing the components of the application--activities (screens), services, broadcast receivers (messages), and content providers (database access)
- Permissions that application must have in order to access protected parts of the Android API
- Permissions that other applications must have in order to interact with the application's components, such as content providers

The following code snippet shows the general structure of the `manifest` file and elements that it can contain:

```
<?xml version="1.0" encoding="utf-8"?>
<manifest>
  <uses-permission />
  <permission />
  <permission-tree />
  <permission-group />
  <instrumentation />
  <uses-sdk />
```

```
<uses-configuration />
<uses-feature />
<supports-screens />
<compatible-screens />
<supports-gl-texture />

<application>
  <activity>
    <intent-filter>
      <action />
        <category />
          <data />
    </intent-filter>
    <meta-data />
  </activity>

  <activity-alias>
    <intent-filter> . . . </intent-filter>
    <meta-data />
  </activity-alias>

  <service>
    <intent-filter> . . . </intent-filter>
    <meta-data/>
  </service>

  <receiver>
    <intent-filter> . . . </intent-filter>
    <meta-data />
  </receiver>
  <provider>
    <grant-uri-permission />
    <meta-data />
    <path-permission />
  </provider>

  <uses-library />
</application>
</manifest>
```

Main Application class

Each Android application defines its main `Application` class. The `Application` class in Android is the base class within an Android application that contains all other components, such as `activities` and `services`. The `Application` class, or any subclass of the `Application` class, is instantiated before any other class when the process for your application/package is created.

We will create an `Application` class for Journaler. Locate the main sources directory. Expand it, and if there is no Kotlin sources directory, create it. Then, create the `package com` and subpackage journaler; to do so, right-click on the Kotlin directory and choose **New | Package**. Once you've created the package structure, right-click on the **journaler** package and choose **New | KotlinFile/Class**. Name it `Journaler`. `Journaler.kt` is created.

Each `Application` class must extend the Android Application class as shown in our example:

```kotlin
package com.journaler

import android.app.Application
import android.content.Context


class Journaler : Application() {

  companion object {
    var ctx: Context? = null
  }

  override fun onCreate() {
    super.onCreate()
    ctx = applicationContext
  }

}
```

For now, our main `Application` class will provide us with static access to application context. What this context is will be explained later. However, Android will not use this class until it's mentioned in manifest. Open the `app` module `android manifest` and add the following block of code:

```xml
<manifest xmlns:android="http://schemas.android.com/apk/
res/android" package="com.journaler">

<application
```

```
            android:name=".Journaler"
            android:allowBackup="false"
            android:icon="@mipmap/ic_launcher"
            android:label="@string/app_name"
            android:roundIcon="@mipmap/ic_launcher_round"
            android:supportsRtl="true"
            android:theme="@style/AppTheme">

    </application>
    </manifest>
```

With `android:name=".Journaler"`, we tell Android which class to use.

Your first screen

We created an application with no screens. We will not waste time, we will create one! Create a new package named `activity` where all our screen classes will be defined, and create your first `Activity` class named `MainActivity.kt`. We will start with one simple class:

```
        package com.journaler.activity

        import android.os.Bundle
        import android.os.PersistableBundle
        import android.support.v7.app.AppCompatActivity
        import com.journaler.R

        class MainActivity : AppCompatActivity() {
          override fun onCreate(savedInstanceState: Bundle?,
          persistentState: PersistableBundle?) {
            super.onCreate(savedInstanceState, persistentState)
            setContentView(R.layout.activity_main)
          }
        }
```

Soon, we will explain the meaning of all these lines. For now, it's important to note that `setContentView(R.layout.activity_main)` assigns UI resource to our screen and `activity_main` is a name of the XML defining it. Since we don't have it yet, we will create it. Locate `res` directory under the `main` directory. If there is no layout folder there, create one and then create a new layout named `activity_main` by right-clicking on `layout` directory and choosing the **New** | **Layout** resource file. Assign `activity_main` as its name and `LinearLayout` as its root element. The content of the file should be similar to this:

```
<?xml version="1.0" encoding="utf-8"?>
<LinearLayout xmlns:android="http://schemas.android.com/
 apk/res/android"
  android:orientation="vertical"
  android:layout_width="match_parent"
  android:layout_height="match_parent">

</LinearLayout>
```

There is one more thing to do before we are ready to run our application: we must tell our manifest about this screen. Open the `main manifest` file and add the following piece of code:

```
<application ... >
  <activity
    android:name=".activity.MainActivity"
    android:configChanges="orientation"
    android:screenOrientation="portrait">
    <intent-filter>
      <action android:name="android.intent.action.MAIN" />
      <category android:name="android.intent.category.LAUNCHER" />
    </intent-filter>
  </activity>
</application>
```

We will explain all these attributes soon; all you need to know for now is that your application is ready to run. However, before that, `commit and push` your work. You don't want to lose it!

Summary

In this chapter, we introduced the basics of Android and gave glimpses of Kotlin. We configured a working environment and made the first screen of our application.

In the next chapter, we will go deeper into the matter of Android. You will learn how to build your application and customize different variants. We will also cover different ways of running the application.

2
Building and Running

At this point, you have successfully created an Android project containing one screen. In the previous chapter, you also learned how to set up your working environment. We showed you how simple it is to use Android tools. You also defined some flavors and build types. Let's take control over it! It's time to do your first build and run it on a device or an emulator. You will try it with all build types and flavor combinations.

This chapter will cover the following points:

- Running your application on emulator and/or real hardware device
- Introduction to Logcat
- Gradle tool

Running your first Android application

We made our first screen and defined some specifics for the application itself. To be sure that what we did so far is ok, we do the build and run our application. We will run the **completeDebug** build variant. If you forgot how to switch to this build variant, we will remind you. Open Android Studio and the `Journaler` project. Open the **Build Variants** pane by clicking on the **Build Variants** pane on the left side of the Android Studio window or by choosing **View | Tool Windows | Build Variants**. The **Build Variants** pane will appear. Choose **completeDebug** from the drop-down list, as shown in the screenshot:

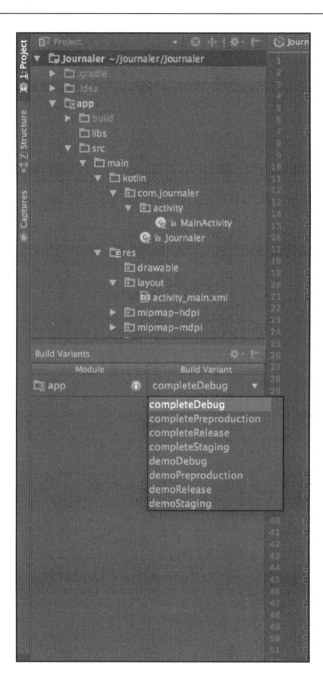

We will use this **Build Variant** as our main build variant for the try out execution, and for production build, we will use the **completeDebug** build variant. After we choose **Build Variant** from the drop-down list, it takes some time for Gradle to build the chosen variant.

We will run our application now. We will do it on an emulator first and then on a real live device. Start your emulator instance by opening the AVD Manager. We will open it by clicking on the AVD Manager icon. It is the fastest way to open it. Double-click on the AVD instance. It will take some time until your emulator is ready. Emulator performs Android system boot and then it loads a default application launcher.

Your emulator is booted and ready to run the application. In order to run the application, click on the Run icon or navigate to **Run | Run 'app'**.

There is a keyboard shortcut for this; on macOS, it is *Ctrl + R*.

When an application runs, a dialog box for **Select Deployment Target** appears. In case you have multiple instances on which an application can run, you can choose one of them as shown in the following screenshot:

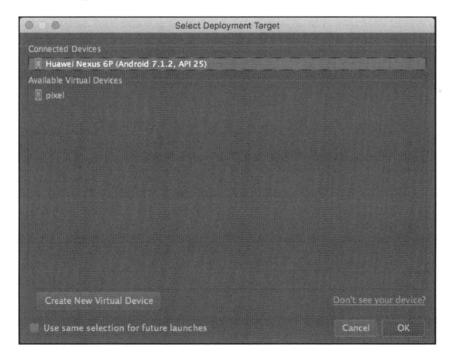

Pick your deployment target and click on **OK**. In case you want to remember your selection, check the **Use same selection for future launches** selection. It takes some time for the application to run, but after a few seconds, your application appears!

Meet the Logcat

Logcat is an important part of everyday development. Its purpose is to display all logs coming from your device. It displays logs from an emulator or a live device connected. Android has several levels of log messages:

- **Assert**
- **Verbose**
- **Debug**
- **Information**
- **Warning**
- **Error**

You can filter log messages by these log levels (for example, when you need to see only errors--application crash stacktrace) or log tag (we will explain this later); or by keyword, regex, or the application package. Before we apply any filter, we will configure Android Studio so the log messages are colored differently.

Choose **Android Studio** | **Preferences**. In the search field, enter `Logcat`. Logcat coloring preferences appears, as shown in the following screenshot:

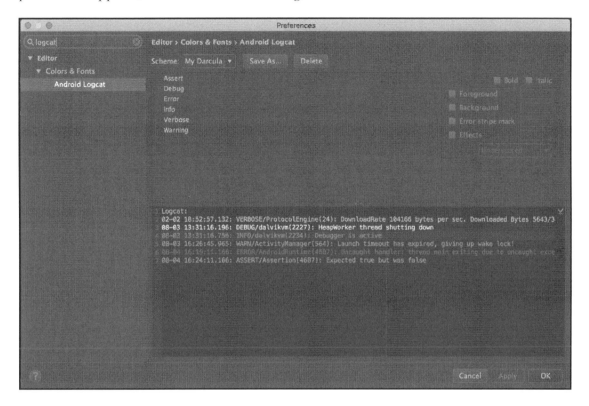

To edit coloring, you must save a copy of the current coloring theme. Choose your theme from the drop-down list and choose **Save As**. Choose some proper name and confirm:

Choose **Assert** from the list and uncheck **Use inherited attributes** to override the color. Make sure that the **Foreground** option is checked and click on **Color** located to the right of checkbox to choose a new color for the log text. We will pick some tone of pink, as shown in the following screenshot:

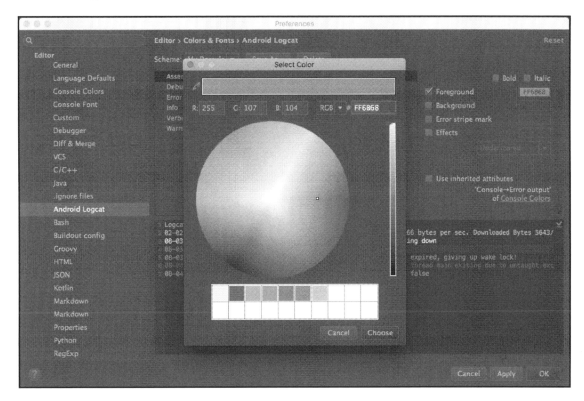

For the **Assert** level, you can enter the hex code manually: FF6B68. For maximal readability, we recommend the following colors:

- **Assert**: #FF6B68
- **Verbose**: #BBBBBB
- **Debug**: #F4F4F4
- **Information**: #6D82E3
- **Warning**: #E57E15
- **Error**: #FF1A11

To apply changes, click on **Apply** and then **OK**.

Open Android Monitor (**View** | **Tool Windows** | **Android Monitor**) and take a look at the messages printed in the **Logcat** pane. They are colored with different tones for each log level, as shown here:

Now we will define our own log messages, which is also a good opportunity to work with the Android lifecycle. We will put proper log messages for each lifecycle event for the `Application` class and the screen (activity) we created.

Open your main `Application` class, `Journaler.kt`. Extend the code like the following:

```kotlin
class Journaler : Application() {

    companion object {
        val tag = "Journaler"
        var ctx: Context? = null
    }

    override fun onCreate() {
        super.onCreate()
        ctx = applicationContext
        Log.v(tag, "[ ON CREATE ]")
    }

    override fun onLowMemory() {
        super.onLowMemory()
        Log.w(tag, "[ ON LOW MEMORY ]")
    }

    override fun onTrimMemory(level: Int) {
        super.onTrimMemory(level)
        Log.d(tag, "[ ON TRIM MEMORY ]: $level")
    }
}
```

Here, we introduced some important changes. We overrode the main lifecycle event for the onCreate() application. We also overrode two additional methods: onLowMemory(), triggered in critical memory situations (actively running processes should trim their memory usage), and onTrimMemory(), when the memory is trimmed.

To log events in our application, we use Log class with static methods, each exposed for a proper log level. Based on this, we have the following methods exposed:

- For **Verbose** level:

```
v(String tag, String msg)
v(String tag, String msg, Throwable tr)
```

- For **Debug** level:

```
d(String tag, String msg)
d(String tag, String msg, Throwable tr)
```

- For **Information** level:

```
i(String tag, String msg)
i(String tag, String msg, Throwable tr)
```

- For **Warning** level:

```
w(String tag, String msg)
w(String tag, String msg, Throwable tr)
```

- For **Error** level:

```
e(String tag, String msg)
e(String tag, String msg, Throwable tr)
```

Methods accept the following parameters:

- Tag: This is used to identify the origin of a log message
- message: This is the message we want to log
- throwable: This represents an exception to log

Beside these log methods, there are some additional methods that you can use:

- wtf(String tag, String msg)
- wtf(String tag, Throwable tr)
- wtf(String tag, String msg, Throwable tr)

Wtf stands for **What a Terrible Failure**! `Wtf` is used to report an exception that should never happen!

We will play some more with the `Log` class. Open the only screen you have created so far and update the `MainActivity` class with the following changes:

```kotlin
class MainActivity : AppCompatActivity() {
  private val tag = Journaler.tag

  override fun onCreate(
    savedInstanceState: Bundle?,
    persistentState: PersistableBundle?
  ) {
    super.onCreate(savedInstanceState, persistentState)
    setContentView(R.layout.activity_main)
    Log.v(tag, "[ ON CREATE ]")
  }

  override fun onPostCreate(savedInstanceState: Bundle?) {
    super.onPostCreate(savedInstanceState)
    Log.v(tag, "[ ON POST CREATE ]")
  }

  override fun onRestart() {
    super.onRestart()
    Log.v(tag, "[ ON RESTART ]")
  }

  override fun onStart() {
    super.onStart()
    Log.v(tag, "[ ON START ]")
  }

  override fun onResume() {
    super.onResume()
    Log.v(tag, "[ ON RESUME ]")
  }

  override fun onPostResume() {
    super.onPostResume()
    Log.v(tag, "[ ON POST RESUME ]")
  }

  override fun onPause() {
    super.onPause()
    Log.v(tag, "[ ON PAUSE ]")
  }
```

```
    override fun onStop() {
      super.onStop()
      Log.v(tag, "[ ON STOP ]")
    }

    override fun onDestroy() {
      super.onDestroy()
      Log.v(tag, "[ ON DESTROY ]")
    }
  }
```

We overrode all important lifecycle methods by the order they execute during the activity's lifecycle. For each event, we print the proper log message. Let's explain the purpose of the lifecycle and each important event.

Here, you can see the official diagram from the Android developers' website, explaining the activity lifecycle:

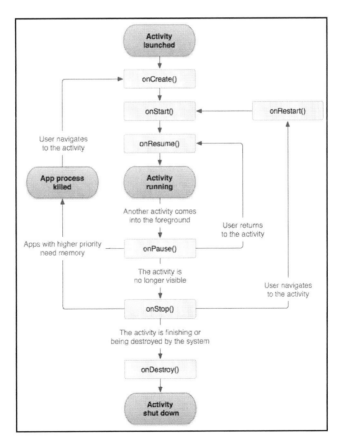

You can find the image at `https://developer.android.com/images/activity_lifecycle.png`:

- `onCreate()`: This is executed when the activity is first created. This is a place where we usually do main UI elements initialization.
- `onRestart()`: This is executed if your activity was stopped at some moment and then resumed. For example, you turn off your phone screen (lock it) and then unlock it again.
- `onStart()`: This is executed when the screen becomes visible to the application user.
- `onResume()`: This is executed when the user starts interaction with the activity.
- `onPause()`: Before we resume our previous activity, this method is executed on the current one. This is a good place to save all the information you will need when you resume again. If there are any unsaved changes, you should save them here.
- `onStop()`: This is executed when an activity is no longer visible to the application user.
- `onDestroy()`: This is executed before an activity is destroyed by Android. This can happen, for example, if somebody executed the `finish()` method of the `Activity` class. To know if the activity is finishing at a particular moment, Android provides a method for that check: `isFinishing()`. If an activity is finishing, the method will return Boolean `true`.

Now, when we wrote some code using the Android lifecycle and put proper log messages, we will execute two use cases and look at the logs printed out by Logcat.

First case

Run your application. Then just go back and leave it. Kill the app. Open **Android Monitor**, and from the device drop-down list, choose your device instance (emulator or real device). From the next drop-down list, choose the **Journaler** application package. Observe the following Logcat output:

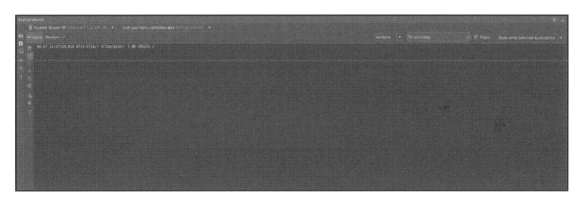

You will notice the log messages we put in our source code.

Let's check how many times during our interaction with the application we entered the onCreate() and onDestroy() methods. Position your cursor on the search field and type on create. Observe the change in content--there is only one entry when we expected two: one for the main Application class and one for the main activity. Why did this happen? We will find out later:

What does our output contain? It contains the following:

06-27: This is the date the event occurred.

11:37:59.914: This is the time the event occurred.

6713-6713/?: This is the process and thread identifier with the package. Process and thread identifiers are the same if the application has only one thread.

`V/Journaler`: This is the log level and tag.

`[ ON CREATE ]`: This is the log message.

Change the filter to `on destroy`. The content changes to the following:

06-27 11:38:07.317 6713-6713/com.journaler.complete.dev V/Journaler: [ON DESTROY]

In your case, you will have different date, time, and pid/tid values.

From the drop-down list, change your filtering from **Verbose** to **Warn**. Keep the value for the filter! You will notice that your Logcat is now empty. It's empty because there is no warning messages with the message text containing `on destroy`. Remove the filter text and return to **Verbose** level.

Run your application. Lock your screen and unlock it a few times in a row. Then, close and kill the **Journaler** application. Observe the following Logcat output:

As you can see, it's noticeably entering lifecycle states for pausing and resuming. Finally, we kill our app and an `onDestroy()` event is triggered. You can see it in Logcat.

If it's easier for you, you can use Logcat from a terminal. Open the terminal and execute the following command line:

```
adb logcat
```

Using the Gradle build tool

During our development, we will need to build different build variants or run tests. Those tests can be executed for only certain build variants, if needed, or for all of them.

In the following examples, we will cover some of the most common Gradle use cases. We will start with cleaning and building.

As you remember, the **Journaler** application has the following build types defined:

- debug
- release
- staging
- preproduction

The following build flavors are also defined in the **Journaler** application:

- demo
- complete
- special

Open terminal. To remove everything we built so far, and all temporally build derivates, execute the following command line:

```
./gradlew clean
```

It takes some time to do the cleaning. Then execute the following command line:

```
./gradlew assemble.
```

This assembles everything--all the build variants that we have in our application. Imagine the time impact it can have if we are dealing with a really big project. Therefore, we will `isolate` the build command. To build only the debug build type, execute the following command line:

```
./gradlew assembleDebug
```

It will be executed much faster than the previous example! This builds all flavors for the debug build type. In order to be more effective, we will instruct Gradle that we are interested only in a complete build flavor for the debug build type. Execute this:

```
./gradlew assembleCompleteDebug
```

This executes much faster. Here, we will mention several more important Gradle commands that are useful:

To run all unit tests execute:

```
./gradlew test
```

In case you want to run unit tests for a specific build variant, execute this command:

```
./gradlew testCompleteDebug
```

In Android, we can run tests on a real device instance or an emulator. Usually, those tests have access to some of Android's components. To execute those (instrumentation) tests, you can use the command shown in the following example:

```
./gradlew connectedCompleteDebug
```

You will find more about tests and testing Android applications in the final chapters of this book.

Debug your application

Now, we know how to log important application messages. During development, we will face situations when only logging messages is not enough when analyzing application behavior or investigating bugs.

For us, it's important to have the ability to debug an application code during its execution on real Android devices or on emulators. So, let's debug something!
Open the main `Application` class and put the break point on line where we log the `onCreate()` method, as shown here:

```
Journaler ×    app ×    Journaler.kt    MainActivity.kt ×    activity_main.xml ×    AndroidManifest.xml ×

Journaler   onCreate()
1    package com.journaler
2
3    import android.app.Application
4    import android.content.Context
5    import android.util.Log
6
7
8    class Journaler : Application() {
9
10       companion object {
11           val tag = "Journaler"
12           var ctx: Context? = null
13       }
14
15       override fun onCreate() {
16           super.onCreate()
17           ctx = applicationContext
18           Log.v(tag, "[ ON CREATE ]")
19       }
20
21       override fun onLowMemory() {
22           super.onLowMemory()
23           Log.w(tag, "[ ON LOW MEMORY ]")
24       }
25
26       override fun onTrimMemory(level: Int) {
27           super.onTrimMemory(level)
28           Log.d(tag, "[ ON TRIM MEMORY ]: $level")
29       }
30
31   }
```

As you can see, we set the break point at line **18**. We will add more break points. Let's add it in our main (and only) activity. Put a break point in each lifecycle event at lines where we perform logging.

We set breakpoints at lines **18**, **23**, **28**, **33**, **38**, and so on. Run the application in debug mode by clicking on the debug icon or by choosing **Run | Debug app**. The application is started in debug mode. Wait a little bit and a debugger will soon enter the first break point we set.

The following screenshot illustrates this:

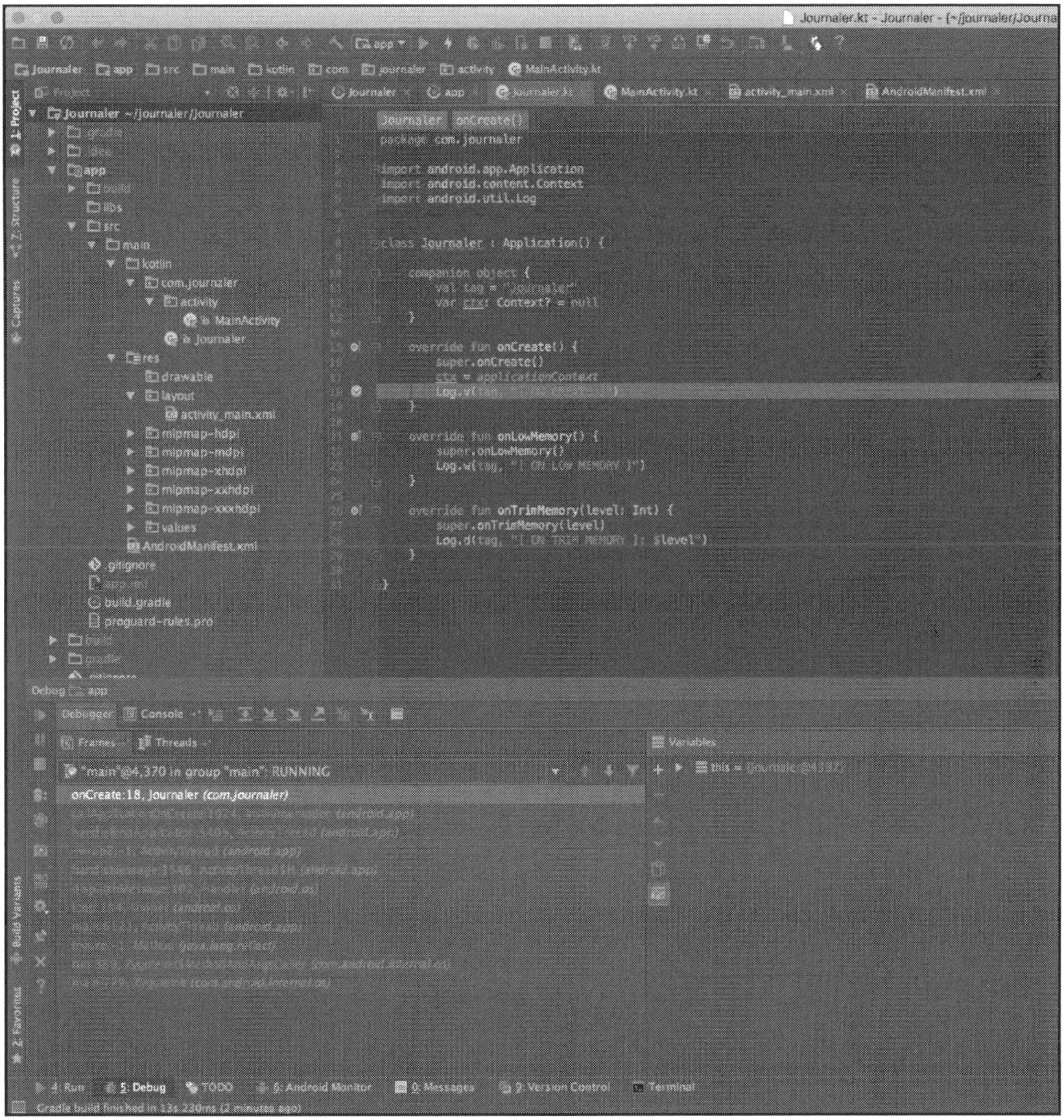

As you can see, the `onCreate()` method of the `Application` class is the first method we enter. Let's check if our applications enter lifecycle methods as expected. Click on the **Resume Program** icon from the **Debugger** pane. You may notice that we did not enter the `onCreate()` method for our main activity! We entered `onStart()` after the main `Application` class `onCreate()` method. Congratulations! You just discovered your first Android bug! Why did this happen? We used the wrong `onCreate()` method version instead of using the following line of code:

```
void onCreate(@Nullable Bundle savedInstanceState)
```

We accidentally overrode this:

```
onCreate(Bundle savedInstanceState, PersistableBundle
persistentState)
```

Thanks to debugging, we discovered this! Stop the debugger by clicking on the **Stop** icon from the **Debugger** pane and fix the code. Change the code lines to this:

```
override fun onCreate(savedInstanceState: Bundle?) {
  super.onCreate(savedInstanceState)
  setContentView(R.layout.activity_main)
  Log.v(tag, "[ ON CREATE 1 ]")
}
override fun onCreate(savedInstanceState: Bundle?,
persistentState: PersistableBundle?) {
  super.onCreate(savedInstanceState, persistentState)
  Log.v(tag, "[ ON CREATE 2 ]")
}
```

We updated our log messages so we can track entering both the `onCreate()` method versions. Save your changes and start the application again in debug mode. Don't forget to set the break point to both `onCreate()` method overrides! Go through the break points one by one. Now we entered all break points in an expected order.

To see all break points, click on the **View Breakpoints** icon. The **Breakpoints** window appears, as shown here:

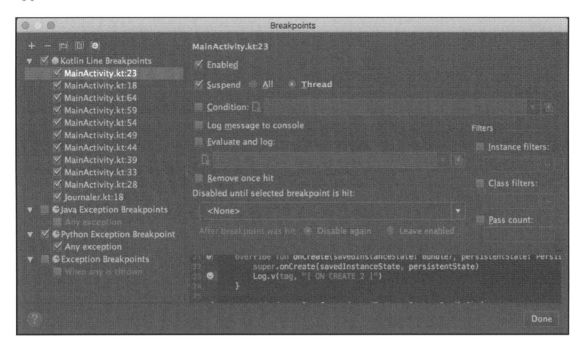

By double clicking on **Breakpoint**, you will be positioned at the line where it is set. Stop the debugger.

Imagine you can continue to develop your application for the next two years. Your application becomes really big, and it also executes some expensive operations. Running it directly in **Debug** mode can be very difficult and time consuming. We will lose a significant amount of time until it enters the break point we are interested in. What can we do about it? Applications running in debug mode are slower, and we have a slow and big application. How to skip the part where we are losing our precious time? We will demonstrate. Run your application by clicking on the **Run** icon or by choosing **Run | Run 'app'**. The application is executed and started on our deployment target (real device or emulator). Attach the debugger to your application by clicking on **Attach debugger** to the Android Process icon or by choosing **Run | Attach debugger** to Android. Choose the **Process** window that appears:

Pick our application process by double clicking on its package name. The **Debugger** pane appears. From your application, try to go back. **Debugger** enters the onPause() method of your main activity. Stop **Debugger**.

Summary

In this chapter, you learned how to build and run your application from Android Studio IDE or directly from the terminal. We also analyzed some logs that we got from the emulator and real devices. And, in the end, we did some debugging.

In the next chapter, we will get familiar with some components of UI--screens, to be more precise. We will show you how to create new screens and how to add some stylish details to them. We will also discuss complex layouts of buttons and images.

3
Screens

One screen with a plain user interface is not exciting at all. However, before you go into eye candy styling and *wow* effects, you need to create more screens containing all the elements a professionally developed application must have. You see all this in modern applications you use in your everyday life. In the previous chapter, we built and ran our project. This skill is important so we can continue with our progress. Now you will add a UI in your application!

In this chapter, we will cover the following topics:

- Analyzing mockup
- Defining application activities
- Android layouts
- Android Context
- Fragments, fragment manager, and stack
- View pager
- Transaction, dialog fragments, and notifications
- Other important UI components

Analyzing the mockup plan

Things are getting hooked! We are ready to begin with some serious development! We will create all of the screens for our application. However, before we create them, we will create and analyze a mockup so we know what exactly we will create. The mockup will represent the basic application wireframe with no design. It will be just a layout for the screens and the relationship between them. To create a good mockup with wireframes, you will need a tool. Any tool capable of drawing lines will do the job. To draw our mockup, we used **Pencil**. Pencil is a free open source application providing GUI prototyping.

Let's take a look at our mockup:

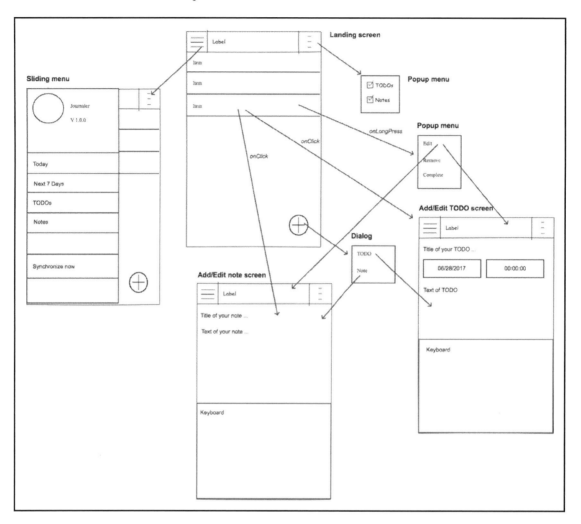

As you can see, the mockup presents a relatively simple application with a few screens. There are different components that will be included in these screens, and we will explain these along with each screen. Let's go through the mockup.

The first screen, titled **Landing screen**, will be our main application screen. Every time we enter the application, this screen will appear. We already defined the `MainActivity` class. This activity will represent the screen. Soon, we will extend the code so the activity follows the mockup exactly as described.

The central part of the screen will be the list containing all the items we created. Each item will contain basic properties, such as title or date and time. We will be able to filter items by type. We will be able to filter only **Notes** or **TODOs**. The difference between **Notes** and **TODOs** is that **TODOs** will represent tasks with the *date* and *time* assigned. We will also support some functionalities such as the **onLongPress** events. The **onLongPress** event on each item will present a **Popup menu** with the **Edit**, **Remove**, or **Complete** options. Clicking on **Edit** will open the screen for updating.

At the bottom-right corner, we will have a **+** button. The purpose of the button is to open the option **Dialog** on which a user can choose if they want to create a **Note** or **TODO** task. Depending on the option, a user can choose one of the screens that appear--**Add note screen** or **Add TODO screen**.

Landing screen also contains the **Sliding menu** button positioned at its top-left corner. Clicking on that button will open the **Sliding menu** with the following items in it:

- An application icon with the application title and version
- A **Today** button to filter only **TODO** items assigned for the current date
- A **Next 7 Days** button to filter **TODO** items assigned in the **Next 7 Days** including the current one
- A **TODOs** button filter only **TODO** items
- The **Notes** button will filter only the **Note** items

Applying some of these filters will affect the checkboxes from the **Popup** menu we get by clicking on the top-right corner of the **Landing screen**. Also, checking and unchecking those will modify the currently applied filter.

The last item in the sliding menu is **Synchronize now**. This button will trigger synchronization and synchronize all unsynchronized items with backend if there are any.

Now we will explain two screens responsible for the creation (or editing) of **Notes** and **TODOs**:

- **Add/Edit note screen**: This is used to create a new note or to update the content of an existing one. **Keyboard** will be opened as edit text field is focused. There is no save or update button since we plan that all changes we make are applied immediately. The top-left and top-right buttons are disabled while we are on this screen.
- **Add/Edit TODO screen**: This is used to create a new **TODO** application or to update the content of an existing one. **Keyboard** will open as in the previous example. There is no save or update button as shown in the previous example, either. The top-left and top-right buttons are disabled too. Following are the title view, we have buttons to pick date and time. By default, they will be set to the current date and time. Opening **keyboard** will push these buttons up.

We covered the basic UI and what we want to achieve by analyzing this mockup. The time has come to create some new screens.

Defining application activities

To sum up, we will have three activities:

- **Landing activity** (`MainActivty.kt`)
- **Add/Edit note screen**
- **Add/Edit TODO screen**

It's common practice in Android development to create an activity that will be a parent class to all other activities because, like this, we will reduce code base and share it at the same time with multiple activites. In most cases, Android developers call it `BaseActivity`. We will define our version of `BaseActivity`. Create a new class called `BaseActivity`; the `BaseActivity.kt` file is created. Make sure the newly created class is located under the `Activity` package of your project.

The `BaseActivity` class must extend the `FragmentActivity` class of Android SDK. We will extend `FragmentActivity` because we plan to use fragments inside our `MainActivity` class. Fragments will be used with **ViewPager** to navigate between different filters (**Today**, **Next 7 Days**, and so on). We plan that when the user clicks on one of those from our sliding menu, **ViewPager** automatically swipes to position with the fragment containing the data filtered by the chosen criteria. We will extend `FragmentActivity` from the package as follows--`android.support.v4.app.FragmentActivity`.

Android provides a way to support multiple API versions. Since we plan to do so, we will use the `FragmentActivity` version from the support library. Like this, we maximize our compatibility! To add support for the Android support library, include the following directive in the `build.gradle` configuration:

```
compile 'com.android.support:appcompat-v7:26+'
```

As you probably remember, we did so!

Let's continue! Since we are introducing a base class for all activities, we have to do some small refactoring to the only activity we have now. We will move the `tag` field from `MainActivity` to `BaseActivity`. Since it must be accessible to children of `BaseActivity`, we will update its visibility to `protected`.

We want each `Activity` class to have its unique tag. We will use activity concretization to choose the value for its tag. So, the `tag` field becomes `abstract` with no default value assigned:

```
protected abstract val tag : String
```

Beside this, we have some more common stuff in all activities. Each activity will have a layout. A layout is Android identified by the ID of the integer type. In the `BaseActivity` class, we will create an `abstract` method, as follows:

```
protected abstract fun getLayout(): Int
```

To optimize the code, we will move `onCreate` from `MainActivity` to `BaseActivity`. Instead of passing the ID of the layout from the Android generated resource directly, we will pass the result value of the `getLayout()` method. We will move all other lifecycle method overrides as well.

Update your classes according to these changes and build and run the application as follows:

```
BasicActivity.kt:
package com.journaler.activity
import android.os.Bundle
import android.support.v4.app.FragmentActivity
import android.util.Log

abstract class BaseActivity : FragmentActivity() {
  protected abstract val tag : String
  protected abstract fun getLayout(): Int

  override fun onCreate(savedInstanceState: Bundle?) {
    super.onCreate(savedInstanceState)
```

```kotlin
    setContentView(getLayout())
    Log.v(tag, "[ ON CREATE ]")
  }

  override fun onPostCreate(savedInstanceState: Bundle?) {
    super.onPostCreate(savedInstanceState)
    Log.v(tag, "[ ON POST CREATE ]")
  }

  override fun onRestart() {
    super.onRestart()
    Log.v(tag, "[ ON RESTART ]")
  }

  override fun onStart() {
    super.onStart()
    Log.v(tag, "[ ON START ]")
  }

  override fun onResume() {
    super.onResume()
    Log.v(tag, "[ ON RESUME ]")
  }

  override fun onPostResume() {
    super.onPostResume()
    Log.v(tag, "[ ON POST RESUME ]")
  }

  override fun onPause() {
    super.onPause()
    Log.v(tag, "[ ON PAUSE ]")
  }

  override fun onStop() {
    super.onStop()
    Log.v(tag, "[ ON STOP ]")
  }

  override fun onDestroy() {
    super.onDestroy()
    Log.v(tag, "[ ON DESTROY ]")
  }
}
MainActivity.kt:
package com.journaler.activity
import com.journaler.R
```

```
class MainActivity : BaseActivity() {
  override val tag = "Main activity"
  override fun getLayout() = R.layout.activity_main
}
```

Now, we are ready to define the rest of the screens. We have to create a screen for adding and editing **Notes** and a screen that does the same for **TODOs**. There is a lot of common between these screens. The only difference for now is that the **TODOs** screen has buttons for date and time. We will create a common class for everything that these screens share. Each concretization will extend it. Create a class called `ItemActivity`. Make sure it's located in the `Activity` package. Create two more classes--`NoteActivity` and `TodoActivity`. `ItemActivity` extends our `BaseActivity` class and `NoteActivity` and `TodoActivity` activity classes extend `ItemActivity` class. You will be asked to override members. Please do so. Give some meaningful value for the tag we will use in logging. To assign a proper layout ID first we must create it!

Locate the layout we created for the main screen. Now, using the same principle, create two more layouts:

- `activity_note.xml`, let it be the `LinearLayout` class if asked
- `activity_todo.xml`, let it be the `LinearLayout` class if asked

Any layout or layout member in Android gets a unique ID as `integer` representation in the `R` class that Android generates during the build. The `R` class for our application is as follows:

```
com.journaler.R
```

To access the layout, use the following line of code:

```
R.layout.layout_you_are_interested_in
```

We use static access. So, let's update our class concretizations to access layout IDs. Classes now look like this:

```
ItemActivity.kt:
abstract class ItemActivity : BaseActivity()
For now, this class is short and simple.
NoteActivity.kt:
package com.journaler.activity
import com.journaler.R
class NoteActivity : ItemActivity(){
  override val tag = "Note activity"
  override fun getLayout() = R.layout.activity_note
}
Pay attention on import for R class!
```

```
TodoActivity.kt:
package com.journaler.activity
import com.journaler.Rclass TodoActivity : ItemActivity(){
  override val tag = "Todo activity"
  override fun getLayout() = R.layout.activity_todo
}
```

Last step is to register our screens (activities) in `view groups`. Open the `manifest` file and add the following:

```
<activity
  android:name=".activity.NoteActivity"
  android:configChanges="orientation"
  android:screenOrientation="portrait" />

<activity
  android:name=".activity.TodoActivity"
  android:configChanges="orientation"
  android:screenOrientation="portrait" />
```

Both activities are locked to `portrait` orientation.

We made progress! We defined our application screens. In the next section, we will populate the screens it with UI components.

Android layouts

We will continue our work by defining layouts for each screen. Layouts in Android are defined in XML. We will mention the most commonly used layout types and populate them with commonly used layout components.

Each layout file has one of the layout types as its top-level container. Layouts can contain other layouts with UI components and so on. We can nest it. Let's mention the most commonly used layout types:

- **Linear layout**: This aligns UI components in a linear order, vertically or horizontally
- **Relative layout**: These UI components are aligned relatively to each other
- **List view layout**: All items are organized in the form of a list
- **Grid view layout**: All items are organized in the form of a grid
- **Scroll view layout**: This is used to enable scrolling when its content becomes higher than the actual height of the screen

Layout elements that we just mentioned are `view groups`. Each view group contains other views. `View groups` extend the `ViewGroup` class. At the top, everything is a `View` class. Classes (views) that are extending the `View` class, but do not extend `ViewGroup`, can't contain other elements (children). Such examples are `Button`, `ImageButton`, `ImageView`, and similar classes. Therefore, it's possible, for example, to define a `RelativeLayout` that contains a `LinearLayout`, which contains other multiple views aligned vertically or horizontally and so on.

We will now highlight some commonly used views:

- `Button`: This is a `Base` class that represents a button linked to the `onClick` action we define
- `ImageButton`: This is a button with an image used as its visual representation
- `ImageView`: This is a view that displays an image loaded from different sources
- `TextView`: This is a view that contains single or multiline non-editable text
- `EditText`: This is a view that contains single or multiline editable text
- `WebView`: This is a view that presents rendered HTML pages loaded from different sources
- `CheckBox`: This is a main two-states choice view

Every `View` and `ViewGroup` supports misc XML attributes. Some attributes are specific to only certain view types. There are also attributes that are the same for all views. We will highlight the most commonly used view attributes through the examples of our screens later in this chapter.

To assign a unique identifier by which you can access a view through the code or other layout members, you must define an ID. To assign an ID to a view, use the syntax like in this example:

```
android:id="@+id/my_button"
```

In this example, we assigned the `my_button` ID to a view. To access it from code, we will use the following:

```
R.id.my_button
```

R is a generated class providing us access to resources. To create an instance of the button, we will use the `findViewById()` method defined in the Android `Activity` class:

```
val x = findViewById(R.id.my_button) as Button
```

Since we used Kotlin, we can access it directly, as shown in this example:

```
my_button.setOnClickListener { ... }
```

 The IDE will ask you about a proper import. Keep in mind that other layout resource files can have an ID with the same name defined. In that case, it can happen that you have a wrong import! If that happens, your application will crash.

The @ symbol at the beginning of the string indicates that the XML parser should parse and expand the rest of the ID string and identify it as an ID resource. The + symbol means that this is a new resource name. When referencing an Android resource ID, you do not need the + symbol, as shown in this example:

```
<ImageView
  android:id="@+id/flowers"
  android:layout_width="fill_parent"
  android:layout_height="fill_parent"
  android:layout_above="@id/my_button"
/>
```

Let's build our UI for the main application screen! We will start with some prerequisites. In the values resource directory, create `dimens.xml` to define some dimensions we will use:

```
<?xml version="1.0" encoding="utf-8"?>
<resources>
  <dimen name="button_margin">20dp</dimen>
  <dimen name="header_height">50dp</dimen>
</resources>
```

Android defines dimensions in the following units:

- **px (pixels)**: This corresponds to actual pixels on the screen
- **in (inches)**: This is based on the physical size of the screen, that is, 1 inch = 2.54 centimeters
- **mm (millimeters)**: This is based on the physical size of the screen
- **pt (points)**: This is the 1/72 of an inch based on the physical size of the screen

And the most important for us is the following:

- **dp (Density-independent Pixels)**: This represents an abstract unit that is based on the physical density of the screen. They are relative to a 160 DPI screen. One dp is one pixel on a 160 DPI screen. The ratio of dp-to-pixel will change with the screen density, but not necessarily in direct proportion.
- **sp (Scale-independent Pixels)**: These are like the dp unit and generally used for font size.

We have to define a header layout that will be included on all screens. Create the `activity_header.xml` file and define it like this:

```xml
<?xml version="1.0" encoding="utf-8"?>
<RelativeLayout    xmlns:android=
"http://schemas.android.com/apk/res/android"
android:layout_width="match_parent"
android:layout_height="@dimen/header_height">
<Button
  android:id="@+id/sliding_menu"
  android:layout_width="@dimen/header_height"
  android:layout_height="match_parent"
  android:layout_alignParentStart="true" />

<TextView
  android:layout_centerInParent="true"
  android:id="@+id/activity_title"
  android:layout_width="wrap_content"
  android:layout_height="wrap_content" />

<Button
  android:id="@+id/filter_menu"
  android:layout_width="@dimen/header_height"
  android:layout_height="match_parent"
  android:layout_alignParentEnd="true" />

</RelativeLayout>
```

Let's explain the most important parts of it. First of all, we have defined `RelativeLayout` as our main container. Since all elements are positioned relatively to the parent and to each other, we will use some special attributes to express these relationships.

For every view, we must have width and height attributes. Values for it can be as follows:

- Dimension defined in the dimension resource file, for example:

```
android:layout_height="@dimen/header_height"
```

- Directly defined dimension value, for example:

```
android:layout_height="50dp"
```

- Match the size of the parent (`match_parent`)
- Or wrap the content of the view (`wrap_content`)

Then, we will populate the layout with children views. We have three children views. We will define two buttons and one text view. Text view is aligned to the center of the layout. Buttons are aligned with edges of the layout--one to the left and the other to the right. To achieve central alignment of the text view, we used the `layout_centerInParent` attribute. The value passed to it is the Boolean true. To align a button at the layout's left edge, we used the `layout_alignParentStart` attribute. For the right edge, we used the `layout_alignParentEnd` attribute. Each child has a proper ID assigned. We will include this in `MainActivity`:

```
<?xml version="1.0" encoding="utf-8"?>
<LinearLayout xmlns:android=
"http://schemas.android.com/apk/res/android"
android:layout_width="match_parent"
android:layout_height="match_parent"
android:orientation="vertical">

<include layout="@layout/activity_header" />

<RelativeLayout
    android:layout_width="match_parent"
    android:layout_height="match_parent">
 <ListView
    android:id="@+id/items"
    android:layout_width="match_parent"
    android:layout_height="match_parent"
    android:background="@android:color/darker_gray" />

 <android.support.design.widget.FloatingActionButton
    android:id="@+id/new_item"
    android:layout_width="wrap_content"
    android:layout_height="wrap_content"
    android:layout_alignParentBottom="true"
    android:layout_alignParentEnd="true"
```

```
        android:layout_margin="@dimen/button_margin" />

    </RelativeLayout>
    </LinearLayout>
```

The main container for `Main activity` is `LinearLayout`. An orientation attribute for `LinearLayout` is mandatory:

```
    android:orientation="vertical"
```

Values that can be assigned to it are vertical and horizontal. As the first child of the `Main activity`, we included the `activity_header` layout. Then we defined `RelativeLayout`, which fills the rest of screen.

`RelativeLayout` has two members, `ListView` that will present all our items. We assigned a background to it. We did not define our own color in the colors resource file, but the one predefined in Android. Last view we have here is `FloatingActionButton`, the same one you can see in the Gmail Android application. The button will be positioned over the list with items at the bottom of the screen aligned to the right. We also set a margin that will surround the button from all sides. Take a look at the attributes we used.

Before we run our application again, we will make a few more changes. Open `BaseActivity` and update its code as follows:

```
    ...
    protected abstract fun getActivityTitle(): Int

    override fun onCreate(savedInstanceState: Bundle?) {
        super.onCreate(savedInstanceState)
        setContentView(getLayout())
        activity_title.setText(getActivityTitle())
        Log.v(tag, "[ ON CREATE ]")
    }
    ...
```

We introduced the `abstract` method that will provide a proper title for each activity. We will `access` the `activity_title` view defined in `activity_header.xml`, which is included in our activity, and assign the value we get by executing the method.

Open `MainActivity` and override the following method:

```
    override fun getActivityTitle() = R.string.app_name
```

Add the same line to ItemActivity. Finally, run the application. Your main screen should look like this:

Let's define layouts for the rest of the screens. For the **Notes**, **Add/Edit note screen**, we will define the following layout:

```xml
<?xml version="1.0" encoding="utf-8"?>
<ScrollView xmlns:android=
 "http://schemas.android.com/apk/res/android"
android:layout_width="match_parent"
android:layout_height="match_parent"
android:fillViewport="true" >

<LinearLayout
   android:layout_width="match_parent"
   android:layout_height="wrap_content"
   android:orientation="vertical">

   <include layout="@layout/activity_header" />

   <EditText
     android:id="@+id/note_title"
     android:layout_width="match_parent"
     android:layout_height="wrap_content"
     android:hint="@string/title"
     android:padding="@dimen/form_padding" />

   <EditText
     android:id="@+id/note_content"
     android:layout_width="match_parent"
     android:layout_height="match_parent"
     android:gravity="top"
     android:hint="@string/your_note_content_goes_here"
     android:padding="@dimen/form_padding" />

</LinearLayout>
</ScrollView>
```

There are a few important things that we must highlight. We will explain them one by one. We introduced ScrollView as our top container for the layout. Since we will populate multiline notes, it will happen that its content goes below the physical limit of the screen. If that happens, we will be able to scroll the content. We used one very important attribute-- fillViewport. This attribute tells the container to stretch to the whole screen. All children use that space.

Using EditText views

We introduced the `EditText` views to enter editable text content. You can see some new attributes here:

- **hint**: This defines the default string value that will be presented to the user
- **padding**: This is the space between the view itself and its content
- **gravity**: This defines direction for the content; in our case, all text will stick to the top of the parent view

 Note that, for all strings and dimensions, we defined proper entries in the `strings.xml` file and the `dimens.xml` file.

The strings resource file now looks like this:

```
<resources>
  <string name="app_name">Journaler</string>
  <string name="title">Title</string>
  <string name="your_note_content_goes_here">Your note content goes
  here.</string>
</resources>
Todos screen will be very similar to this:
<?xml version="1.0" encoding="utf-8"?>
<ScrollView xmlns:android=
"http://schemas.android.com/apk/res/android"
android:layout_width="match_parent"
android:layout_height="match_parent"
android:fillViewport="true">

<LinearLayout
  android:layout_width="match_parent"
  android:layout_height="wrap_content"
  android:orientation="vertical">

<include layout="@layout/activity_header" />

<EditText
  android:id="@+id/todo_title"
  android:layout_width="match_parent"
  android:layout_height="wrap_content"
  android:hint="@string/title"
  android:padding="@dimen/form_padding" />

<LinearLayout
```

```
        android:layout_width="match_parent"
        android:layout_height="wrap_content"
        android:orientation="horizontal"
        android:weightSum="1">

    <Button
        android:id="@+id/pick_date"
        android:text="@string/pick_a_date"
        android:layout_width="0dp"
        android:layout_height="wrap_content"
        android:layout_weight="0.5" />

    <Button
        android:id="@+id/pick_time"
        android:text="@string/pick_time"
        android:layout_width="0dp"
        android:layout_height="wrap_content"
        android:layout_weight="0.5" />

</LinearLayout>

<EditText
        android:id="@+id/todo_content"
        android:layout_width="match_parent"
        android:layout_height="match_parent"
        android:gravity="top"
        android:hint="@string/your_note_content_goes_here"
        android:padding="@dimen/form_padding" />
</LinearLayout>
</ScrollView>
```

Again, the top container is `ScrollView`. Compared to the previous screen, we have introduced some differences. We added the container to hold buttons for date and time picking. The orientation is horizontal. We set the parent container attribute, `weightSum`, to define the weight value that can be divided by children views so each child takes the amount of space defined by its own weight. So, `weightSum` is one. First button has a `layout_weight` of `0.5`. It will consume 50% of the horizontal space. The second button has the same value. We achieved view splitting in two halves. Locate the bottom of your XML and click on **Design** to switch to **Design** view. Your buttons should look like this:

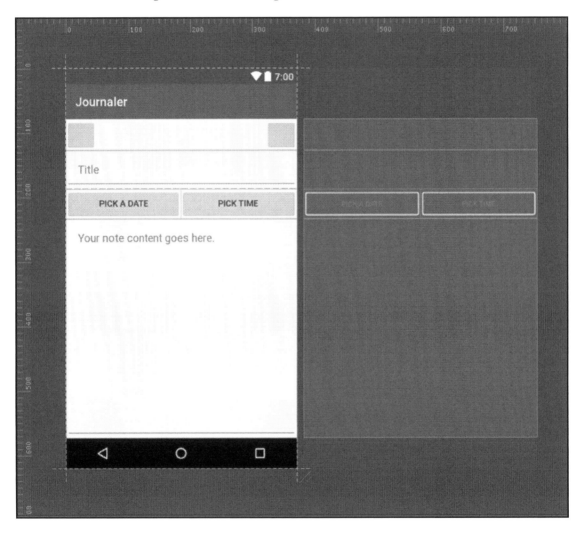

We defined layouts for our screens. To express how these screens should look, we relied on many different attributes. This is just a small portion of the available attributes we can use. To make this section complete, we will present you with some other important attributes that you will use in everyday development.

The margins attribute

Margins accept dimension resources or direct dimension values in one of the following supported units:

- `layout_margin`
- `layout_marginTop`
- `layout_marginBottom`
- `layout_marginStart`
- `layout_marginEnd`

The padding attribute

Padding accepts dimension resources or direct dimension values in one of the following supported units:

- `padding`
- `paddingTop`
- `paddingBottom`
- `paddingStart`
- `paddingEnd`

Checking out the gravity attribute

View Gravity:

- **gravity (direction of the content inside the view)**: This accepts the following-- `top`, `left`, `right`, `start`, `end`, `center`, `center_horizontal`, `center_vertical`, and many other
- **layout_gravity (direction of the content inside the view parent)**: This accepts the following-- `top`, `left`, `right`, `left`, `start`, `end`, `center`, `center_horizontal`, `center_vertical`, and many others

It's possible to combine values for gravity as follows:

```
android:gravity="top|center_horizontal"
```

Looking at other attributes

We just saw the most important attributes we will use. It is time to see other attributes you may find handy. Other attributes are as follows:

- `src`: This is the resource to use:

  ```
  android:src="@drawable/icon"
  ```

- `background`: Background for the view, hex color, or color resource is as follows:

  ```
  android:background="#ddff00"
  android:background="@color/colorAccent"
  ```

- `onClick`: This is the method to be invoked when a user clicks on the view (usually a button)
- `visibility`: This is the visibility of the view, which accepts the following parameters--gone (invisible and does not consume any layout space), invisible (invisible but consumes layout space), and visible
- `hint`: This is the hint text for the view, and it accepts a string value or a string resource
- `text`: This is the text for the view, and it accepts a string value or a string resource
- `textColor`: This is the color for the text, hex color, or color resource
- `textSize`: This is the size for the text in supported units--direct unit value or dimension resource
- `textStyle`: This is the style resource that defines attributes to assign to view, as follows:

  ```
  style="@style/my_theme"
  . . .
  ```

In this section, we covered working with attributes. Without them, we can't develop our UI. In the rest of this chapter, we will introduce you to Android Context.

Understanding Android Context

All our main screens now have their layouts defined. We will now explain Android Context since each screen we just created represents one `Context` instance. If you go through the class definition and follow class extension, you will realize that each activity we create extends the `Context` class.

`Context` represents the current state of the application or object. It is used to access specific classes and resources of the application. For example, consider the following lines of code:

```
resources.getDimension(R.dimen.header_height)
getString(R.string.app_name)
```

Access we showed is provided by the `Context` class, which shows our activities are extending. `Context` is needed when we have to launch another activity, start a service, or send broadcast messages. We will show use of these methods when the time is proper. We already mentioned that each screen (`Activity`) of an Android application represents a `Context` instance. Activities are not the only classes that represent context. Except activities, we have the service context type too.

Android Context has the following purposes:

- Showing a dialog
- Starting an activity
- Inflating layout
- Starting a service
- Binding to a service
- Sending a broadcast message
- Registering for broadcast messages
- And, like we already showed in the preceding example, loading resources

`Context` is an important part of Android and one of the most frequently used classes of the framework. Later in this book, you will meet other `Context` classes. However, before that, we will be focused on fragments and their explanation.

Understanding fragments

We have mentioned that the central part of our main screen will contain a list of filtered items. We want to have several pages with a different set of filters applied. A user will be able to swipe left or right to change the filtered content and navigate through the following pages:

- All displayed
- Items for **Today**
- Items for **Next 7 Days**
- Only **Notes**
- Only **TODO**s

To achieve this functionality, we will need to define fragments. What are fragments and what is their purpose?

A fragment is a portion of the interface of an `Activity` instance. You can use fragments to create multiplane screens or screens with view paging, like in our case.

Just like activities, fragments have their own lifecycle. Fragment lifecycle is presented in the following diagram:

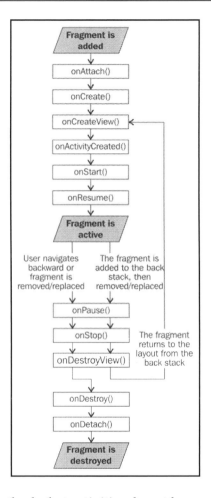

There are some additional methods that activities do not have:

- onAttach(): This is executed when a fragment is associated to an activity.
- onCreateView(): This instantiates and returns a fragment's view instance.
- onActivityCreated(): This executes when an activity's onCreate() is executed.
- onDestroyView(): This executes when a view is destroyed; it is convenient when some cleanup is needed.
- onDetach(): This is executed when a fragment is unassociated from an activity. To demonstrate the use of fragments, we will put the central part of our MainActivity into one single fragment. Later, we will move it to ViewPager and add more pages to it.

Create a new package called `fragment`. Then, create a new class called `BaseFragment`. Update your `BaseFragment` class according to this example:

```
package com.journaler.fragment

import android.os.Bundle
import android.support.v4.app.Fragment
import android.util.Log
import android.view.LayoutInflater
import android.view.View
import android.view.ViewGroup

abstract class BaseFragment : Fragment() {
  protected abstract val logTag : String
  protected abstract fun getLayout(): Int

override fun onCreateView(
  inflater: LayoutInflater?, container: ViewGroup?,
  savedInstanceState: Bundle?
  ): View? {
    Log.d(logTag, "[ ON CREATE VIEW ]")
    return inflater?.inflate(getLayout(), container, false)
  }

 override fun onPause() {
    super.onPause()
    Log.v(logTag, "[ ON PAUSE ]")
 }

 override fun onResume() {
    super.onResume()
    Log.v(logTag, "[ ON RESUME ]")
 }

 override fun onDestroy() {
    super.onDestroy()
    Log.d(logTag, "[ ON DESTROY ]")
 }

 }
```

Pay attention to imports:

```
import android.support.v4.app.Fragment
```

We want maximal compatibility, so we are importing fragments from the Android support library.

As you can see, we did something similar to what we did with `BaseActivity`. Create a new fragment, a class named `ItemsFragment`. Update its code according to this example:

```
package com.journaler.fragment
import com.journaler.R

class ItemsFragment : BaseFragment() {
  override val logTag = "Items fragment"
  override fun getLayout(): Int {
    return R.layout.fragment_items
  }
}
```

We introduced a new layout that actually contains the list view we had in `activity_main`. Create a new layout resource called `fragment_items`:

```
<?xml version="1.0" encoding="utf-8"?>
<RelativeLayout xmlns:android=
 "http://schemas.android.com/apk/res/android"
android:layout_width="match_parent"
android:layout_height="match_parent">

<ListView
   android:id="@+id/items"
   android:layout_width="match_parent"
   android:layout_height="match_parent"
   android:background="@android:color/darker_gray" />

<android.support.design.widget.FloatingActionButton
   android:id="@+id/new_item"
   android:layout_width="wrap_content"
   android:layout_height="wrap_content"
   android:layout_alignParentBottom="true"
   android:layout_alignParentEnd="true"
   android:layout_margin="@dimen/button_margin" />

</RelativeLayout>
```

You already saw this. It is just a part we extracted from the `activity_main` layout. Instead of this, we put the following in the `activity_main` layout:

```
<?xml version="1.0" encoding="utf-8"?>
<LinearLayout xmlns:android=
 "http://schemas.android.com/apk/res/android"
 android:layout_width="match_parent"
 android:layout_height="match_parent"
 android:orientation="vertical">
<include layout="@layout/activity_header" />
```

```
<FrameLayout
    android:id="@+id/fragment_container"
    android:layout_width="match_parent"
    android:layout_height="match_parent" />
</LinearLayout>
```

FrameLayout will be our fragment container. To show the new fragment in fragment_containerFrameLayout, update the code of MainActivity as follows:

```
class MainActivity : BaseActivity() {

    override val tag = "Main activity"
    override fun getLayout() = R.layout.activity_main
    override fun getActivityTitle() = R.string.app_name

    override fun onCreate(savedInstanceState: Bundle?) {
        super.onCreate(savedInstanceState)
        val fragment = ItemsFragment()
        supportFragmentManager
                .beginTransaction()
                .add(R.id.fragment_container, fragment)
                .commit()
    }
}
```

We accessed supportFragmentManager. If we did not choose to use the Android support library, we would use fragmentManager. Then, we start fragment transaction, to which, we add a new fragment instance that will be associated to fragment_container FrameLayout. The commit method executes this transaction. If we run our application now, we will not notice anything different, but, if we take a look at the logs, we may notice that the fragment lifecycle has been executed:

```
V/Journaler: [ ON CREATE ]
V/Main activity: [ ON CREATE ]
D/Items fragment: [ ON CREATE VIEW ]
V/Main activity: [ ON START ]
V/Main activity: [ ON POST CREATE ]
V/Main activity: [ ON RESUME ]
V/Items fragment: [ ON RESUME ]
V/Main activity: [ ON POST RESUME ]
```

We added a simple fragment to our interface. In the next section, you will learn more about fragment manager and its purpose. Then, we will do something very interesting--we will create a ViewPager.

Fragment manager

The component that is responsible for interacting with fragments from your current activity is **fragment manager**. We can use the `FragmentManager` form in two different imports:

- `android.app.FragmentManager`
- `android.support.v4.app.Fragment`

Import from the Android support library is recommended.

To perform a series of edit operations, start the fragment transaction using the `beginTransaction()` method. It will return an instance of transaction. To add a fragment (usually the first), use the `add` method, like in our example. The method takes the same arguments, but replaces the current fragment if already added. If we are planning to navigate backwards through fragments, it is needed to add the transaction to back stack by using the `addToBackStack` method. It takes a name parameter or null if we do not want to assign a name.

Finally, we schedule a transaction by executing `commit()`. This is a not momental operation. It schedules operations on the application's main thread. When the main thread is ready, the transaction will be executed. Think about it when planning and implementing your code!

Fragments stack

To illustrate examples of fragments and the back stack, we will extend our application further. We will create a fragment to display a user manual containing the text, `Lorem ipsum`. First we need to create a new fragment. Create a new layout named `fragment_manual`. Update the layout as shown in this example:

```
<?xml version="1.0" encoding="utf-8"?>
<LinearLayout xmlns:android=
 "http://schemas.android.com/apk/res/android"
android:layout_width="match_parent"
android:layout_height="match_parent"
android:orientation="vertical">

<TextView
  android:layout_width="match_parent"
  android:layout_height="match_parent"
  android:layout_margin="10dp"
  android:text="@string/lorem_ipsum_sit_dolore"
  android:textSize="14sp" />
```

```
</LinearLayout>
```

This is a simple layout containing the text view stretched across the whole parent view. The fragment that will use this layout will be called `ManualFragment`. Create a class for the fragment and make sure it has the following content:

```
package com.journaler.fragment
import com.journaler.R

class ManualFragment : BaseFragment() {
  override val logTag = "Manual Fragment"
  override fun getLayout() = R.layout.fragment_manual
}
```

Finally, let's add it to the fragment back stack. Update the `onCreate()` method of `MainActivity` as follows:

```
override fun onCreate(savedInstanceState: Bundle?) {
  super.onCreate(savedInstanceState)
  val fragment = ItemsFragment()
  supportFragmentManager
          .beginTransaction()
          .add(R.id.fragment_container, fragment)
          .commit()
  filter_menu.setText("H")
  filter_menu.setOnClickListener {
    val userManualFrg = ManualFragment()
    supportFragmentManager
            .beginTransaction()
            .replace(R.id.fragment_container, userManualFrg)
            .addToBackStack("User manual")
            .commit()
  }
}
```

Build and run the application. The top-right header button will have label H; click on it. The fragment containing the `Lorem ipsum` text fills the view. Tap on the back button and the fragment disappears. This means that you successfully added and removed the fragment from the back stack.

We have to try one more thing--click on the same button two to three times in the row. Click on the back button. Then again. And again. You will go through the back stack until you reach the first fragment. If you tap on the back button once more, you will leave the application. Observe your Logcat.

Do you remember the order in which lifecycle methods are executed? You can recognize that each time a new fragment is added to the top, the one below pauses. When we start going back by pressing the back button, the fragment on the top pauses and the one below resumes. Fragments that are removed from the back stack enter the `onDestroy()` method at the end.

Creating View Pager

As we mentioned, we want our items to display on several pages that can be swiped. To do so, we need `ViewPager`. `ViewPager` makes it possible to swipe between different fragments as a part of the fragment collection. We will make some changes to our code. Open the `activity_main` layout and update it like this:

```
<?xml version="1.0" encoding="utf-8"?>
<LinearLayout xmlns:android=
 "http://schemas.android.com/apk/res/android"
android:layout_width="match_parent"
android:layout_height="match_parent"
android:orientation="vertical">
<android.support.v4.view.ViewPager  xmlns:android=
"http://schemas.android.com/apk/res/android"
    android:id="@+id/pager"
    android:layout_width="match_parent"
    android:layout_height="match_parent" />

</LinearLayout>
```

Instead of `FrameLayout`, we put the `ViewPager` view. Then, open the `MainActivity` class and update it like this:

```
class MainActivity : BaseActivity() {
  override val tag = "Main activity"
  override fun getLayout() = R.layout.activity_main
  override fun getActivityTitle() = R.string.app_name

  override fun onCreate(savedInstanceState: Bundle?) {
    super.onCreate(savedInstanceState)
    pager.adapter = ViewPagerAdapter(supportFragmentManager)
}

private class ViewPagerAdapter(manager: FragmentManager) :
FragmentStatePagerAdapter(manager) {
  override fun getItem(position: Int): Fragment {
    return ItemsFragment()
```

```
    }

    override fun getCount(): Int {
      return 5
    }
  }
}
```

The main part of our work is to define the `adapter` class for the pager. We must extend the `FragmentStatePagerAdapter` class; its constructor accepts the fragment manager that will deal with fragment transactions. To complete work properly, override the `getItem()` methods that returns an instance of the fragment and `getCount()` that returns the total number of expected fragments. The rest of the code is very clear--we access to pager (the ID of `ViewPager` we assigned) and assign to it a new instance of the adapter.

Run your application and try swiping left and right. While you're swiping, observe Logcat and the lifecycle logs.

Making animations with transitions

To animate transactions between fragments, it's needed to assign some animation resources to the transaction instance. As you remember, after we begin the fragment transaction, we get one transaction instance. We can then access this instance and execute the method as follows:

- `setCustomAnimations (int enter, int exit, int popEnter, int popExit)`

Or, we can use this method:

- `setCustomAnimations (int enter, int exit)`

Here, each parameter represents the animation used in this transaction. We can define our own animation resources or use one of the predefined ones:

Dialog fragments

If you need to display any of your fragments floating above the rest of application's UI, then `DialogFragment` is perfect for you. All you need to do is define the fragment very similarly to what we did so far. Define the class that is extending `DialogFragment`. Override the `onCreateView()` method so you can define the layout. You can override `onCreate()` as well. The last thing you have to do is to display it as follows:

```
val dialog = MyDialogFragment()
dialog.show(supportFragmentManager, "dialog")
```

In this example, we passed the instance and the name for the transaction to the fragment manager.

Notifications

If the content you are planning to present to the end user is short, then, instead of dialogs, you should try notifications. We can customize notifications in many different ways. Here, we will present some basic customizations. Creating and displaying notifications is easy. It requires more knowledge of Android than we have learned so far. Don't worry; we will do our best to explain it. You will face many of these classes in the later chapters.

We will demonstrate how to use notifications as follows:

1. Define a `notificationBuilder` and pass a small icon, content title, and content text as follows:

```
val notificationBuilder = NotificationCompat.Builder(context)
        .setSmallIcon(R.drawable.icon)
        .setContentTitle("Hello!")
        .setContentText("We love Android!")
```

2. Define `Intent` for activity of your application. (More about intents, will be discussed in the next chapter):

```
val result = Intent(context, MyActivity::class.java)
```

3. Now define the stack builder object that will contain the back stack for the activity as follows:

```
val builder = TaskStackBuilder.create(context)
```

5. Add back stack for the intent:

```
builder.addParentStack(MyActivity::class.java)
```

6. Add intent at the top of the stack:

```
builder.addNextIntent(result)
val resultPendingIntent = builder.getPendingIntent(
  0,
  PendingIntent.FLAG_UPDATE_CURRENT )Define ID for the
  notification and notify:
val id = 0
notificationBuilder.setContentIntent(resultPendingIntent)
val manager = getSystemService(NOTIFICATION_SERVICE) as
NotificationManager
manager.notify(id, notificationBuilder.build())
```

Other important UI components

Android Framework is large and powerful. So far, we have covered `View` classes, which are most frequently used. However, there are a lot of `View` classes that we did not cover. Some of them will be covered later, but some that are not so frequently used will be just mentioned. Anyway, it's good to know that these views exist and it is a good starting point for your further learning. Let's give some examples to give you an idea:

- **ConstraintLayout**: This views and positions child elements in a flexible way
- **CoordinatorLayout**: This is a very advanced version of FrameLayout
- **SurfaceView**: This is a view used for drawing (especially when high performance is needed)
- **VideoView**: This is set to play video content

Summary

In this chapter, you learned how to create screens divided into sections, and now you are able to create basic and complex layouts containing buttons and images. You also learned how to create dialogs and notifications. In the following chapter, you will connect all your screens and navigation actions.

4
Connecting Screen Flow

Hello fellow readers! We have come to an important point in our application development--connecting our screens. As you know, we created screens in the previous chapter, and, in this chapter, we will connect them by using Android's powerful framework. We will continue with our work, and, with Android, we will do more serious stuff with our UI. Prepare yourself and concentrate on every aspect of this chapter. It will be very interesting! We promise!

In this chapter, we will cover the following topics:

- Creating an application bar
- Using drawer navigation
- Android intents
- Passing information between activities and fragments

Creating an application bar

We are continuing our journey through Android Application Development. So far, we have created a base for our application, defined the ground for a UI, and created major screens; however, these screens are not connected. In this chapter, we will connect them and make fantastic interaction.

Since everything starts from our `MainActivity` class, we will apply some improvements before we set some actions to trigger other screens. We have to *wrap* it with an application bar. What is an application bar? It's a piece of the UI that is used to access other parts of the application and provide visual structure with interactive elements. We already have one, but it's not the usual Android application bar. At this point, our application is has a modified application bar, and we want it to have a standard Android application bar.

Here, we will show you exactly how to create one.

Start by replacing a top-level activity extension to `AppCompatActivity`. We need to access features that are needed for an application bar. `AppCompatActivity` will add these additional features to standard `FragmentActivity`. Your `BaseActivity` definition should now look like this:

```
abstract class BaseActivity : AppCompatActivity() {
...
```

Then update the theme application that is used, so the application bar can be used. Open **Android Manifest** and set a new theme as follows:

```
...
<application
  android:name=".Journaler"
  android:allowBackup="false"
  android:icon="@mipmap/ic_launcher"
  android:label="@string/app_name"
  android:roundIcon="@mipmap/ic_launcher_round"
  android:supportsRtl="true"
  android:theme="@style/Theme.AppCompat.Light.NoActionBar">
...
```

Now open your `activity_main` layout. Remove the header included directive and add `Toolbar`:

```
<?xml version="1.0" encoding="utf-8"?>
<LinearLayout xmlns:android=
  "http://schemas.android.com/apk/res/android"
android:layout_width="match_parent"
android:layout_height="match_parent"
android:orientation="vertical">

<android.support.v7.widget.Toolbar
  android:id="@+id/toolbar"
  android:layout_width="match_parent"
  android:layout_height="50dp"
  android:background="@color/colorPrimary"
  android:elevation="4dp" />

<android.support.v4.view.ViewPager
  android:id="@+id/pager"
  android:layout_width="match_parent"
  android:layout_height="match_parent" />

</LinearLayout>
```

Apply the same change to all layouts. When you finish it, update your `BaseActivity` code to use the new `Toolbar`. Your `onCreate()` method should now look like this:

```
override fun onCreate(savedInstanceState: Bundle?) {
  super.onCreate(savedInstanceState)
  setContentView(getLayout())
  setSupportActionBar(toolbar)
Log.v(tag, "[ ON CREATE ]")
  }
```

We assigned an application bar by calling the `setSupportActionBar()` method and passing the toolbar's ID from the layout. If you run the application, it will look like this:

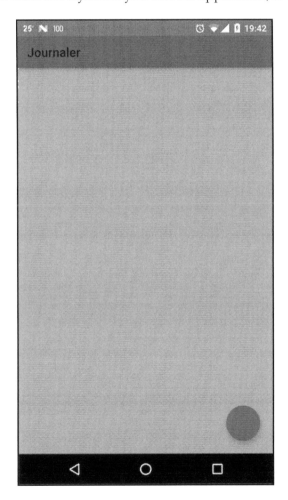

We lost the buttons we had in our header! Don't worry, we will get them back! We will create a menu that will handle actions instead of buttons. In Android, a menu is an interface that is used to manage the items, and you can define your own menu resource. In the `/res` directory, create a `menu` folder. Right-click on the `menu` folder and choose the **New** | **New menu resource** file. Call it **main**. A new XML file opens. Update its content according to this example:

```xml
<?xml version="1.0" encoding="utf-8"?>
<menu xmlns:android="http://schemas.android.com/apk/res/android"
xmlns:app="http://schemas.android.com/apk/res-auto">

<item
  app:showAsAction="ifRoom"
  android:orderInCategory="1"
  android:id="@+id/drawing_menu"
  android:icon="@android:drawable/ic_dialog_dialer"
  android:title="@string/mnu" />

<item
  app:showAsAction="ifRoom"
  android:orderInCategory="2"
  android:id="@+id/options_menu"
  android:icon="@android:drawable/arrow_down_float"
  android:title="@string/mnu" />
</menu>
```

We set common attributes, the icon, and the order. To make sure your icons will be visible, use the following:

```
app:showAsAction="ifRoom"
```

By doing this, items in the menu will be expanded if there is any space available; otherwise, they will be accessible through the context menu. Other options of spacing in Android that you can choose are as follows:

- **Always**: This button is always placed in an application bar
- **Never**: This button is never placed in an application bar
- **collapseAction View**: This button can be shown as a widget
- **withText**: This button is displayed with text

To assign a menu to the application bar, add the following to `BaseActivity`:

```
override fun onCreateOptionsMenu(menu: Menu): Boolean {
  menuInflater.inflate(R.menu.main, menu)
  return true
}
```

Finally, connect actions to menu items and extend `MainActivity` by adding the following piece of code:

```
override fun onOptionsItemSelected(item: MenuItem): Boolean {
  when (item.itemId) {
    R.id.drawing_menu -> {
      Log.v(tag, "Main menu.")
      return true
    }
    R.id.options_menu -> {
      Log.v(tag, "Options menu.")
      return true
    }
    else -> return super.onOptionsItemSelected(item)
  }
}
```

Here, we overrode the `onOptionsItemSelected()` method and handled cases for menu item ID. On each selection, we added a log message. Now run your application. You should see these menu items:

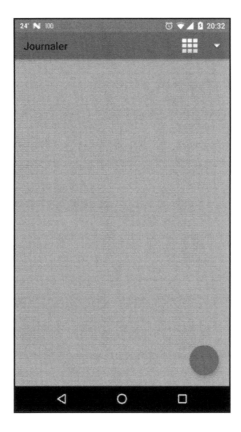

Click a few times on each item and observe Logcat. You should see logs similar to this:

```
V/Main activity: Main menu.
V/Main activity: Options menu.
V/Main activity: Options menu.
V/Main activity: Options menu.

V/Main activity: Main menu.

V/Main activity: Main menu.
```

We successfully switched our header to the application bar. It is quite different to the header we had in the application wireframe. This is not important at the moment since we will do some significant styling in the next chapters. Our application bar will look different.

In the following section, we will deal with the navigation drawer, and we will begin to assemble our application's navigation.

Using the navigation drawer

As you probably remember, in our mockup we have presented that there will be links to filtered data (**Notes** and **Todos**). We will filter these by using the navigation drawer. Every modern application uses a navigation drawer. It's a piece of the UI that displays the application's navigation options. To define the drawer, we have to put the DrawerLayout view in our layout. Open activity_main and apply the following modification:

```xml
<?xml version="1.0" encoding="utf-8"?>
<android.support.v4.widget.DrawerLayout    xmlns:android=
"http://schemas.android.com/apk/res/android"
 android:id="@+id/drawer_layout"
 android:layout_width="match_parent"
 android:layout_height="match_parent">

<LinearLayout
  android:layout_width="match_parent"
  android:layout_height="match_parent"
  android:orientation="vertical">

<android.support.v7.widget.Toolbar
  android:id="@+id/toolbar"
  android:layout_width="match_parent"
  android:layout_height="50dp"
  android:background="@color/colorPrimary"
  android:elevation="4dp" />

<android.support.v4.view.ViewPager xmlns:android=
"http://schemas.android.com/apk/res/android"
  android:id="@+id/pager"
  android:layout_width="match_parent"
  android:layout_height="match_parent" />

</LinearLayout>

<ListView
   android:id="@+id/left_drawer"
   android:layout_width="240dp"
```

```
      android:layout_height="match_parent"
      android:layout_gravity="start"
      android:background="@android:color/darker_gray"
      android:choiceMode="singleChoice"
      android:divider="@android:color/transparent"
      android:dividerHeight="1dp" />
  </android.support.v4.widget.DrawerLayout>
```

The main content of the screen must be the first child of `DrawerLayout`. The navigation drawer uses the second child as the content of the drawer. In our case, it's `ListView`. To tell the navigation drawer if navigation should be positioned left or right, use the `layout_gravity` attribute. If we plan to use the navigation drawer positioned to the right, we should set the attribute value to `end`.

Now we have an empty navigation drawer, and we have to populate it with some buttons. Create a new layout file for each navigation item. Call it `adapter_navigation_drawer`. Define it as a simple linear layout with only one button inside:

```
<?xml version="1.0" encoding="utf-8"?>
<LinearLayout xmlns:android=
"http://schemas.android.com/apk/res/android"
  android:layout_width="match_parent"
  android:layout_height="match_parent"
  android:orientation="vertical">

<Button
  android:id="@+id/drawer_item"
  android:layout_width="match_parent"
  android:layout_height="wrap_content" />

</LinearLayout>
```

Then, create a new package called `navigation`. In this package, create a new Kotlin `data` class, like this:

```
package com.journaler.navigation
data class NavigationDrawerItem(
  val title: String,
  val onClick: Runnable
)
```

We defined a drawer item entity. Now create one more class:

```
class NavigationDrawerAdapter(
    val ctx: Context,
    val items: List<NavigationDrawerItem>
) : BaseAdapter() {
```

```
override fun getView(position: Int, v: View?, group: ViewGroup?):
View {
  val inflater = LayoutInflater.from(ctx)
  var view = v
  if (view == null) {
    view = inflater.inflate(
      R.layout.adapter_navigation_drawer, null
    ) as LinearLayout
  }

  val item = items[position]
  val title = view.findViewById<Button>(R.id.drawer_item)
  title.text = item.title
  title.setOnClickListener {
    item.onClick.run()
  }

  return view
}

override fun getItem(position: Int): Any {
  return items[position]
}

override fun getItemId(position: Int): Long {
  return 0L
}

override fun getCount(): Int {
  return items.size
}

}
```

This class shown here extends Android's `BaseAdapter` and overrides methods needed for the adapter to provide view instances. All views that the adapter creates will be assigned to expand `ListView` in our navigation drawer.

Finally, we will assign this adapter. To do that, we need to update our `MainActivity` class by executing the following piece of code:

```
class MainActivity : BaseActivity() {
...
override fun onCreate(savedInstanceState: Bundle?) {
  super.onCreate(savedInstanceState)
  pager.adapter = ViewPagerAdapter(supportFragmentManager)

  val menuItems = mutableListOf<NavigationDrawerItem>()
```

```
val today = NavigationDrawerItem(
  getString(R.string.today),
    Runnable {
      pager.setCurrentItem(0, true)
    }
  )

val next7Days = NavigationDrawerItem(
    getString(R.string.next_seven_days),
      Runnable {
        pager.setCurrentItem(1, true)
      }
  )

 val todos = NavigationDrawerItem(
    getString(R.string.todos),
      Runnable {
        pager.setCurrentItem(2, true)
      }
  )

 val notes = NavigationDrawerItem(
    getString(R.string.notes),
      Runnable {
        pager.setCurrentItem(3, true)
      }
  )

menuItems.add(today)
menuItems.add(next7Days)
menuItems.add(todos)
menuItems.add(notes)

val navgationDraweAdapter =
  NavigationDrawerAdapter(this, menuItems)
left_drawer.adapter = navgationDraweAdapter
}
override fun onOptionsItemSelected(item: MenuItem): Boolean {
  when (item.itemId) {
    R.id.drawing_menu -> {
      drawer_layout.openDrawer(GravityCompat.START)
      return true
    }
    R.id.options_menu -> {
      Log.v(tag, "Options menu.")
      return true
    }
    else -> return super.onOptionsItemSelected(item)
```

```
            }
        }
    }
```

In this code example, we instantiated several `NavigationDrawerItem` instances, then, we assigned a title to the buttons and `Runnable` actions that we will execute. Each `Runnable` will jump to a specific page of our view pager. We passed all instances to the adapter as one single mutable list. You may have also noticed that we changed the line for the `drawing_menu` item. By clicking on it, we will expand our navigation drawer. Please follow these steps:

1. Build your application and run it.
2. Click on the menu button at the top-right position of the main screen or expand the navigation drawer by swiping from the far-left side of the screen to the right.
3. Click on buttons.
4. You will notice that the view pager is animating its page positions below the navigation drawer.

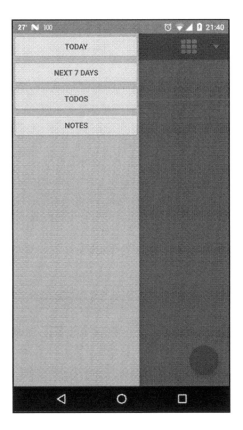

Connecting activities

As you remember, other than `MainActivity`, we also have some more activities. In our application, we created activities to create/edit **Notes** and **TODOs**. Our plan is to connect them to the button click events, and then, when the user clicks on the button, the proper screen will open. We will start by defining an `enum` that represents an operation that we will perform in an opened activity. When we open it, we can view, create, or update **Note** or **Todo**. Create a new package called `model` and `enum` with the name `MODE`. Make sure you have the following `enum` values:

```
enum class MODE(val mode: Int) {
  CREATE(0),
  EDIT(1),
  VIEW(2);

  companion object {
    val EXTRAS_KEY = "MODE"

    fun getByValue(value: Int): MODE {
      values().forEach {
        item ->

        if (item.mode == value) {
          return item
        }
      }
      return VIEW
    }
  }
}
```

We added a few additions here. In `enum`'s companion object, we defined the extras key definition. Soon, you will need it, and you will understand its purpose. We also created a method that will give us an `enum` based on its value.

As you probably remember, both activities for working with **Notes** and **Todos** share the same class. Open `ItemActivity` and extend it as follows:

```
abstract class ItemActivity : BaseActivity() {
  protected var mode = MODE.VIEW
  override fun getActivityTitle() = R.string.app_name
  override fun onCreate(savedInstanceState: Bundle?) {
    super.onCreate(savedInstanceState)
    val modeToSet = intent.getIntExtra(MODE.EXTRAS_KEY,
    MODE.VIEW.mode)
    mode = MODE.getByValue(modeToSet)
```

```
        Log.v(tag, "Mode [ $mode ]")
      }
    }
```

We introduced a field mode of the type we just defined that will tell us if we are viewing, creating, or editing a **Note** or **Todo** item. Then, we overrode the onCreate() method. This is important! When we click on the button and open the activity, we will pass some values to it. This code snippet retrieves the value we passed. To achieve that, we access the Intent instance (in the next section, we will explain intents) and the integer field called MODE (value of MODE.EXTRAS_KEY). The method that gives us this value is called getIntExtra(). There is a version of the method for every type. If there is no value, MODE.VIEW.mode is returned. Finally, we set mode to a value we obtained by getting the MODE instance from the integer value.

The last piece of the puzzle is triggering an activity opening. Open ItemsFragment and extend it as follows:

```
class ItemsFragment : BaseFragment() {
  ...
  override fun onCreateView(
    inflater: LayoutInflater?,
    container: ViewGroup?,
    savedInstanceState: Bundle?
  ): View? {
      val view = inflater?.inflate(getLayout(), container, false)
      val btn = view?.findViewById<FloatingActionButton>
      (R.id.new_item)
      btn?.setOnClickListener {
        val items = arrayOf(
          getString(R.string.todos),
          getString(R.string.notes)
        )
        val builder =
        AlertDialog.Builder(this@ItemsFragment.context)
        .setTitle(R.string.choose_a_type)
        .setItems(
          items,
          { _, which ->
           when (which) {
           0 -> {
             openCreateTodo()
           }
           1 -> {
             openCreateNote()
           }
           else -> Log.e(logTag, "Unknown option selected
```

```
                 [ $which ]")
              }
            }
         )

      builder.show()
    }

    return view
  }

  private fun openCreateNote() {
    val intent = Intent(context, NoteActivity::class.java)
    intent.putExtra(MODE.EXTRAS_KEY, MODE.CREATE.mode)
    startActivity(intent)
  }

  private fun openCreateTodo() {
    val intent = Intent(context, TodoActivity::class.java)
    intent.putExtra(MODE.EXTRAS_KEY, MODE.CREATE.mode)
    startActivity(intent)
  }

}
```

We accessed the `FloatingActionButton` instance and assigned a click listener. On clicking, we will create a dialog with two options. Each of these options will trigger a proper method for activity opening. The implementation of both methods is very similar. As an example, we will focus on `openCreateNote()`.

We will create a new `Intent` instance. In Android, `Intent` represents our intention to do something. To start an activity, we must pass the context and the class of the activity we want to start. We must also assign some values to it. Those values will be passed to an activity instance. In our case, we are passing the integer value for the `MODE.CREATE`. `startActivity()` method that will execute the intent and a screen will appear.

Run the application, click on the rounded button at the bottom-right corner of your screen, and choose an option from the dialog, as shown in the following screenshot:

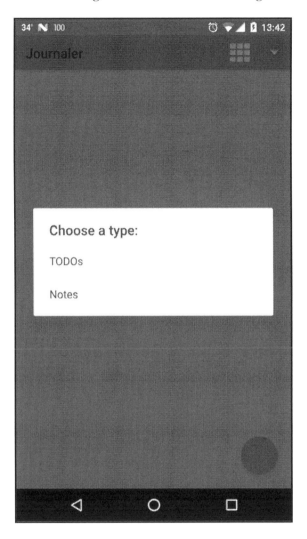

This will take you to this screen:

This will take you further to add your own data with date and time:

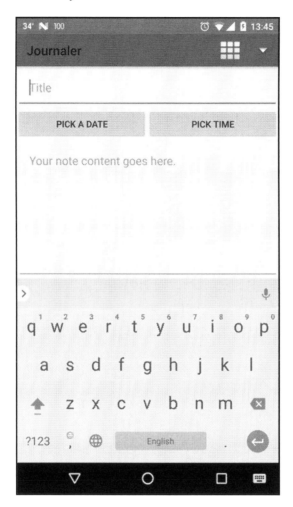

Looking deeper into Android Intents

The most operations you plan to perform in Android are defined through the `Intent` class. `Intents` can be used to start activities like we did, start services (processes running in background), or send broadcast messages.

`Intent` usually accepts an action and data that we want to pass to some class. Action attributes we can set are, for example, `ACTION_VIEW`, `ACTION_EDIT`, `ACTION_MAIN`.

Except action and data, we can set a category for the intent. The category gives additional information to the action we set. We can also set the type for the intent and the component that stands for the explicit component class name we will use.

There are two types of `intents`:

- Explicit intents
- Implicit intents

Explicit intents have an explicit component set that provides an explicit class to be run. Implicit intents do not have an explicit component, but the system decides what to do with it based on the data and attributes we assigned. Intent resolution process is responsible for handling such `intents`.

Combinations of these parameters are endless. We will give some examples so you can better understand the purpose of `intents`:

- Opening a web page:

```
val intent = Intent(Intent.ACTION_VIEW,
Uri.parse("http://google.com"))
startActivity(intent)
Sharing:
val intent = Intent(Intent.ACTION_SEND)
intent.type = "text/plain"
intent.putExtra(Intent.EXTRA_TEXT, "Check out this cool app!")
startActivity(intent)
```

- Capturing an image from a camera:

```
val takePicture = Intent(MediaStore.ACTION_IMAGE_CAPTURE)
if (takePicture.resolveActivity(packageManager) != null) {
 startActivityForResult(takePicture, REQUEST_CAPTURE_PHOTO +
 position)
} else {
   logger.e(tag, "Can't take picture.")
}
```

- Picking an image from the gallery:

```
val pickPhoto = Intent(
  Intent.ACTION_PICK,
  MediaStore.Images.Media.EXTERNAL_CONTENT_URI
  )
  startActivityForResult(pickPhoto, REQUEST_PICK_PHOTO +
position)
```

As you can see, `intents` are a crucial part of the Android Framework. In the next section, we will extend our code to make more use of `intents`.

Passing information between activities and fragments

To pass information between our activities, we will use the Android Bundle. Bundle can contain multiple values of different types. We will illustrate the use of Bundle by extending our code. Open `ItemsFragemnt` and update it as follows:

```
private fun openCreateNote() {
  val intent = Intent(context, NoteActivity::class.java)
  val data = Bundle()
  data.putInt(MODE.EXTRAS_KEY, MODE.CREATE.mode)
  intent.putExtras(data)
  startActivityForResult(intent, NOTE_REQUEST)
}
private fun openCreateTodo() {
   val date = Date(System.currentTimeMillis())
   val dateFormat = SimpleDateFormat("MMM dd YYYY", Locale.ENGLISH)
   val timeFormat = SimpleDateFormat("MM:HH", Locale.ENGLISH)

   val intent = Intent(context, TodoActivity::class.java)
   val data = Bundle()
   data.putInt(MODE.EXTRAS_KEY, MODE.CREATE.mode)
```

```
        data.putString(TodoActivity.EXTRA_DATE, dateFormat.format(date))
        data.putString(TodoActivity.EXTRA_TIME,
        timeFormat.format(date))
        intent.putExtras(data)
        startActivityForResult(intent, TODO_REQUEST)
    }

    override fun onActivityResult(requestCode: Int, resultCode: Int,
    data: Intent?) {
        super.onActivityResult(requestCode, resultCode, data)
        when (requestCode) {
            TODO_REQUEST -> {
                if (resultCode == Activity.RESULT_OK) {
                    Log.i(logTag, "We created new TODO.")
                } else {
                    Log.w(logTag, "We didn't created new TODO.")
                }
            }
            NOTE_REQUEST -> {
                if (resultCode == Activity.RESULT_OK) {
                    Log.i(logTag, "We created new note.")
                } else {
                    Log.w(logTag, "We didn't created new note.")
                }
            }
        }
    }
```

Here, we introduced some important changes. First of all, we started our **Note** and **Todo** activities as sub activities. This means that our `MainActivity` class depends on the result of the work of those activities. When starting the sub activity instead of the `startActivity()` method, we used `startActivityForResult()`. Parameters we passed are the intent and request number. To get a result of the execution, we overrode the `onActivityResult()` method. As you can see, we checked which activity finished and if that execution produced a successful result.

We also changed the way we pass the information. We created the `Bundle` instance and assigned multiple values, like in case of the **Todo** activity. We added mode, date, and time. Bundle is assigned to intent using the `putExtras()` method. To use these extras, we updated our activities too. Open `ItemsActivity` and apply changes, like this:

```
abstract class ItemActivity : BaseActivity() {
    protected var mode = MODE.VIEW
    protected var success = Activity.RESULT_CANCELED
    override fun getActivityTitle() = R.string.app_name
```

```
  override fun onCreate(savedInstanceState: Bundle?) {
    super.onCreate(savedInstanceState)
    val data = intent.extras
    data?.let{
      val modeToSet = data.getInt(MODE.EXTRAS_KEY, MODE.VIEW.mode)
      mode = MODE.getByValue(modeToSet)
    }
    Log.v(tag, "Mode [ $mode ]")
  }

  override fun onDestroy() {
    super.onDestroy()
    setResult(success)
  }

}
```

Here, we introduced the field holding result of activity work. We also updated the way we handle the passed information. As you can see, if there are any extras available, we will obtain an integer value for the mode. And, finally, the onDestroy() method sets the result of the work that will be available for parent activity.

Open TodoActivity and apply the following changes:

```
class TodoActivity : ItemActivity() {

companion object {
  val EXTRA_DATE = "EXTRA_DATE"
  val EXTRA_TIME = "EXTRA_TIME"
}

override val tag = "Todo activity"

override fun getLayout() = R.layout.activity_todo

override fun onCreate(savedInstanceState: Bundle?) {
  super.onCreate(savedInstanceState)
  val data = intent.extras
  data?.let {
    val date = data.getString(EXTRA_DATE, "")
    val time = data.getString(EXTRA_TIME, "")
    pick_date.text = date
    pick_time.text = time
  }
}

}
```

We have obtained values for date and time extras and set them to date/time picker buttons. Run your application and open the **Todo** activity. Your **Todo** screen should look like this:

When you leave the **Todo** activity and return back to the main screen, observe your Logcat. There will be a log with the following content:

W/Items fragment--we didn't create a new TODO.

Since we have not created any **Todo** items yet, we passed a proper result. We canceled the creation process by going back to the main screen. In the later chapters, and the ones following, we will create **Notes** and **Todos** with success.

Summary

We used this chapter to connect our interface and establish a real application flow. We established a connection between screens by setting proper actions to UI elements. We passed the data from point to point. All this in a very easy way! We have something that is working, but it looks ugly. In the next chapter, we will make sure it looks pretty! We will style it and add some nice visual effects. Prepare yourself to meet Android's powerful UI API.

5
Look and Feel

Nowadays, applications have a breathtaking visual appearance. This is something that makes your application unique and original. An eye pleasing appearance will make your application stand out in a field of similar applications, but it will also strongly appeal to your users and they are more likely to install and keep your app on their devices. In this chapter, we will show you how to make your application beautiful. We will introduce you to the secrets of Android UI theming! Our focus will only be on the visual aspect of Android applications.

In this chapter, we will cover the following topics:

- Themes and styles in Android
- Working with assets
- Custom fonts and coloring
- Button designs
- Animations and animation sets

Themes in the Android Framework

In the last chapter, we established a connection between the main UI elements. Our application does not look like one until it gets some color. To get colors, we will start with the main application theme. We will extend one of the existing Android themes and override it with colors we like.

Open `styles.xml`. Here, you will set the default theme defined for our application needs. We will also have several colors overridden. However, we will change the `parent` theme and customize it according to our wishes. We will update the theme according to the following example:

```xml
<resources>

    <style name="AppTheme"
      parent="Theme.AppCompat.Light.NoActionBar">
      <item name="android:colorPrimary">@color/colorPrimary</item>
      <item name="android:statusBarColor">@color/colorPrimary</item>
      <item name="android:colorPrimaryDark">
       @color/colorPrimaryDark</item>
      <item name="android:colorAccent">@color/colorAccent</item>
      <item name="android:textColor">@android:color/black</item>
    </style>

</resources>
```

We defined a theme that inherits from the `AppCompat` theme. The primary color represents the color for the application branding. The color's darker variant is `colorPrimaryDark`, while the UI controls colors that will be colored in `colorAccent`. We will also set the primary text color to black. The status bar will also use our primary branding color.

Open the `colors.xml` file and define the colors we will use for the theme as follows:

```xml
<?xml version="1.0" encoding="utf-8"?>
<resources>
    <color name="colorPrimary">#ff6600</color>
    <color name="colorPrimaryDark">#197734</color>
    <color name="colorAccent">#ffae00</color>
</resources>
```

Before you run the application to see your theme, make sure that the theme is actually applied. Update the `manifest` file with the following lines of code:

```xml
<application
android:theme="@style/AppTheme"
```

Also, update the color for the floating action button of `fragment_items` as follows:

```
<android.support.design.widget.FloatingActionButton
    android:backgroundTint="@color/colorPrimary"
    android:id="@+id/new_item"
    android:layout_width="wrap_content"
    android:layout_height="wrap_content"
    android:layout_alignParentBottom="true"
    android:layout_alignParentEnd="true"
    android:layout_margin="@dimen/button_margin" />
```

The background tint attribute will make sure that the button has the same color as the status bar. Build and run the application. Congratulations, you have successfully branded your application in orange!

Styles in Android

The theme we just defined represents style. All styles are defined in the `styles.xml` file. We will create several styles to demonstrate how easy it is for you to create styles and how powerful they are. You can define styles for buttons, text, or any other view. You can inherit styles too.

For the purpose of styling, we will define the color palette that we will use in the application. Open your `colors.xml` file and extend it as follows:

```
<color name="green">#11c403</color>
<color name="green_dark">#0e8c05</color>
<color name="white">#ffffff</color>
<color name="white_transparent_40">#64ffffff</color>
<color name="black">#000000</color>
<color name="black_transparent_40">#64000000</color>
<color name="grey_disabled">#d5d5d5</color>
<color name="grey_text">#444d57</color>
<color name="grey_text_transparent_40">#64444d57</color>
<color name="grey_text_middle">#6d6d6d</color>
<color name="grey_text_light">#b9b9b9</color>
<color name="grey_thin_separator">#f1f1f1</color>
<color name="grey_thin_separator_settings">#eeeeee</color>
<color name="vermilion">#f3494c</color>
<color name="vermilion_dark">#c64145</color>
<color name="vermilion_transparent_40">#64f3494c</color>
<color name="plum">#121e2a</color>
```

Pay attention to transparent colors! Observe the case of white color. Pure white color has the code #ffffff while the 40% transparent white has the code #64ffffff. To achieve transparency, you can use the following values:

0% = #00
10% = #16
20% = #32
30% = #48
40% = #64
50% = #80
60% = #96
70% = #112
80% = #128
90% = #144

Now that we have defined the color palette we will create our first styles. Open styles.xml and extend it:

```xml
<style name="simple_button">
    <item name="android:textSize">16sp</item>
    <item name="android:textAllCaps">false</item>
    <item name="android:textColor">@color/white</item>
</style>

<style name="simple_button_green" parent="simple_button">
    <item name="android:background">
    @drawable/selector_button_green</item>
</style>
```

We defined two styles. First that defines simple button. It has white text with letters of 16sp in size. The second extends a first and adds the attribute for the background. We will create a selector so we can demonstrate you styles we defined. Since we do not have this resource yet, create selector_button_green xml in the drawable resource folder:

```xml
<?xml version="1.0" encoding="utf-8"?>
<selector xmlns:android=
  "http://schemas.android.com/apk/res/android">

 <item android:drawable="@color/grey_disabled"
  android:state_enabled="false" />
 <item android:drawable="@color/green_dark"
  android:state_selected="true" />
 <item android:drawable="@color/green_dark"
  android:state_pressed="true" />
 <item android:drawable="@color/green" />
```

```
</selector>
```

We defined a selector. Selector is XML that describes visual behavior or the different states. We added a different color for the button's disabled state, color for states when the button is pressed, released, or when we do not have any interaction with it.

To see what the buttons will look like, open `activity_todo` layout and for each button set the style:

```
style="@style/simple_button_green"
```

Then, run the application and open the **Todo** screen. Your screen should look like this:

If you press the buttons you will notice that the color has changed to a darker green. In the next sections, we will even more improve these buttons even more by adding rounded edges but before that let's create some more styles:

- Add styles for input fields and for navigation drawers to your `styles.xml`:

```
<style name="simple_button_grey" parent="simple_button">
 <item name="android:background">
  @drawable/selector_button_grey</item>
</style>

<style name="edit_text_transparent">
  <item name="android:textSize">14sp</item>
  <item name="android:padding">19dp</item>
  <item name="android:textColor">@color/white</item>
  <item name="android:textColorHint">@color/white</item>
  <item name="android:background">
  @color/black_transparent_40</item>
</style>

<style name="edit_text_gery_text"
  parent="edit_text_transparent">
 <item name="android:textAlignment">textStart</item>
 <item name="android:textColor">@color/white</item>
 <item name="android:background">@color/grey_text_light</item>
</style>
```

- For input fields, we defined the color for the hint. Also we introduced one more selector drawable, `selector_button_grey`:

```
<?xml version="1.0" encoding="utf-8"?>
<selector xmlns:android=
 "http://schemas.android.com/apk/res/android">

 <item android:drawable="@color/grey_disabled"
 android:state_enabled="false" />
 <item android:drawable="@color/grey_text_middle"
 android:state_selected="true" />
 <item android:drawable="@color/grey_text_middle"
 android:state_pressed="true" />
 <item android:drawable="@color/grey_text" />
</selector>
```

- For `note_title` on both screens (**Note** and **Todo**) add the style:

```
style="@style/edit_text_transparent"
```

- For `note_content` add:

  ```
  style="@style/edit_text_gery_text"
  ```

- For `adapter_navigation_drawer` layout apply the style to a button:

  ```
  style="@style/simple_button_grey"
  ```

That's it! You styled your application! Now run it and take a look at all screens and navigation drawers:

What do you think? Does the UI look nicer now? Observe the next screenshot too:

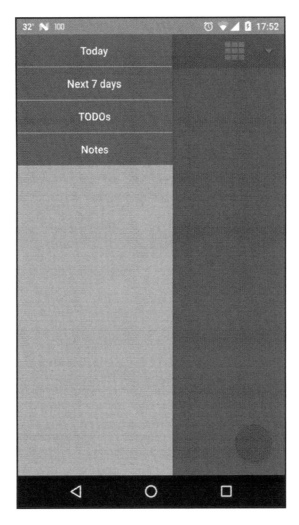

Application now seems nice. Feel free to adjust the attributes and colors according to your desire. We are not done yet. We need some fonts to apply! In the next sections, we will deal with that.

Working with assets

The time has come that your application needs to work with raw resources. A good example of that is fonts. Each font application we use will be an individual file stored in the assets folder. The assets folder is a subdirectory of main directory or directory that represents the build variant. Besides fonts, it's common that here you store txt files, mp3, waw, mid, and similar. You can't store these types of files in the res directory.

Using custom fonts

Fonts are assets. So to provide some fonts for your application we need to copy them first. There are a lot of good free font resources. For example, Google Fonts. Download some fonts and copy them to your assets directory. If there is no assets directory create one. We will place our fonts in the assets/fonts directory.

In our examples, we will use Exo. Exo comes with the following font files:

- Exo2-Black.ttf
- Exo2-BlackItalic.ttf
- Exo2-Bold.ttf
- Exo2-BoldItalic.ttf
- Exo2-ExtraBold.ttf
- Exo2-ExtraBoldItalic.ttf
- Exo2-ExtraLight.ttf
- Exo2-ExtraLightItalic.ttf
- Exo2-Italic.ttf
- Exo2-Light.ttf
- Exo2-LightItalic.ttf
- Exo2-Medium.ttf
- Exo2-MediumItalic.ttf
- Exo2-Regular.ttf
- Exo2-SemiBold.ttf
- Exo2-SemiBoldItalic.ttf
- Exo2-Thin.ttf
- Exo2-ThinItalic.ttf

Copying `font` files into the `assets` directory will not give us support for those fonts out of the box. We need to use them through our code. We will create the code that will apply fonts for us.

Open `BaseActivity` and extend it:

```
abstract class BaseActivity : AppCompatActivity() {
companion object {
  private var fontExoBold: Typeface? = null
  private var fontExoRegular: Typeface? = null

  fun applyFonts(view: View, ctx: Context) {
    var vTag = ""
    if (view.tag is String) {
      vTag = view.tag as String
    }
    when (view) {
      is ViewGroup -> {
        for (x in 0..view.childCount - 1) {
          applyFonts(view.getChildAt(x), ctx)
        }
      }
      is Button -> {
        when (vTag) {
          ctx.getString(R.string.tag_font_bold) -> {
            view.typeface = fontExoBold
          }
          else -> {
            view.typeface = fontExoRegular
          }
        }
      }
      is TextView -> {
        when (vTag) {
          ctx.getString(R.string.tag_font_bold) -> {
          view.typeface = fontExoBold
          }
           else -> {
             view.typeface = fontExoRegular
           }
        }
      }
      is EditText -> {
        when (vTag) {
          ctx.getString(R.string.tag_font_bold) -> {
            view.typeface = fontExoBold
          }
          else -> {
```

```
                    view.typeface = fontExoRegular
                 }
              }
           }
        }
     }
  }
...
override fun onPostCreate(savedInstanceState: Bundle?) {
    super.onPostCreate(savedInstanceState)
    Log.v(tag, "[ ON POST CREATE ]")
    applyFonts()
}
...
protected fun applyFonts() {
    initFonts()
    Log.v(tag, "Applying fonts [ START ]")
    val rootView = findViewById(android.R.id.content)
    applyFonts(rootView, this)
    Log.v(tag, "Applying fonts [ END ]")
}

private fun initFonts() {
    if (fontExoBold == null) {
        Log.v(tag, "Initializing font [ Exo2-Bold ]")
        fontExoBold = Typeface.createFromAsset(assets, "fonts/Exo2-
        Bold.ttf")
    }
    if (fontExoRegular == null) {
        Log.v(tag, "Initializing font [ Exo2-Regular ]")
        fontExoRegular = Typeface.createFromAsset(assets,
        "fonts/Exo2-Regular.ttf")
    }
 }
}
```

We extended our base activity to handle fonts. When the activity enters `onPostCreate()`, the `applyFonts()` method will be called. `applyFonts()` then does the following:

- Calls the `initFonts()` method which creates `TypeFace` instances from the assets. `TypeFace` is used as the representation of a font and its visual properties. We instantiated typefaces for `ExoBold` and `ExoRegular`.

- What happens next is that we are obtaining `root` view for our current activity and passing it to the `applyFonts()` method from the companion object. If the view is a `view group` we iterate through its children until the ordinary view is reached. View has a property `typeface` to which we set our `typeface` instance. You will notice also that we are retrieving the class property called `tag` from each view. In Android we can set tags to our views. Tags can be instances of any class. In our case, we are checking if the tag is `String` with the value of string resource by the name `tag_font_bold`.

To set tags, create a new `xml` in the `values` directory called **tags** and populate it with the following content:

```
<?xml version="1.0" encoding="utf-8"?>
<resources>
  <string name="tag_font_regular">FONT_REGULAR</string>
  <string name="tag_font_bold">FONT_BOLD</string>
</resources>
To apply it open styles.xml and add tag to simple_button style:
<item name="android:tag">@string/tag_font_bold</item>
```

Now all application's buttons will have the bold font version applied. Now build your application and run it. You will notice that the font has changed!

Applying coloring

We defined the color palette for our application. We applied each color by accessing its resource. Sometimes we do not have a particular color resource available. It can happen that we obtained the color dynamically through the backend (in a response to some API call) or we want the color to be defined from the code because of some other reasons.

Android is very powerful when you need to deal with colors from your code. We will cover some examples and show you what you can do.

To get color from an existing resource you can do the following:

```
val color = ContextCompat.getColor(contex, R.color.plum)
```

Before we used to do this:

```
val color = resources.getColor(R.color.plum)
```

But it is deprecated from Android version 6.

When you obtained a color you can apply it on some view:

```
pick_date.setTextColor(color)
```

Another way to obtain a color is by accessing `Color` class static methods. Let's start with parsing some color string:

```
val color = Color.parseColor("#ff0000")
```

We must note that there is already a certain number of predefined colors available:

```
val color = Color.RED
```

So we don't need to parse `#ff0000`. There are some other colors as well:

```
public static final int BLACK
public static final int BLUE
public static final int CYAN
public static final int DKGRAY
public static final int GRAY
public static final int GREEN
public static final int LTGRAY
public static final int MAGENTA
public static final int RED
public static final int TRANSPARENT
public static final int WHITE
public static final int YELLOW
```

Sometimes you will have only parameters about red, green, or blue and based on that to create a color:

```
Color red = Color.valueOf(1.0f, 0.0f, 0.0f);
```

We must note that this method is available from API version 26!

If RGB is not your desired color space then you can pass it as a parameter:

```
val colorSpace = ColorSpace.get(ColorSpace.Named.NTSC_1953)
val color = Color.valueOf(1f, 1f, 1f, 1f, colorSpace)
```

As you can see there are a lot of possibilities when you deal with the color. If standard color resources are not enough for you to manage your colors you can do it in an advanced way. We encourage you to play with it and try on some user interfaces.

For example, if you are using the `AppCompat` library once you get `Color` instance you can use it like in the following example:

```
counter.setTextColor(
    ContextCompat.getColor(context, R.color.vermilion)
)
```

Consider the following screenshot:

Make your buttons look pretty

We colored our buttons and defined states for them. We colored each state differently. We have colors for disabled state, for enabled, and pressed states. Now we will go one step further. We will make our buttons rounded and color them with a gradient instead of a solid color. We will prepare a layout for a new button style. Open the `activity_todo` layout and modify the buttons container:

```
<LinearLayout
  android:background="@color/grey_text_light"
  android:layout_width="match_parent"
  android:layout_height="wrap_content"
  android:orientation="horizontal"
  android:weightSum="1">
  ...

</LinearLayout>
```

We set the background the same as the one we used for the edit text field. Buttons will be rounded so we want them on the same background as the rest of the screen. Now, let's define some additional dimensions and the colors we will use. We need to define the radius for a button with rounded corners:

```
<dimen name="button_corner">10dp</dimen>
```

Since we plan to use gradient colors we must add a second color for gradients. Add these colors to your `colors.xml`:

```
<color name="green2">#208c18</color>
<color name="green_dark2">#0b5505</color>
```

Now when we have defined this we will need to update our style for green buttons:

```
<style name="simple_button_green" parent="simple_button">
    <item name="android:layout_margin">5dp</item>
    <item name="android:background">
    @drawable/selector_button_green</item>
</style>
```

We added a margin so that buttons are separated from each other. We need now rectangular rounded drawables. Create three drawable resources `rect_rounded_green`, `rect_rounded_green_dark`, and `rect_rounded_grey_disabled`. Make sure they are defined like this:

- `rect_rounded_green`:

```
<shape xmlns:android=
  "http://schemas.android.com/apk/res/android">
   <gradient
   android:angle="270"
   android:endColor="@color/green2"
   android:startColor="@color/green" />

   <corners android:radius="@dimen/button_corner" />
</shape>
```

- `rect_rounded_green_dark`:

```
<shape xmlns:android="http://schemas.android.com/apk/res/android">
  <gradient
  android:angle="270"
  android:endColor="@color/green_dark2"
  android:startColor="@color/green_dark" />

 <corners android:radius="@dimen/button_corner" />
</shape>
```

- `rect_rounded_grey_disabled`:

```
<shape xmlns:android=
"http://schemas.android.com/apk/res/android">

<solid android:color="@color/grey_disabled" />
<corners android:radius="@dimen/button_corner" />
</shape>
```

- We defined gradients containing attributes for:
    - gradient angle (of 270 degrees)
    - start color (we used our color resource)
    - end color (we used our color resource too)

Also, each drawable resource has a value for its corner's radius. Last step is to update our selector. Open `selector_button_green` and update it:

```xml
<?xml version="1.0" encoding="utf-8"?>
<selector xmlns:android=
"http://schemas.android.com/apk/res/android">

<item
android:drawable="@drawable/rect_rounded_grey_disabled"
android:state_enabled="false" />

<item
android:drawable="@drawable/rect_rounded_green_dark"
android:state_selected="true" />

<item
android:drawable="@drawable/rect_rounded_green_dark"
android:state_pressed="true" />

<item
android:drawable="@drawable/rect_rounded_green" />

</selector>
```

Build your app and run it. Open the **Todo** screen and take a look at it. Buttons are now much nicer with smooth rounded edges. Buttons are separated from each other by margins and if you press a finger on them you will see the secondary gradient with the darker green we defined:

Setting animations

We consider our layout to be nice. It is pretty. But can it be more entertaining? Sure it can! If we make our layout more interactive we will achieve a better user experience and attract users to use it. We will achieve that by adding some animations. Animations can be defined through the code or by animating view properties. We will improve each of the screens by adding simple and effective opening animations.

Animations defined as resources are located in the `anim` resources directory. We will need a few animation resources there--`fade_in`, `fade_out`, `bottom_to_top`, `top_to_bottom`, `hide_to_top`, `hide_to_bottom`. Create them and define them according to these examples:

- `fade_in`:

```xml
<?xml version="1.0" encoding="utf-8"?>
<alpha xmlns:android=
"http://schemas.android.com/apk/res/android"
android:duration="300"
android:fromAlpha="0.0"
android:interpolator="@android:anim/accelerate_interpolator"
android:toAlpha="1.0" />
```

- `fade_out`:

```xml
<?xml version="1.0" encoding="utf-8"?>
<alpha xmlns:android=
"http://schemas.android.com/apk/res/android"
android:duration="300"
android:fillAfter="true"
android:fromAlpha="1.0"
android:interpolator="@android:anim/accelerate_interpolator"
android:toAlpha="0.0" />
-  bottom_to_top:
<set xmlns:android=
 "http://schemas.android.com/apk/res/android"
android:fillAfter="true"
android:fillEnabled="true"
android:shareInterpolator="false">

<translate
android:duration="900"
android:fromXDelta="0%"
android:fromYDelta="100%"
android:toXDelta="0%"
android:toYDelta="0%" />

</set>
```

- `top_to_bottom`:

```xml
<set xmlns:android="http://schemas.android.com/apk/res/android"
android:fillAfter="true"
android:fillEnabled="true"
android:shareInterpolator="false">
```

```
  <translate
    android:duration="900"
    android:fromXDelta="0%"
    android:fromYDelta="-100%"
    android:toXDelta="0%"
    android:toYDelta="0%" />
</set>
```

- hide_to_top:

```
  <set xmlns:android="http://schemas.android.com/apk/res/android"
    android:fillAfter="true"
    android:fillEnabled="true"
    android:shareInterpolator="false">

 <translate
    android:duration="900"
    android:fromXDelta="0%"
    android:fromYDelta="0%"
    android:toXDelta="0%"
    android:toYDelta="-100%" />

</set>
```

- hide_to_bottom:

```
    <set xmlns:android=
      "http://schemas.android.com/apk/res/android"
       android:fillAfter="true"
       android:fillEnabled="true"
       android:shareInterpolator="false">

    <translate
      android:duration="900"
      android:fromXDelta="0%"
      android:fromYDelta="0%"
      android:toXDelta="0%"
      android:toYDelta="100%" />

    </set>
```

Take a look at this example and the attributes you can define. In the fade animation example, we animated an `alpha` property for the view. We set the animation duration, from, and to alpha values and the interpolator we will use for the animation. In Android, for your animations you can choose one of these interpolators:

- `accelerate_interpolator`
- `accelerate_decelerate_interpolator`
- `bounce_interpolator`
- `cycle_interpolator`
- `anticipate_interpolator`
- `anticipate_overshot_interpolator`
- and many others, all defined in--`@android:anim/...`

For other animations we defined the translation with `from` and `to` parameters.

Before we use these animations we will adjust some backgrounds so there is no gap in our layouts before the animation starts. For `activity_main`, add the background for **Toolbar parent** view:

```
android:background="@android:color/darker_gray"
```

For `activity_note` and `activity_todo` nest toolbar in one more parent so the final color is the same as the color for the title field below the toolbar:

```
<LinearLayout
    android:layout_width="match_parent"
    android:layout_height="wrap_content"
    android:background="@color/black_transparent_40"
    android:orientation="vertical">

  <LinearLayout
    android:layout_width="match_parent"
    android:layout_height="wrap_content"
    android:background="@color/black_transparent_40"
    android:orientation="vertical">

  <android.support.v7.widget.Toolbar
    android:id="@+id/toolbar"
    android:layout_width="match_parent"
    android:layout_height="50dp"
    android:background="@color/colorPrimary"
    android:elevation="4dp" />
```

Finally we will apply our animations. We will use fade in and out animations for our screens, opening and closing. Open `BaseActivity` and modify it like this:

```
override fun onCreate(savedInstanceState: Bundle?) {
    super.onCreate(savedInstanceState)
    overridePendingTransition(R.anim.fade_in, R.anim.fade_out)
    setContentView(getLayout())
    setSupportActionBar(toolbar)
    Log.v(tag, "[ ON CREATE ]")
}
```

We overrode transition effects by using the `overridePendingTransition()` method that takes enter and exit animations as parameters.

Update your `onResume()` and `onPause()` methods too:

```
override fun onResume() {
    super.onResume()
    Log.v(tag, "[ ON RESUME ]")
    val animation = getAnimation(R.anim.top_to_bottom)
    findViewById(R.id.toolbar).startAnimation(animation)
}

override fun onPause() {
    super.onPause()
    Log.v(tag, "[ ON PAUSE ]")
    val animation = getAnimation(R.anim.hide_to_top)
    findViewById(R.id.toolbar).startAnimation(animation)

}
```

We created an instance of animation and applied it on the view using the `startAnimation()` method. `getAnimation()` method is ours. We defined it. So, add the implementation to `BaseActivity`:

```
protected fun getAnimation(animation: Int): Animation =
AnimationUtils.loadAnimation(this, animation)
```

Since we are using Kotlin, to make it available to all activities, not just the ones that are extending `BaseActivity` change method to be extension function like this:

```
fun Activity.getAnimation(animation: Int): Animation =
AnimationUtils.loadAnimation(this, animation)
```

Build your application again and run it. Open and close screens multiple times to see how our animations are working.

Animation sets in Android

In previous sections, we worked with animations from resources defined in XML. In this section, we will play with various view attributes and with animation sets. We will illustrate the purpose and use with simple and effective examples.

Let's demonstrate the first animation from the code. Open `ItemsFragment`. Add the following method:

```
private fun animate(btn: FloatingActionButton, expand: Boolean =
true) {
    btn.animate()
            .setInterpolator(BounceInterpolator())
            .scaleX(if(expand){ 1.5f } else { 1.0f })
            .scaleY(if(expand){ 1.5f } else { 1.0f })
            .setDuration(2000)
            .start()
    }
```

What this method will do? This method will animate scaling for the button with bounce interpolation. If the expand parameter is `true`, we will scale up, otherwise we will scale down.

Apply it to our floating action button. Extend the button click listener:

```
btn?.setOnClickListener {
animate(btn)
...

    }
```

And set the main dialog to cancellable with on an cancel action set:

```
val builder = AlertDialog.Builder(this@ItemsFragment.context)
                .setTitle(R.string.choose_a_type)
                .setCancelable(true)
                .setOnCancelListener {
                    animate(btn, false)
                }
.setItems ( ... )

...
builder.show()
```

Build and run the application. Click on the **add item** button and then close the dialog by tapping outside of it. We have a wonderful scale animation!

To have floating action button complete add PNG resource for plus sign and apply it to the button:

```
<android.support.design.widget.FloatingActionButton
...
android:src="@drawable/add"
android:scaleType="centerInside"
...
/>
```

With the icon added to the button the animation looks perfect! Let's make it even more perfect! We will create an animation set containing multiple animations!

```
private fun animate(btn: FloatingActionButton, expand: Boolean =
true) {
    val animation1 = ObjectAnimator.ofFloat(btn, "scaleX",
    if(expand){ 1.5f } else { 1.0f })
    animation1.duration = 2000
    animation1.interpolator = BounceInterpolator()

    val animation2 = ObjectAnimator.ofFloat(btn, "scaleY",
    if(expand){ 1.5f } else { 1.0f })
    animation2.duration = 2000
    animation2.interpolator = BounceInterpolator()

    val animation3 = ObjectAnimator.ofFloat(btn, "alpha",
    if(expand){ 0.3f } else { 1.0f })
    animation3.duration = 500
    animation3.interpolator = AccelerateInterpolator()

    val set = AnimatorSet()
    set.play(animation1).with(animation2).before(animation3)
    set.start()
}
```

The `AnimatorSet` class gives us the ability to create complex animations. In this case, we defined animations for scaling along the *x* axis and for scaling along the *y* axis. This two animations will be animated at the same time giving us the effect of scaling in both directions. After we scale view we will reduce (or increase) view's capacity. As you can see, we can chain or order animation's execution.

Build your project and run. You can see new animation behavior.

Summary

This chapter was a rather interactive one. First we showed you how to add, define, change, and adjust a theme in Android. Then we submerged into Android styles and assets. In this chapter, we also adopted some custom fonts and coloring. In the end, we made some seriously beautiful buttons and swift animations. In the next chapter, you will start learning about the system part of the Android Framework. We will start with permissions.

6
Permissions

Hello again! Can you believe that one important part of this book is already behind us? We are finished with the user interface, and, now, we are heading into a more complex part of the book--the system.

In this chapter, and the ones following, we will dig deep into the structure of the Android system. You will learn about permissions, database handling, preferences, concurrency, services, messaging, the backend, APIs, and high performances.

However, you shouldn't let yourself be fooled; this book and its content does not cover the entire framework. That is simply impossible; Android is such a vast framework that it can take you years to completely master it. Here, we are merely penetrating into the world of Android and Kotlin.

However, don't be discouraged! In this book, we will give you knowledge and skills needed for mastering both Kotlin and Android. In this chapter, precisely, we will discuss permissions in Android. You will learn what are permissions, what are they used for, and, most importantly, why we need (with strong emphasis on need) to use them.

In this chapter, we will cover the following topics:

- Permissions from Android Manifest
- Requesting permissions
- Permission handling in the Kotlin way

Permissions from Android Manifest

Android applications operate in their own process and are separated from the rest of the operating system. Because of this, in order to perform some system specific operations, it's required to request them. An example of such permission requests are requests to use Bluetooth, retrieve the current GPS location, send SMS messages, or read from or write to file system. Permissions grant access to various device features. There are several ways to deal with permissions. We will start with a very base using manifest.

First of all, we must determine what permissions are needed. It can happen that during the installation procedure, a user decides not to install an application because there are too many permissions. For example, a user can ask himself why an application requires the send SMS functionality when an application itself is just a simple image gallery application.

For **Journaler**, the application we are developing in this book, we will need the following permissions:

- Read the GPS coordinates because we want each note we create to have coordinates associated if we want to
- We will need access to the internet, so we can later execute API calls
- Boot complete event, we will need it so the application service can do synchronization with the backend each time we reboot our phone
- Reading and writing external storage so we can read the data or store it
- Access network state so we know if there is a connection to the internet available
- Use vibration so we can vibrate when we received something from the backend

Open the `AndroidManifest.xml` file and update it with the following permissions:

```
<manifest xmlns:android=
 "http://schemas.android.com/apk/res/android"
 package="com.journaler">

  <uses-permission android:name="android.permission.INTERNET" />
  <uses-permission android:name=
   "android.permission.RECEIVE_BOOT_COMPLETED" />
  <uses-permission android:name=
   "android.permission.READ_EXTERNAL_STORAGE" />
  <uses-permission android:name=
   "android.permission.WRITE_EXTERNAL_STORAGE" />
  <uses-permission android:name=
   "android.permission.ACCESS_NETWORK_STATE" />
  <uses-permission android:name=
   "android.permission.ACCESS_FINE_LOCATION" />
  <uses-permission android:name=
```

```
  "android.permission.ACCESS_COARSE_LOCATION" />
 <uses-permission android:name="android.permission.VIBRATE" />
  <application ... >
    ...
  </application

  ...

</manifest>
```

Names for permissions we just requested are pretty much self-explanatory and they are
covering all the points we mentioned. Besides these permissions, you can request some
others as well. Take a look at the following names for each. You will be surprised what you
can actually request:

```
<uses-permission android:name=
"android.permission.ACCESS_CHECKIN_PROPERTIES" />
<uses-permission  android:name=
"android.permission.ACCESS_LOCATION_EXTRA_COMMANDS" />
<uses-permission android:name=
"android.permission.ACCESS_MOCK_LOCATION" />
<uses-permission android:name=
"android.permission.ACCESS_SURFACE_FLINGER" />
<uses-permission android:name=
"android.permission.ACCESS_WIFI_STATE" />
<uses-permission android:name=
"android.permission.ACCOUNT_MANAGER" />
<uses-permission android:name=
"android.permission.AUTHENTICATE_ACCOUNTS" />
<uses-permission android:name=
"android.permission.BATTERY_STATS" />
<uses-permission android:name=
"android.permission.BIND_APPWIDGET" />
<uses-permission android:name=
"android.permission.BIND_DEVICE_ADMIN" />
<uses-permission android:name=
"android.permission.BIND_INPUT_METHOD" />
<uses-permission android:name=
"android.permission.BIND_REMOTEVIEWS" />
<uses-permission android:name=
"android.permission.BIND_WALLPAPER" />
<uses-permission android:name=
"android.permission.BLUETOOTH" />
<uses-permission android:name=
"android.permission.BLUETOOTH_ADMIN" />
<uses-permission android:name=
"android.permission.BRICK" />
<uses-permission android:name=
```

```
"android.permission.BROADCAST_PACKAGE_REMOVED" />
<uses-permission android:name=
"android.permission.BROADCAST_SMS" />
<uses-permission android:name=
"android.permission.BROADCAST_STICKY" />
<uses-permission android:name=
 "android.permission.BROADCAST_WAP_PUSH" />
<uses-permission android:name=
 "android.permission.CALL_PHONE"/>
<uses-permission android:name=
 "android.permission.CALL_PRIVILEGED" />
<uses-permission android:name=
 "android.permission.CAMERA"/>
<uses-permission android:name=
 "android.permission.CHANGE_COMPONENT_ENABLED_STATE" />
<uses-permission android:name=
"android.permission.CHANGE_CONFIGURATION" />
<uses-permission android:name=
"android.permission.CHANGE_NETWORK_STATE" />
<uses-permission android:name=
"android.permission.CHANGE_WIFI_MULTICAST_STATE" />
<uses-permission android:name=
"android.permission.CHANGE_WIFI_STATE" />
<uses-permission android:name=
"android.permission.CLEAR_APP_CACHE" />
<uses-permission android:name=
"android.permission.CLEAR_APP_USER_DATA" />
<uses-permission android:name=
"android.permission.CONTROL_LOCATION_UPDATES" />
<uses-permission android:name=
"android.permission.DELETE_CACHE_FILES" />
<uses-permission android:name=
"android.permission.DELETE_PACKAGES" />
<uses-permission android:name=
"android.permission.DEVICE_POWER" />
<uses-permission android:name=
"android.permission.DIAGNOSTIC" />
<uses-permission android:name=
"android.permission.DISABLE_KEYGUARD" />
<uses-permission android:name=
"android.permission.DUMP" />
<uses-permission android:name=
"android.permission.EXPAND_STATUS_BAR" />
<uses-permission android:name="
android.permission.FACTORY_TEST" />
<uses-permission android:name=
"android.permission.FLASHLIGHT" />
<uses-permission android:name=
```

```
 "android.permission.FORCE_BACK" />
<uses-permission android:name=
 "android.permission.GET_ACCOUNTS" />
<uses-permission android:name=
 "android.permission.GET_PACKAGE_SIZE" />
<uses-permission android:name=
 "android.permission.GET_TASKS" />
<uses-permission android:name=
 "android.permission.GLOBAL_SEARCH" />
<uses-permission android:name=
 "android.permission.HARDWARE_TEST" />
<uses-permission android:name=
 "android.permission.INJECT_EVENTS" />
<uses-permission android:name=
 "android.permission.INSTALL_LOCATION_PROVIDER" />
<uses-permission android:name=
 "android.permission.INSTALL_PACKAGES" />
<uses-permission android:name=
 "android.permission.INTERNAL_SYSTEM_WINDOW" />
<uses-permission android:name=
 "android.permission.KILL_BACKGROUND_PROCESSES" />
<uses-permission android:name=
 "android.permission.MANAGE_ACCOUNTS" />
<uses-permission android:name=
 "android.permission.MANAGE_APP_TOKENS" />
<uses-permission android:name=
 "android.permission.MASTER_CLEAR" />
<uses-permission android:name=
 "android.permission.MODIFY_AUDIO_SETTINGS" />
<uses-permission android:name=
 "android.permission.MODIFY_PHONE_STATE" />
<uses-permission android:name=
 "android.permission.MOUNT_FORMAT_FILESYSTEMS" />
<uses-permission android:name=
 "android.permission.MOUNT_UNMOUNT_FILESYSTEMS" />
<uses-permission android:name=
 "android.permission.NFC" />
<uses-permission android:name=
 "android.permission.PROCESS_OUTGOING_CALLS" />
<uses-permission android:name=
 "android.permission.READ_CALENDAR" />
<uses-permission android:name=
 "android.permission.READ_CONTACTS" />
<uses-permission android:name=
"android.permission.READ_FRAME_BUFFER" />
<uses-permission android:name=
"android.permission.READ_HISTORY_BOOKMARKS" />
<uses-permission android:name=
```

```
"android.permission.READ_INPUT_STATE" />
<uses-permission android:name=
"android.permission.READ_LOGS" />
<uses-permission android:name=
"android.permission.READ_PHONE_STATE" />
<uses-permission android:name=
"android.permission.READ_SMS" />
<uses-permission android:name=
"android.permission.READ_SYNC_SETTINGS" />
<uses-permission android:name=
"android.permission.READ_SYNC_STATS" />
<uses-permission android:name=
"android.permission.REBOOT" />
<uses-permission android:name=
"android.permission.RECEIVE_MMS" />
<uses-permission android:name=
"android.permission.RECEIVE_SMS" />
<uses-permission android:name=
"android.permission.RECEIVE_WAP_PUSH" />
<uses-permission android:name=
"android.permission.RECORD_AUDIO" />
<uses-permission android:name=
"android.permission.REORDER_TASKS" />
<uses-permission android:name=
"android.permission.RESTART_PACKAGES" />
<uses-permission android:name=
"android.permission.SEND_SMS" />
<uses-permission android:name=
"android.permission.SET_ACTIVITY_WATCHER" />
<uses-permission android:name=
 "android.permission.SET_ALARM" />
<uses-permission android:name=
 "android.permission.SET_ALWAYS_FINISH" />
<uses-permission android:name=
 "android.permission.SET_ANIMATION_SCALE" />
<uses-permission android:name=
 "android.permission.SET_DEBUG_APP" />
<uses-permission android:name=
 "android.permission.SET_ORIENTATION" />
<uses-permission android:name=
 "android.permission.SET_POINTER_SPEED" />
<uses-permission android:name=
 "android.permission.SET_PROCESS_LIMIT" />
<uses-permission android:name=
 "android.permission.SET_TIME" />
<uses-permission android:name=
 "android.permission.SET_TIME_ZONE" />
<uses-permission android:name=
```

```
 "android.permission.SET_WALLPAPER" />
<uses-permission android:name=
 "android.permission.SET_WALLPAPER_HINTS" />
<uses-permission android:name=
 "android.permission.SIGNAL_PERSISTENT_PROCESSES" />
<uses-permission android:name=
 "android.permission.STATUS_BAR" />
<uses-permission android:name=
 "android.permission.SUBSCRIBED_FEEDS_READ" />
<uses-permission android:name=
 "android.permission.SUBSCRIBED_FEEDS_WRITE" />
<uses-permission android:name=
 "android.permission.SYSTEM_ALERT_WINDOW" />
<uses-permission android:name=
 "android.permission.UPDATE_DEVICE_STATS" />
<uses-permission android:name=
 "android.permission.USE_CREDENTIALS" />
<uses-permission android:name=
 "android.permission.USE_SIP" />
<uses-permission android:name=
 "android.permission.WAKE_LOCK" />
<uses-permission android:name=
 "android.permission.WRITE_APN_SETTINGS" />
<uses-permission android:name=
 "android.permission.WRITE_CALENDAR" />
<uses-permission android:name=
 "android.permission.WRITE_CONTACTS" />
<uses-permission android:name=
 "android.permission.WRITE_GSERVICES" />
<uses-permission android:name=
 "android.permission.WRITE_HISTORY_BOOKMARKS" />
<uses-permission android:name=
 "android.permission.WRITE_SECURE_SETTINGS" />
<uses-permission android:name=
 "android.permission.WRITE_SETTINGS" />
<uses-permission android:name=
 "android.permission.WRITE_SMS" />
<uses-permission android:name=
 "android.permission.WRITE_SYNC_SETTINGS" />
<uses-permission android:name=
 "android.permission.BIND_ACCESSIBILITY_SERVICE"/>
<uses-permission android:name=
 "android.permission.BIND_TEXT_SERVICE"/>
<uses-permission android:name=
 "android.permission.BIND_VPN_SERVICE"/>
<uses-permission android:name=
 "android.permission.PERSISTENT_ACTIVITY"/>
<uses-permission android:name=
```

```
  "android.permission.READ_CALL_LOG"/>
<uses-permission android:name=
 "com.android.browser.permission.READ_HISTORY_BOOKMARKS"/>
<uses-permission android:name=
 "android.permission.READ_PROFILE"/>
<uses-permission android:name=
 "android.permission.READ_SOCIAL_STREAM"/>
<uses-permission android:name=
 "android.permission.READ_USER_DICTIONARY"/>
<uses-permission android:name=
 "com.android.alarm.permission.SET_ALARM"/>
<uses-permission android:name=
 "android.permission.SET_PREFERRED_APPLICATIONS"/>
<uses-permission android:name=
 "android.permission.WRITE_CALL_LOG"/>
<uses-permission android:name=
 "com.android.browser.permission.WRITE_HISTORY_BOOKMARKS"/>
<uses-permission android:name=
 "android.permission.WRITE_PROFILE"/>
<uses-permission android:name=
 "android.permission.WRITE_SOCIAL_STREAM"/>
<uses-permission android:name=
 "android.permission.WRITE_USER_DICTIONARY"/>
```

Requesting permissions

After the Android SDK version, 23 permissions are required to be requested at runtime (not for all of them). This means that we need to request them from the code as well. We will demonstrate how to do that from our application. We will request required permissions for the GPS location obtaining as a user opens the application. The user will get a dialog to approve permission if there is not any approved. Open your BaseActivity class and extend it as follows:

```
abstract class BaseActivity : AppCompatActivity() {
  companion object {
  val REQUEST_GPS = 0
  ... }
  ...
  override fun onCreate(savedInstanceState: Bundle?) {
    super.onCreate(savedInstanceState)
    ...
    requestGpsPermissions() }
...
  private fun requestGpsPermissions() {
    ActivityCompat.requestPermissions(
```

```
        this@BaseActivity,
        arrayOf(
          Manifest.permission.ACCESS_FINE_LOCATION,
          Manifest.permission.ACCESS_COARSE_LOCATION ),
          REQUEST_GPS ) }
          ...
    override fun onRequestPermissionsResult(
      requestCode:
      Int, permissions: Array<String>, grantResults: IntArray ) {
        if (requestCode == REQUEST_GPS) {
          for (grantResult in grantResults)
          { if (grantResult == PackageManager.PERMISSION_GRANTED)
          { Log.i( tag, String.format( Locale.ENGLISH, "Permission
          granted [ %d ]", requestCode ) )
          }
          else {
            Log.e( tag, String.format( Locale.ENGLISH, "Permission
            not granted [ %d ]", requestCode ) )
          } } } } }
```

So what exactly is going on in this code? We will explain all lines from top to bottom.

In the companion object, we defined the ID for our request. We will wait for the result for that ID. In the onCreate() method, we called the requestGpsPermissions() method that actually makes the permission request under the ID we defined. The result of the permission request will be available in the onRequestPermissionsResult() overrode method. As you can see, we are logging permission request results. The application can now retrieve the GPS data.

The principle is the same for all other Android permissions. Build your application and run it. You will be asked about permissions as shown in the following screenshot:

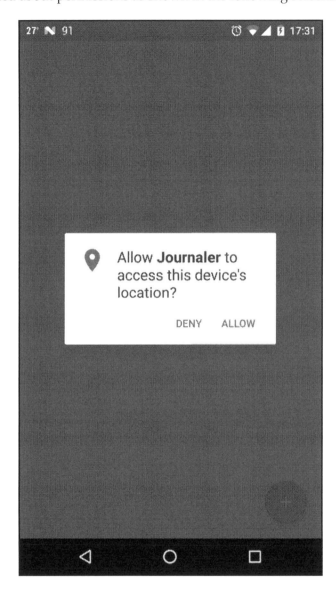

Doing it the Kotlin way

What happens if our application requires a lot of permissions that must be handled through the code? It happens that we have a lot of code handling different permission requests. This means that we have a lot of boilerplate code! Luckily for us, we are using Kotlin. Kotlin will be our tool to make things simpler!

Create a new package called `permission`. Then create two new Kotlin files as follows:

`PermissionCompatActivity` and `PermissionRequestCallback`.

Let's define the permission request callback as follows:

```
package com.journaler.permission

interface PermissionRequestCallback {
  fun onPermissionGranted(permissions: List<String>)
  fun onPermissionDenied(permissions: List<String>)
}
```

This will be the `callback` that will be fired when permissions are resolved. Then, define our permission `compat` activity:

```
package com.journaler.permission

import android.content.pm.PackageManager
import android.support.v4.app.ActivityCompat
import android.support.v7.app.AppCompatActivity
import android.util.Log
import java.util.concurrent.ConcurrentHashMap
import java.util.concurrent.atomic.AtomicInteger

abstract class PermissionCompatActivity : AppCompatActivity() {

  private val tag = "Permissions extension"
  private val latestPermissionRequest = AtomicInteger()
  private val permissionRequests = ConcurrentHashMap<Int,
  List<String>>()
  private val permissionCallbacks =
   ConcurrentHashMap<List<String>, PermissionRequestCallback>()

  private val defaultPermissionCallback = object :
  PermissionRequestCallback {
    override fun onPermissionGranted(permissions: List<String>) {
        Log.i(tag, "Permission granted [ $permissions ]")
    }
    override fun onPermissionDenied(permissions: List<String>) {
```

```
         Log.e(tag, "Permission denied [ $permissions ]")
      }
  }

fun requestPermissions(
   vararg permissions: String,
   callback: PermissionRequestCallback = defaultPermissionCallback
) {
   val id = latestPermissionRequest.incrementAndGet()
   val items = mutableListOf<String>()
   items.addAll(permissions)
   permissionRequests[id] = items
   permissionCallbacks[items] = callback
   ActivityCompat.requestPermissions(this, permissions, id)
}

override fun onRequestPermissionsResult(
   requestCode: Int,
   permissions: Array<String>,
   grantResults: IntArray
) {
   val items = permissionRequests[requestCode]
   items?.let {
      val callback = permissionCallbacks[items]
      callback?.let {
        var success = true
         for (x in 0..grantResults.lastIndex) {
            val result = grantResults[x]
            if (result != PackageManager.PERMISSION_GRANTED) {
               success = false
               break
            }
         }
         if (success) {
            callback.onPermissionGranted(items)
         } else {
            callback.onPermissionDenied(items)
         }
      }
   }
}
```

The idea behind this class is the following--we exposed end-user to the `requestPermissions()` method that accepts a variable number of arguments representing permissions we are interested in. We can pass the `callback` (the interface we just defined) that is optional. If we do not pass our own `callback`, the default one will be used. After permissions are resolved, we fire `callback`s. We consider permissions resolving successful, only if all permissions are granted.

Let's update our `BaseActivity` class as follows:

```
abstract class BaseActivity : PermissionCompatActivity() {
...
override fun onCreate(savedInstanceState: Bundle?) {
    ...
    requestPermissions(
       Manifest.permission.ACCESS_FINE_LOCATION,
       Manifest.permission.ACCESS_COARSE_LOCATION
    )
  }
  ...
}
```

As you can see, we removed all previous permissions-related code from the `BaseActivity` class and replaced it with a single `requestPermission()` call.

Summary

This chapter was maybe short, but the information that you learned was extremely valuable. Permissions are needed for every Android application. They are there to protect both the users and the developers. And, as you have seen, there are quite a lot different permissions that you can use depending on your needs.

In the next chapter, we will continue with the system part, and you will learn about database handling.

7
Working with Databases

In the previous chapter, we obtained crucial permissions needed to access Android system features. In our case, we obtained location permissions. In this chapter, we will move on by inserting data into the database. We will insert location data that we will get from Android's location provider. For that purpose, we will define proper database schema and management classes. We will also define classes to access the location provider to obtain location data.

In this chapter, we will cover the following topics:

- Introduction to SQLite
- Describing database
- CRUD operations

Introduction to SQLite

To persist data for our application, we will need a database. In Android, for offline data storage, you can use SQLite.

SQLite is supported out of the box, which means that it comes included with the Android Framework.

Benefits

Benefits of SQLite are that it is powerful, fast, and reliable with a huge community that uses it. If you find any problem, it will be easy to find a solution since somebody from the community has most likely already solved such issues. SQLite is a self-contained, embedded, full-featured, public-domain SQL database engine.

We will use SQLite to store all our **Todos** and **Notes**. To do that, we will define our database, the mechanism for accessing it, and data management. We will not expose a naked database instance directly, but we will wrap it properly so it is easy to insert, update, query, or remove data.

Describing our database

First thing we will do is describe our database by defining its tables and columns with proper data types. We will also define simple models that will represent our data. To do so, create a new package called `database`:

```
com.journaler.database
```

Then, create a new Kotlin class called `DbModel`. The `DbModel` class will represent the matrix for all database models of our application and will contain only the ID, since the ID is a mandatory field and will be used as a primary key. Make sure your `DbModel` class looks like this:

```
package com.journaler.database

abstract class DbModel {
  abstract var id: Long
}
```

Now, when we define our starting point, we will define data classes that will actually contain data. Inside our existing package called `model`, create new classes--`DbEntry`, `Note`, and `Todo`. `Note` and `Todo` will extend `Entry`, which extends the `DbModel` class.

The `Entry` class code is as follows:

```
package com.journaler.model

import android.location.Location
import com.journaler.database.DbModel

abstract class Entry(
  var title: String,
  var message: String,
  var location: Location
) : DbModel()
Note class:
package com.journaler.model

import android.location.Location
```

```
class Note(
  title: String,
  message: String,
  location: Location
) : Entry(
    title,
    message,
    location
    ) {
     override var id = 0L
    }
```

You will notice that we put the current geolocation as the information stored in our note along with `title` and note `message` content. We also overrode the ID. Since the newly instantiated `note` is not yet stored into the database, its ID will be zero. After we store it, it will be updated to the ID value obtained from the database.

The `Todo` class:

```
package com.journaler.model

import android.location.Location

class Todo(
  title: String,
  message: String,
  location: Location,
  var scheduledFor: Long
) : Entry(
    title,
    message,
    location
) {
override var id = 0L
}
```

The `Todo` class will have one additional field than the `Note` class--`timestamp` for the time when `todo` is scheduled.

Now, after we define our data models, we will describe our database. We have to define the database helper class responsible for database initialization. The database helper class must extend Android's `SQLiteOpenHelper` class. Create the `DbHelper` class and make sure it extends the `SQLiteOpenHelper` class:

```kotlin
package com.journaler.database

import android.database.sqlite.SQLiteDatabase
import android.database.sqlite.SQLiteOpenHelper
import android.util.Log
import com.journaler.Journaler

class DbHelper(val dbName: String, val version: Int) :
SQLiteOpenHelper(
  Journaler.ctx, dbName, null, version
) {

  companion object {
    val ID: String = "_id"
    val TABLE_TODOS = "todos"
    val TABLE_NOTES = "notes"
    val COLUMN_TITLE: String = "title"
    val COLUMN_MESSAGE: String = "message"
    val COLUMN_SCHEDULED: String = "scheduled"
    val COLUMN_LOCATION_LATITUDE: String = "latitude"
    val COLUMN_LOCATION_LONGITUDE: String = "longitude"
  }

  private val tag = "DbHelper"

  private val createTableNotes =  """
    CREATE TABLE if not exists $TABLE_NOTES
      (
        $ID integer PRIMARY KEY autoincrement,
        $COLUMN_TITLE text,
        $COLUMN_MESSAGE text,
        $COLUMN_LOCATION_LATITUDE real,
        $COLUMN_LOCATION_LONGITUDE real
      )
    """

  private val createTableTodos =  """
    CREATE TABLE if not exists $TABLE_TODOS
      (
        $ID integer PRIMARY KEY autoincrement,
        $COLUMN_TITLE text,
        $COLUMN_MESSAGE text,
```

```
            $COLUMN_SCHEDULED integer,
            $COLUMN_LOCATION_LATITUDE real,
            $COLUMN_LOCATION_LONGITUDE real
        )
    """

    override fun onCreate(db: SQLiteDatabase) {
     Log.d(tag, "Database [ CREATING ]")
     db.execSQL(createTableNotes)
     db.execSQL(createTableTodos)
     Log.d(tag, "Database [ CREATED ]")
    }

    override fun onUpgrade(db: SQLiteDatabase?, oldVersion: Int,
    newVersion: Int) {
      // Ignore for now.
    }

}
```

Our class `companion` object contains definitions for table and column names. We also defined SQLs for tables creation. Finally, SQLs are executed in the `onCreate()` method. In the next section, we will go further with database management and finally insert some data.

CRUD operations

CRUD operations are operations for creating, updating, selecting, or removing data. They are defined with an interface called `Crud` and it will be generic. Create a new interface in the `database` package. Make sure it covers all CRUD operations:

```
interface Crud<T> where T : DbModel {

  companion object {
   val BROADCAST_ACTION = "com.journaler.broadcast.crud"
   val BROADCAST_EXTRAS_KEY_CRUD_OPERATION_RESULT = "crud_result"
  }

 /**
  * Returns the ID of inserted item.
  */
 fun insert(what: T): Long

 /**
  * Returns the list of inserted IDs.
  */
```

```
fun insert(what: Collection<T>): List<Long>

/**
* Returns the number of updated items.
*/
fun update(what: T): Int

/**
* Returns the number of updated items.
*/
fun update(what: Collection<T>): Int

/**
* Returns the number of deleted items.
*/
fun delete(what: T): Int

/**
* Returns the number of deleted items.
*/
fun delete(what: Collection<T>): Int

/**
* Returns the list of items.
*/
fun select(args: Pair<String, String>): List<T>

/**
* Returns the list of items.
*/
fun select(args: Collection<Pair<String, String>>): List<T>

/**
* Returns the list of items.
*/
fun selectAll(): List<T>

}
```

For executing CRUD operations, there are two method versions. First version is the one that accepts *collections of instances* and the second that *accepts a single item*. Let's create CRUD concretization by creating a Kotlin object called Db. Creating an object makes our concretization a perfect singleton. The Db object must implement the Crud interface:

```
package com.journaler.database

import android.content.ContentValues
import android.location.Location
```

```
import android.util.Log
import com.journaler.model.Note
import com.journaler.model.Todo

object Db {

  private val tag = "Db"
  private val version = 1
  private val name = "students"

  val NOTE = object : Crud<Note> {
    // Crud implementations
  }

  val TODO = object : Crud<NoteTodo {
      // Crud implementations
  }
}
```

Insert CRUD operation

The insert operation will add new data into the database. What follows is its implementation:

```
val NOTE = object : Crud<Note> {
  ...
  override fun insert(what: Note): Long {
    val inserted = insert(listOf(what))
    if (!inserted.isEmpty()) return inserted[0]
    return 0
  }

  override fun insert(what: Collection<Note>): List<Long> {
    val db = DbHelper(name, version).writableDatabase
    db.beginTransaction()
    var inserted = 0
    val items = mutableListOf<Long>()
    what.forEach { item ->
      val values = ContentValues()
      val table = DbHelper.TABLE_NOTES
      values.put(DbHelper.COLUMN_TITLE, item.title)
      values.put(DbHelper.COLUMN_MESSAGE, item.message)
      values.put(DbHelper.COLUMN_LOCATION_LATITUDE,
        item.location.latitude)
      values.put(DbHelper.COLUMN_LOCATION_LONGITUDE,
        item.location.longitude)
```

```kotlin
            val id = db.insert(table, null, values)
              if (id > 0) {
                items.add(id)
                Log.v(tag, "Entry ID assigned [ $id ]")
                  inserted++
                }
              }
              val success = inserted == what.size
              if (success) {
                  db.setTransactionSuccessful()
              } else {
                  items.clear()
              }
               db.endTransaction()
               db.close()
               return items
            }
            ...
        }
    ...
    val TODO = object : Crud<Todo> {
      ...
      override fun insert(what: Todo): Long {
        val inserted = insert(listOf(what))
        if (!inserted.isEmpty()) return inserted[0]
        return 0
      }

      override fun insert(what: Collection<Todo>): List<Long> {
        val db = DbHelper(name, version).writableDatabase
        db.beginTransaction()
        var inserted = 0
        val items = mutableListOf<Long>()
        what.forEach { item ->
          val table = DbHelper.TABLE_TODOS
          val values = ContentValues()
          values.put(DbHelper.COLUMN_TITLE, item.title)
          values.put(DbHelper.COLUMN_MESSAGE, item.message)
          values.put(DbHelper.COLUMN_LOCATION_LATITUDE,
          item.location.latitude)
          values.put(DbHelper.COLUMN_LOCATION_LONGITUDE,
          item.location.longitude)
          values.put(DbHelper.COLUMN_SCHEDULED, item.scheduledFor)
            val id = db.insert(table, null, values)
            if (id > 0) {
              item.id = id
              Log.v(tag, "Entry ID assigned [ $id ]")
              inserted++
```

```
          }
        }
        val success = inserted == what.size
        if (success) {
            db.setTransactionSuccessful()
        } else {
            items.clear()
        }
        db.endTransaction()
        db.close()
        return items
      }
    ...
  }
  ...
```

Update CRUD operation

The update operation will update the existing data in our database. What follows is its implementation:

```
val NOTE = object : Crud<Note> {
    ...
    override fun update(what: Note) = update(listOf(what))

    override fun update(what: Collection<Note>): Int {
      val db = DbHelper(name, version).writableDatabase
      db.beginTransaction()
      var updated = 0
      what.forEach { item ->
        val values = ContentValues()
        val table = DbHelper.TABLE_NOTES
        values.put(DbHelper.COLUMN_TITLE, item.title)
        values.put(DbHelper.COLUMN_MESSAGE, item.message)
        values.put(DbHelper.COLUMN_LOCATION_LATITUDE,
        item.location.latitude)
        values.put(DbHelper.COLUMN_LOCATION_LONGITUDE,
        item.location.longitude)
        db.update(table, values, "_id = ?",
        arrayOf(item.id.toString()))
            updated++
      }
      val result = updated == what.size
      if (result) {
        db.setTransactionSuccessful()
      } else {
```

```
          updated = 0
        }
       db.endTransaction()
       db.close()
       return updated
      }
      ...
    }
    ...
  val TODO = object : Crud<Todo> {
    ...
    override fun update(what: Todo) = update(listOf(what))

    override fun update(what: Collection<Todo>): Int {
      val db = DbHelper(name, version).writableDatabase
      db.beginTransaction()
      var updated = 0
      what.forEach { item ->
        val table = DbHelper.TABLE_TODOS
        val values = ContentValues()
        values.put(DbHelper.COLUMN_TITLE, item.title)
        values.put(DbHelper.COLUMN_MESSAGE, item.message)
        values.put(DbHelper.COLUMN_LOCATION_LATITUDE,
        item.location.latitude)
       values.put(DbHelper.COLUMN_LOCATION_LONGITUDE,
       item.location.longitude)
       values.put(DbHelper.COLUMN_SCHEDULED, item.scheduledFor)
       db.update(table, values, "_id = ?",
       arrayOf(item.id.toString()))
          updated++
       }
       val result = updated == what.size
       if (result) {
         db.setTransactionSuccessful()
       } else {
         updated = 0
       }
       db.endTransaction()
       db.close()
       return updated
      }
      ...
    }
    ...
```

Delete CRUD operation

The delete operation will remove the existing data from the database. What follows is its implementation:

```
val NOTE = object : Crud<Note> {
  ...
  override fun delete(what: Note): Int = delete(listOf(what))
      override fun delete(what: Collection<Note>): Int {
      val db = DbHelper(name, version).writableDatabase
      db.beginTransaction()
      val ids = StringBuilder()
      what.forEachIndexed { index, item ->
      ids.append(item.id.toString())
        if (index < what.size - 1) {
           ids.append(", ")
        }
      }
      val table = DbHelper.TABLE_NOTES
      val statement = db.compileStatement(
        "DELETE FROM $table WHERE ${DbHelper.ID} IN ($ids);"
      )
      val count = statement.executeUpdateDelete()
      val success = count > 0
      if (success) {
        db.setTransactionSuccessful()
        Log.i(tag, "Delete [ SUCCESS ][ $count ][ $statement ]")
      } else {
         Log.w(tag, "Delete [ FAILED ][ $statement ]")
      }
       db.endTransaction()
       db.close()
       return count
    }
    ...
  }
  ...
  val TODO = object : Crud<Todo> {
    ...
    override fun delete(what: Todo): Int = delete(listOf(what))
    override fun delete(what: Collection<Todo>): Int {
      val db = DbHelper(name, version).writableDatabase
      db.beginTransaction()
      val ids = StringBuilder()
      what.forEachIndexed { index, item ->
      ids.append(item.id.toString())
        if (index < what.size - 1) {
            ids.append(", ")
```

```
          }
      }
      val table = DbHelper.TABLE_TODOS
      val statement = db.compileStatement(
        "DELETE FROM $table WHERE ${DbHelper.ID} IN ($ids);"
      )
      val count = statement.executeUpdateDelete()
      val success = count > 0
      if (success) {
        db.setTransactionSuccessful()
        Log.i(tag, "Delete [ SUCCESS ][ $count ][ $statement ]")
      } else {
        Log.w(tag, "Delete [ FAILED ][ $statement ]")
      }
       db.endTransaction()
       db.close()
       return count
      }
      ...
    }
    ...
```

Select CRUD operation

The select operation will read and return data from the database. What follows is its implementation:

```
val NOTE = object : Crud<Note> {
    ...
    override fun select(
        args: Pair<String, String>
    ): List<Note> = select(listOf(args))

    override fun select(args: Collection<Pair<String, String>>):
    List<Note> {
      val db = DbHelper(name, version).writableDatabase
      val selection = StringBuilder()
      val selectionArgs = mutableListOf<String>()
      args.forEach { arg ->
          selection.append("${arg.first} == ?")
          selectionArgs.add(arg.second)
      }
      val result = mutableListOf<Note>()
      val cursor = db.query(
          true,
          DbHelper.TABLE_NOTES,
```

```
            null,
            selection.toString(),
            selectionArgs.toTypedArray(),
            null, null, null, null
        )
        while (cursor.moveToNext()) {
        val id = cursor.getLong(cursor.getColumnIndexOrThrow
        (DbHelper.ID))
        val titleIdx = cursor.getColumnIndexOrThrow
        (DbHelper.COLUMN_TITLE)
        val title = cursor.getString(titleIdx)
        val messageIdx = cursor.getColumnIndexOrThrow
        (DbHelper.COLUMN_MESSAGE)
        val message = cursor.getString(messageIdx)
        val latitudeIdx = cursor.getColumnIndexOrThrow(
            DbHelper.COLUMN_LOCATION_LATITUDE
        )
        val latitude = cursor.getDouble(latitudeIdx)
        val longitudeIdx = cursor.getColumnIndexOrThrow(
            DbHelper.COLUMN_LOCATION_LONGITUDE
        )
        val longitude = cursor.getDouble(longitudeIdx)
        val location = Location("")
        location.latitude = latitude
        location.longitude = longitude
        val note = Note(title, message, location)
        note.id = id
        result.add(note)
     }
        cursor.close()
        return result
    }

    override fun selectAll(): List<Note> {
      val db = DbHelper(name, version).writableDatabase
      val result = mutableListOf<Note>()
      val cursor = db.query(
         true,
         DbHelper.TABLE_NOTES,
         null, null, null, null, null, null, null
      )
      while (cursor.moveToNext()) {
             val id = cursor.getLong(cursor.getColumnIndexOrThrow
             (DbHelper.ID))
             val titleIdx = cursor.getColumnIndexOrThrow
             (DbHelper.COLUMN_TITLE)
             val title = cursor.getString(titleIdx)
             val messageIdx = cursor.getColumnIndexOrThrow
```

```
            (DbHelper.COLUMN_MESSAGE)
        val message = cursor.getString(messageIdx)
        val latitudeIdx = cursor.getColumnIndexOrThrow(
          DbHelper.COLUMN_LOCATION_LATITUDE
        )
        val latitude = cursor.getDouble(latitudeIdx)
        val longitudeIdx = cursor.getColumnIndexOrThrow(
          DbHelper.COLUMN_LOCATION_LONGITUDE
        )
        val longitude = cursor.getDouble(longitudeIdx)
        val location = Location("")
        location.latitude = latitude
        location.longitude = longitude
        val note = Note(title, message, location)
        note.id = id
        result.add(note)
      }
      cursor.close()
      return result
    }
    ...
  }
  ...
val TODO = object : Crud<Todo> {
  ...
  override fun select(args: Pair<String, String>): List<Todo> =
  select(listOf(args))

  override fun select(args: Collection<Pair<String, String>>):
  List<Todo> {
    val db = DbHelper(name, version).writableDatabase
    val selection = StringBuilder()
    val selectionArgs = mutableListOf<String>()
    args.forEach { arg ->
      selection.append("${arg.first} == ?")
      selectionArgs.add(arg.second)
    }
    val result = mutableListOf<Todo>()
    val cursor = db.query(
      true,
      DbHelper.TABLE_NOTES,
      null,
      selection.toString(),
      selectionArgs.toTypedArray(),
      null, null, null, null
    )
    while (cursor.moveToNext()) {
        val id = cursor.getLong(cursor.getColumnIndexOrThrow
```

```
        (DbHelper.ID))
        val titleIdx = cursor.getColumnIndexOrThrow
        (DbHelper.COLUMN_TITLE)
        val title = cursor.getString(titleIdx)
        val messageIdx = cursor.getColumnIndexOrThrow
        (DbHelper.COLUMN_MESSAGE)
        val message = cursor.getString(messageIdx)
        val latitudeIdx = cursor.getColumnIndexOrThrow(
            DbHelper.COLUMN_LOCATION_LATITUDE
        )
        val latitude = cursor.getDouble(latitudeIdx)
        val longitudeIdx = cursor.getColumnIndexOrThrow(
            DbHelper.COLUMN_LOCATION_LONGITUDE
        )
        val longitude = cursor.getDouble(longitudeIdx)
        val location = Location("")
        val scheduledForIdx = cursor.getColumnIndexOrThrow(
            DbHelper.COLUMN_SCHEDULED
        )
        val scheduledFor = cursor.getLong(scheduledForIdx)
        location.latitude = latitude
        location.longitude = longitude
        val todo = Todo(title, message, location, scheduledFor)
        todo.id = id
        result.add(todo)
    }
  cursor.close()
  return result
}
override fun selectAll(): List<Todo> {
val db = DbHelper(name, version).writableDatabase
val result = mutableListOf<Todo>()
val cursor = db.query(
  true,
  DbHelper.TABLE_NOTES,
  null, null, null, null, null, null, null
)
while (cursor.moveToNext()) {
        val id = cursor.getLong(cursor.getColumnIndexOrThrow
        (DbHelper.ID))
        val titleIdx = cursor.getColumnIndexOrThrow
        (DbHelper.COLUMN_TITLE)
        val title = cursor.getString(titleIdx)
        val messageIdx = cursor.getColumnIndexOrThrow
        (DbHelper.COLUMN_MESSAGE)
        val message = cursor.getString(messageIdx)
        val latitudeIdx = cursor.getColumnIndexOrThrow(
            DbHelper.COLUMN_LOCATION_LATITUDE
```

```
            )
            val latitude = cursor.getDouble(latitudeIdx)
            val longitudeIdx = cursor.getColumnIndexOrThrow(
                DbHelper.COLUMN_LOCATION_LONGITUDE
            )
            val longitude = cursor.getDouble(longitudeIdx)
            val location = Location("")
            val scheduledForIdx = cursor.getColumnIndexOrThrow(
                DbHelper.COLUMN_SCHEDULED
            )
            val scheduledFor = cursor.getLong(scheduledForIdx)
            location.latitude = latitude
            location.longitude = longitude
            val todo = Todo(title, message, location, scheduledFor)
            todo.id = id
            result.add(todo)
        }
        cursor.close()
        return result
    }
    ...
    }
    ...
```

Each CRUD operation will obtain a database instance by using our DbHelper class. We will not expose it directly, but utilize it by our CRUD mechanism. After each operation, the database will be closed. We can only get a readable database or, like in our case, a WritableDatabase instance by accessing writableDatabase. Each CRUD operation is performed as an SQL transaction. This means that we will start it by calling beginTransaction() on the database instance. The transaction is completed by calling endTransaction(). If we do not call setTransactionSuccessful() before it, no changes will apply. As we already mentioned, there are two versions of each CRUD operation--one that contains the main implementation and the second that just passes instances to the other. To perform the insert into the database, it's important to note that we will use the insert() method on the database instance that accepts the table name into which we are inserting, and content values (ContentValues class) that represent the data. The update and delete operations are similar. We use the update() and delete() methods. In our case, for data removal, we used compileStatement() containing the delete SQL query.

The code we provided here is a bit complex. We directly pointed only to database related matter. So, be patient, read the code slowly, and take your time to investigate it. We encourage you to create your own version of database management classes in your own way by utilizing the Android database classes we have already mentioned.

Tying things together

We have one more step! It's the practical use of our database classes and performing CRUD operations. We will extend the application to create notes, and we will focus on insertion.

Before we insert anything into the database, we must provide a mechanism to obtain the current user location since it's required for both `notes` and `todos`. Create a new class called `LocationProvider` and locate it in the `location` package as follows:

```
object LocationProvider {
  private val tag = "Location provider"
  private val listeners =  CopyOnWriteArrayList
  <WeakReference<LocationListener>>()

  private val locationListener = object : LocationListener {
  ...
  }

  fun subscribe(subscriber: LocationListener): Boolean {
    val result = doSubscribe(subscriber)
    turnOnLocationListening()
    return result
  }

  fun unsubscribe(subscriber: LocationListener): Boolean {
    val result = doUnsubscribe(subscriber)
    if (listeners.isEmpty()) {
        turnOffLocationListening()
    }
    return result
  }

  private fun turnOnLocationListening() {
  ...
  }

  private fun turnOffLocationListening() {
  ...
  }
```

```
    private fun doSubscribe(listener: LocationListener): Boolean {
    ...
    }

    private fun doUnsubscribe(listener: LocationListener): Boolean {
     ...
    }
}
```

We exposed the main structure for the `LocationProvider` object. Let's take a look at the rest of the implementation:

The `locationListener` instance code is as follows:

```
private val locationListener = object : LocationListener {
    override fun onLocationChanged(location: Location) {
        Log.i(
                tag,
                String.format(
                        Locale.ENGLISH,
                        "Location [ lat: %s ][ long: %s ]",
                        location.latitude, location.longitude
                )
        )
        val iterator = listeners.iterator()
        while (iterator.hasNext()) {
            val reference = iterator.next()
            val listener = reference.get()
            listener?.onLocationChanged(location)
        }
    }

    override fun onStatusChanged(provider: String, status: Int,
    extras: Bundle) {
        Log.d(
                tag,
                String.format(Locale.ENGLISH, "Status changed [ %s
                ][ %d ]", provider, status)
        )
        val iterator = listeners.iterator()
        while (iterator.hasNext()) {
            val reference = iterator.next()
            val listener = reference.get()
            listener?.onStatusChanged(provider, status, extras)
        }
    }

    override fun onProviderEnabled(provider: String) {
```

```
            Log.i(tag, String.format("Provider [ %s ][ ENABLED ]",
            provider))
            val iterator = listeners.iterator()
            while (iterator.hasNext()) {
                val reference = iterator.next()
                val listener = reference.get()
                listener?.onProviderEnabled(provider)
            }
        }

    override fun onProviderDisabled(provider: String) {
            Log.i(tag, String.format("Provider [ %s ][ ENABLED ]",
            provider))
            val iterator = listeners.iterator()
            while (iterator.hasNext()) {
                val reference = iterator.next()
                val listener = reference.get()
                listener?.onProviderDisabled(provider)
            }
        }
    }
```

`LocationListener` is Android's interface whose purpose is to be executed on `location` events. We created our concretization that will basically notify all subscribed parties about those events. The most important for us is `onLocationChanged()`:

```
    turnOnLocationListening():

private fun turnOnLocationListening() {
    Log.v(tag, "We are about to turn on location listening.")
    val ctx = Journaler.ctx
    if (ctx != null) {
        Log.v(tag, "We are about to check location permissions.")

        val permissionsOk =
        ActivityCompat.checkSelfPermission(ctx,
        Manifest.permission.ACCESS_FINE_LOCATION) ==
        PackageManager.PERMISSION_GRANTED
        &&
        ActivityCompat.checkSelfPermission(ctx,
        Manifest.permission.ACCESS_COARSE_LOCATION) ==
        PackageManager.PERMISSION_GRANTED

        if (!permissionsOk) {
            throw IllegalStateException(
            "Permissions required [ ACCESS_FINE_LOCATION ]
             [ ACCESS_COARSE_LOCATION ]"
            )
```

```
    }
    Log.v(tag, "Location permissions are ok.
    We are about to request location changes.")
    val locationManager =
    ctx.getSystemService(Context.LOCATION_SERVICE)
    as LocationManager

    val criteria = Criteria()
    criteria.accuracy = Criteria.ACCURACY_FINE
    criteria.powerRequirement = Criteria.POWER_HIGH
    criteria.isAltitudeRequired = false
    criteria.isBearingRequired = false
    criteria.isSpeedRequired = false
    criteria.isCostAllowed = true

    locationManager.requestLocationUpdates(
            1000, 1F, criteria, locationListener,
            Looper.getMainLooper()
    )
    } else {
      Log.e(tag, "No application context available.")
  }
}
```

To turn on location listening, we must check if permissions are properly fulfilled. If that is the case, then we are obtaining Android's `LocationManager` and defined `Criteria` for location updates. We defined our criteria to be very precise and accurate. Finally, we request location updates by passing the following arguments:

- `long minTime`
- `float minDistance`
- `Criteria criteria`
- `LocationListener listener`
- `Looper looper`

As you can see, we passed our `LocationListener` concretization that will notify all subscribed third parties about `location` events:

```
turnOffLocationListening():private fun turnOffLocationListening()
{
  Log.v(tag, "We are about to turn off location listening.")
  val ctx = Journaler.ctx
  if (ctx != null) {
    val locationManager =
    ctx.getSystemService(Context.LOCATION_SERVICE)
```

```
    as LocationManager

    locationManager.removeUpdates(locationListener)
    } else {
        Log.e(tag, "No application context available.")
    }
}
```

- We stopped listening for location by simply removing our listener
  instance.doSubscribe():

```
private fun doSubscribe(listener: LocationListener): Boolean {
  val iterator = listeners.iterator()
  while (iterator.hasNext()) {
    val reference = iterator.next()
    val refListener = reference.get()
    if (refListener != null && refListener === listener) {
        Log.v(tag, "Already subscribed: " + listener)
        return false
    }
  }
  listeners.add(WeakReference(listener))
  Log.v(tag, "Subscribed, subscribers count: " + listeners.size)
  return true
}
```

- The doUnsubscribe() method code is as follows:

```
private fun doUnsubscribe(listener: LocationListener): Boolean {
  var result = true
  val iterator = listeners.iterator()
  while (iterator.hasNext()) {
      val reference = iterator.next()
      val refListener = reference.get()
      if (refListener != null && refListener === listener) {
          val success = listeners.remove(reference)
          if (!success) {
              Log.w(tag, "Couldn't un subscribe, subscribers
              count: " + listeners.size)
          } else {
              Log.v(tag, "Un subscribed, subscribers count: " +
              listeners.size)
          }
          if (result) {
              result = success
          }
      }
}
```

```
            return result
    }
```

These two methods are responsible for subscribing and unsubscribing in location updates to interested third parties.

We have all we need. Open the `NoteActivity` class and extend it as follows:

```
class NoteActivity : ItemActivity() {
  private var note: Note? = null
  override val tag = "Note activity"
  private var location: Location? = null
  override fun getLayout() = R.layout.activity_note
 private val textWatcher = object : TextWatcher {
    override fun afterTextChanged(p0: Editable?) {
        updateNote()
    }

    override fun beforeTextChanged(p0: CharSequence?, p1: Int, p2:
    Int, p3: Int) {}
    override fun onTextChanged(p0: CharSequence?, p1: Int, p2:
    Int, p3: Int) {}
  }

  private val locationListener = object : LocationListener {
    override fun onLocationChanged(p0: Location?) {
        p0?.let {
            LocationProvider.unsubscribe(this)
            location = p0
            val title = getNoteTitle()
            val content = getNoteContent()
            note = Note(title, content, p0)
            val task = object : AsyncTask<Note, Void, Boolean>() {
                override fun doInBackground(vararg params: Note?):
                Boolean {
                    if (!params.isEmpty()) {
                        val param = params[0]
                        param?.let {
                            return Db.NOTE.insert(param) > 0
                        }
                    }
                    return false
                }

                override fun onPostExecute(result: Boolean?) {
                    result?.let {
                        if (result) {
                            Log.i(tag, "Note inserted.")
```

```
                            } else {
                                Log.e(tag, "Note not inserted.")
                            }
                        }
                    }
                }
            task.execute(note)
            }
        }

    override fun onStatusChanged(p0: String?, p1: Int, p2:
    Bundle?) {}
    override fun onProviderEnabled(p0: String?) {}
    override fun onProviderDisabled(p0: String?) {}
    }

    override fun onCreate(savedInstanceState: Bundle?) {
        super.onCreate(savedInstanceState)
        note_title.addTextChangedListener(textWatcher)
        note_content.addTextChangedListener(textWatcher)
    }

    private fun updateNote() {
        if (note == null) {
            if (!TextUtils.isEmpty(getNoteTitle()) &&
            !TextUtils.isEmpty(getNoteContent())) {
                LocationProvider.subscribe(locationListener)
            }
        } else {
            note?.title = getNoteTitle()
            note?.message = getNoteContent()
            val task = object : AsyncTask<Note, Void, Boolean>() {
                override fun doInBackground(vararg params: Note?):
            Boolean {
                if (!params.isEmpty()) {
                    val param = params[0]
                    param?.let {
                        return Db.NOTE.update(param) > 0
                    }
                }
                    return false
            }

            override fun onPostExecute(result: Boolean?) {
                result?.let {
                    if (result) {
                        Log.i(tag, "Note updated.")
                    } else {
```

```
                        Log.e(tag, "Note not updated.")
                    }
                }
            }
        }
        task.execute(note)
    }
}

private fun getNoteContent(): String {
    return note_content.text.toString()
}

private fun getNoteTitle(): String {
    return note_title.text.toString()
}

}
```

What did we do here? Let's go from top to bottom and explain everything! We added two fields--one that contains the current `Note` instance we are editing and one that holds information about the current user's location. Then, we defined a `TextWatcher` instance. `TextWatcher` is a listener that we will assign to our `EditText` views, and, on each change, the proper update method will be triggered. That method will create a new `note` class and persist it into a database if it does not exist, or perform a data update if it exists.

Since we will not insert note until there is no location data available, we defined our `locationListener` to put received location into the location field and to unsubscribe itself. Then, we will get the current value for the `note` title and its main content and create a new `note` instance. Since the database operations can take some time, we will execute them asynchronously. For that purpose, we will use the `AsyncTask` class. The `AsyncTask` class is Android's class that is intended to be used for the most async operations. Class defines input type, progress type, and result type. In our case, input type is `Note`. We do not have a progress type, but we have a result type `Boolean`, that is, if the operation is successful or not.

The main work is done in the `doInBackground()` concretization while the result is handled in `onPostExecute()`. As you can see, we are performing insertion in the background using classes we recently defined for database management.

If you keep looking, the next thing we do is assign `textWatcher` to `EditText` views in the `onCreate()` method. Then, we define our most important method--`updateNote()`. It will update an existing note or insert a new one if it does not exist. Again, we used `AsyncTask` to perform an operation in the background.

Build your application and run it. Try to insert `note`. Observe your Logcat. You will notice database-related logs as your type:

```
I/Note activity: Note inserted.
I/Note activity: Note updated.
I/Note activity: Note updated.
I/Note activity: Note updated.
```

If you can see these logs, you have successfully implemented your first database in Android. We encourage you to extend the code for the rest of the CRUD operations. Make sure `NoteActivity` supports the `select` and `delete` operations.

Summary

In this chapter, we demonstrated how to persist complex data in Android. Databases are the heart of every application, so **Journaler** is not an exception. We covered all CRUD operations performed on the SQLite database and gave a proper implementation for each of them. In our next chapter, we will demonstrate another persistence mechanism for less complex data. We will deal with Android shared preferences, and we will use them to keep simple and small data for our application.

8

Android Preferences

In the previous chapter, we were dealing with complex data that was stored in the SQLite database. This time, we will deal with a much simpler form of data. We will cover one particular case of use to demonstrate the use of Android shared preferences.

Let's say that we want to remember the last page position of our `ViewPager` class and to open it every time an application is started. We will use shared preferences to remember it and persist that information on each view page position change and retrieve it when it is needed.

In this rather short chapter, we will cover the following topics:

- What are Android's preferences and how can you use them?
- Defining your own preferences manager

What are Android preferences?

Preferences for our application that are persisted and retrieved by Android's shared preferences mechanism are called **shared preferences**. Shared preferences themselves represent XML data that is accessed and modified by Android and its API. Android handles all the work for us regarding retrieving and saving preferences. It also provides the mechanism for these preferences to be private, hidden from the public access. Android SDK has a great set of classes for preferences management. Also, there are abstractions available so you are not limited to default XMLs, but you can create your own persistence layer.

How can you use them?

To use shared preferences, you have to obtain the `SharedPreferences` instance from the current context:

```
val prefs = ctx.getSharedPreferences(key, mode)
```

Here, `key` represents a `String` that will name this shared preferences instance. The XML file in the system will have that name as well. These are modes (operation modes) that can be available from `Context class`:

- `MODE_PRIVATE`: This is a default mode, and the created file can only be accessed by our calling application
- `MODE_WORLD_READABLE`: This is deprecated
- `MODE_WORLD_WRITEABLE`: This is deprecated

Then, we can store values or retrieve them as follows:

```
val value = prefs.getString("key", "default value")
```

There is a similar `getter` method for all common data types.

Editing (storing) preferences

We will start this section by providing an example of preferences editing:

```
preferences.edit().putString("key", "balue").commit()
```

 The `commit()` method executes the operation immediately, while the `apply()` method executes it in the background.
Never obtain or manipulate your shared preferences from an application's main thread if you use the `commit()` method.
Make sure that all writing and reading is performed in the background. You can use `AsyncTask` for that purpose or, instead of `commit()`, use `apply()`.

Removing preferences

To remove preferences, there is a `remove` method available, shown here:

```
prefs.edit().remove("key").commit()
```

Do not remove your preferences by overwriting them with empty data. For example, overwriting integers with null or strings with empty string.

Defining your own preferences manager

To achieve the mission from the beginning of this chapter, we will create a proper mechanism to obtaining shared preferences.

Create a new package called `preferences`. We will put all `preferences` related code in that package. For shared preferences management, we will need the following three classes:

- `PreferencesProviderAbstract`: This is basic abstraction to provide access to SharedPreferences
- `PreferencesProvider`: This is a `PreferencesProviderAbstract` implementation
- `PreferencesConfiguration`: This class is responsible for describing preferences we try to instantiate

Benefit of using this approach is a unified approach to shared preferences access in our application.

Let's define each class as follows:

- The `PreferencesProviderAbstract` class code is as follows:

```
package com.journaler.perferences

import android.content.Context
import android.content.SharedPreferences

abstract class PreferencesProviderAbstract {
  abstract fun obtain(configuration: PreferencesConfiguration,
  ctx: Context): SharedPreferences
}
```

- The `PreferencesConfiguration` class code is as follows:

```
package com.journaler.perferences
data class PreferencesConfiguration
(val key: String, val mode: Int)
```

- The `PreferencesProvider` class code is as follows:

```
package com.journaler.perferences

import android.content.Context
import android.content.SharedPreferences

class PreferencesProvider : PreferencesProviderAbstract() {
  override fun obtain(configuration: PreferencesConfiguration,
  ctx: Context): SharedPreferences {
    return ctx.getSharedPreferences(configuration.key,
    configuration.mode)
  }
}
```

As you can see, we created a simple mechanism to obtain shared preferences. We will incorporate it. Open the `MainActivity` class and extend it according to this piece of code:

```
class MainActivity : BaseActivity() {
  ...
  private val keyPagePosition = "keyPagePosition"
  ...
  override fun onCreate(savedInstanceState: Bundle?) {
    super.onCreate(savedInstanceState)

    val provider = PreferencesProvider()
    val config = PreferencesConfiguration("journaler_prefs",
    Context.MODE_PRIVATE)
    val preferences = provider.obtain(config, this)

    pager.adapter = ViewPagerAdapter(supportFragmentManager)
    pager.addOnPageChangeListener(object :
    ViewPager.OnPageChangeListener {
        override fun onPageScrollStateChanged(state: Int) {
            // Ignore
        }

        override fun onPageScrolled(position: Int, positionOffset:
        Float, positionOffsetPixels: Int) {
            // Ignore
        }
```

```
    override fun onPageSelected(position: Int) {
      Log.v(tag, "Page [ $position ]")
      preferences.edit().putInt(keyPagePosition, position).apply()
    }
  })

  val pagerPosition = preferences.getInt(keyPagePosition, 0)
  pager.setCurrentItem(pagerPosition, true)
  ...
}
...
}
```

We created the `preferences` instance that is used to persist and read the view pager position. Build and run your application; swipe to one of the pages and then kill your application and run it again. If you take a look at Logcat, you will see something like this (filter it by `Page`):

```
V/Main activity: Page [ 1 ]
V/Main activity: Page [ 2 ]
V/Main activity: Page [ 3 ]
After we restarted the application:
V/Main activity: Page [ 3 ]
V/Main activity: Page [ 2 ]
V/Main activity: Page [ 1 ]
V/Main activity: Page [ 0 ]
```

We opened the application again after closing, and swiped back to the page with index 0.

Summary

In this chapter, you learned how to use the Android shared preferences mechanism for persisting application preferences. As you can see, it is very easy to create application preferences and use them in your application. In the next chapter, we will focus on concurrency in Android. We will learn about the mechanisms Android offers and give examples of how to use them.

9
Concurrency in Android

In this chapter, we will explain concurrency in Android. We will give examples and advice and apply concurrency to our **Journaler** application. We already touched on some basics by demonstrating the use of the `AsyncTask` class, but now we will dig deeper.

In this chapter, we will cover the following topics:

- Handlers and threads
- `AsyncTask`
- Android Looper
- Delayed execution

Introduction to Android concurrency

A default execution for our application is performed on the main application thread. This execution must be performant! If it happens that something is performing too long, then we get ANR--an Android application not responding message. To avoid ANRs, we run our code in the background. Android provides mechanisms so we can do that efficiently. Running operations asynchronously gives not just good performance, but great user experience.

Main thread

All user interface updates are performed from one thread. This is the main thread. All events are collected in a queue and processed by the `Looper` class instance.

The following image explains the relationship between classes involved:

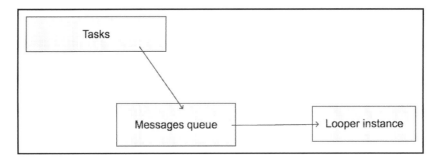

It is important to note that the main thread updates are all the UI you see. However, it can be done from other threads as well. Doing this directly from some other thread will cause an exception and your application can crash. To avoid this, execute all thread-related code on the main thread by calling the `runOnUiThread()` method from your current activity context.

Handlers and threads

In Android, threading can be performed in the standard way by using threads. It is not recommended to just fire naked threads without any control. So, for this purpose, you can use the `ThreadPools` and `Executor` classes.

To demonstrate this, we will update our application. Create a new package called `execution` with a class called `TaskExecutor`. Make sure it looks like this:

```
package com.journaler.execution

import java.util.concurrent.BlockingQueue
import java.util.concurrent.LinkedBlockingQueue
import java.util.concurrent.ThreadPoolExecutor
import java.util.concurrent.TimeUnit

class TaskExecutor private constructor(
    corePoolSize: Int,
    maximumPoolSize: Int,
    workQueue: BlockingQueue<Runnable>?

) : ThreadPoolExecutor(
    corePoolSize,
    maximumPoolSize,
    0L,
```

```
        TimeUnit.MILLISECONDS,
        workQueue
    ) {

    companion object {
        fun getInstance(capacity: Int): TaskExecutor {
            return TaskExecutor(
                    capacity,
                    capacity * 2,
                    LinkedBlockingQueue<Runnable>()
            )
        }
    }
} }
```

We extended the `ThreadPoolExecutor` class and `companion` object with the member method for executor instantiation. Let's apply it to our existing code. We will switch from the `AsyncTask` class we used to `TaskExecutor`. Open the `NoteActivity` class and update it as follows:

```
class NoteActivity : ItemActivity() {
    ...
    private val executor = TaskExecutor.getInstance(1)
    ...
    private val locationListener = object : LocationListener {
        override fun onLocationChanged(p0: Location?) {
            p0?.let {
                LocationProvider.unsubscribe(this)
                location = p0
                val title = getNoteTitle()
                val content = getNoteContent()
                note = Note(title, content, p0)
                executor.execute {
                    val param = note
                    var result = false
                    param?.let {
                        result = Db.insert(param)
                    }
                    if (result) {
                        Log.i(tag, "Note inserted.")
                    } else {
                        Log.e(tag, "Note not inserted.")
                    }
                }
            }
        }

        override fun onStatusChanged(p0: String?, p1: Int, p2: Bundle?)
```

```
      {}
      override fun onProviderEnabled(p0: String?) {}
      override fun onProviderDisabled(p0: String?) {}
    }
      ...
   private fun updateNote() {
    if (note == null) {
       if (!TextUtils.isEmpty(getNoteTitle()) &&
       !TextUtils.isEmpty(getNoteContent())) {
          LocationProvider.subscribe(locationListener)
        }
     } else {
        note?.title = getNoteTitle()
        note?.message = getNoteContent()
        executor.execute {
          val param = note
          var result = false
          param?.let {
             result = Db.update(param)
          }
          if (result) {
             Log.i(tag, "Note updated.")
          } else {
             Log.e(tag, "Note not updated.")
          }
        }
      }
    }
   }
 ... }
```

As you can see, we replaced `AsyncTask` with the executor. Our executor will handle only one thread at a time.

Other than the standard thread approach, Android also provides Handlers as one of the options for developers. Handlers are not a replacement for threads, but an addition! A Handler instance registers itself with its parent thread. It represents a mechanism to send data to that particular thread. We can send instances of the `Message` or `Runnable` class. Let's illustrate its use with an example. We will update the **Notes** screen with an indicator that will be green if everything is performed correctly. If database persisting fails, it will be red. Its default color will be grey. Open the `activity_note.xml` file and extend it with the indicator. The indicator will be plain view, as shown here:

```
<?xml version="1.0" encoding="utf-8"?>
<ScrollView xmlns:android=
 "http://schemas.android.com/apk/res/android"
android:layout_width="match_parent"
android:layout_height="match_parent"
```

```
    android:fillViewport="true">

    <LinearLayout
        android:layout_width="match_parent"
        android:layout_height="wrap_content"
        android:background="@color/black_transparent_40"
        android:orientation="vertical">

        ...

        <RelativeLayout
            android:layout_width="match_parent"
            android:layout_height="wrap_content">

            <View
                android:id="@+id/indicator"
                android:layout_width="40dp"
                android:layout_height="40dp"
                android:layout_alignParentEnd="true"
                android:layout_centerVertical="true"
                android:layout_margin="10dp"
                android:background="@android:color/darker_gray" />

            <EditText
                android:id="@+id/note_title"
                style="@style/edit_text_transparent"
                android:layout_width="match_parent"
                android:layout_height="wrap_content"
                android:hint="@string/title"
                android:padding="@dimen/form_padding" />

        </RelativeLayout>
          ...
      </LinearLayout>

  </ScrollView>
```

Now, when we add the indicator, it will change its color depending on the database insertion result. Update your `NoteActivity` class source code like this:

```
    class NoteActivity : ItemActivity() {
      ...
     private var handler: Handler? = null
     ....
     override fun onCreate(savedInstanceState: Bundle?) {
       super.onCreate(savedInstanceState)
       handler = Handler(Looper.getMainLooper())
       ...
```

```
        }
        ...
        private val locationListener = object : LocationListener {
          override fun onLocationChanged(p0: Location?) {
            p0?.let {
                ...
                executor.execute {
                    ...
                    handler?.post {
                        var color = R.color.vermilion
                        if (result) {
                            color = R.color.green
                        }
                        indicator.setBackgroundColor(
                                ContextCompat.getColor(
                                        this@NoteActivity,
                                        color
                                )
                        )
                    }
                }
            }
          }

          override fun onStatusChanged(p0: String?, p1: Int, p2: Bundle?)
          {}
          override fun onProviderEnabled(p0: String?) {}
          override fun onProviderDisabled(p0: String?) {}
        }
        ...
        private fun updateNote() {
          if (note == null) {
              ...
          } else {
              ...
              executor.execute {
                  ...
                  handler?.post {
                      var color = R.color.vermilion
                      if (result) {
                          color = R.color.green
                      }
                      indicator.setBackgroundColor
                      (ContextCompat.getColor(
                          this@NoteActivity,
                          color
                      ))
                  }
```

```
            }
          }
      } }
```

Build your application and run it. Create a new note. You will notice that the indicator changed color to green after you entered a title and the message content.

We will make some more changes and do the same thing with the `Message` class instance. Update your code according to this example:

```
class NoteActivity : ItemActivity() {
  ...
  override fun onCreate(savedInstanceState: Bundle?) {
    super.onCreate(savedInstanceState)
    handler = object : Handler(Looper.getMainLooper()) {
        override fun handleMessage(msg: Message?) {
            msg?.let {
                var color = R.color.vermilion
                if (msg.arg1 > 0) {
                    color = R.color.green
                }
                indicator.setBackgroundColor
                (ContextCompat.getColor(
                    this@NoteActivity,
                    color
                ))
             }
            super.handleMessage(msg)
          }
        }
      ...
    }
  ...
  private val locationListener = object : LocationListener {
  override fun onLocationChanged(p0: Location?) {
      p0?.let {
          ...
          executor.execute {
              ...
              sendMessage(result)
          }
      }
  }

  override fun onStatusChanged(p0: String?, p1: Int, p2: Bundle?)
  {}
  override fun onProviderEnabled(p0: String?) {}
  override fun onProviderDisabled(p0: String?) {}
```

```
        }
      ...
      private fun updateNote() {
        if (note == null) {
          ...
        } else {
          ...
          executor.execute {
            ...
            sendMessage(result)
          }
        }
      }
      ...
      private fun sendMessage(result: Boolean) {
        val msg = handler?.obtainMessage()
        if (result) {
          msg?.arg1 = 1
        } else {
          msg?.arg1 = 0
        }
        handler?.sendMessage(msg)
      }
      ...
    }
```

Pay attention to the Handler instantiation and the `sendMessage()` method. We obtained the `Message` instance using the `obtainMessage()` method from our `Handler` class. As the message argument, we passed an integer datatype. Depending on its value, we will update the indicator color.

AsyncTask

As you have may have noticed, we are already using the `AsyncTask` class in our application. Now, we will go one step forward with it--we will run it on the executor. Why would we do that?

First of all, by default, all `AsyncTasks` are executed in sequence by Android. To execute it in parallel, we need to execute it on the executor.

Wait! There is more. Now, when we execute tasks in parallel, imagine you executed a few of them. Let's say we start with two. That's fine. They will perform their operations and report us when completed. Then, imagine we run four of them. They will work too, in most cases, if the operations they execute are not too heavy. However, at some point, we run fifty AsyncTasks in parallel.

Then, your application is slowing down! Everything will slow down because there is no control over the execution of tasks. We must manage tasks so the performance is preserved. So, let's do that! We will continue on the same class we were updating so far. Change your NoteActivity as follows:

```kotlin
class NoteActivity : ItemActivity() {
    ...
    private val threadPoolExecutor = ThreadPoolExecutor(
        3, 3, 1, TimeUnit.SECONDS, LinkedBlockingQueue<Runnable>()
)

private class TryAsync(val identifier: String) : AsyncTask<Unit,
Int, Unit>() {
    private val tag = "TryAsync"

    override fun onPreExecute() {
        Log.i(tag, "onPreExecute [ $identifier ]")
        super.onPreExecute()
    }

    override fun doInBackground(vararg p0: Unit?): Unit {
        Log.i(tag, "doInBackground [ $identifier ][ START ]")
        Thread.sleep(5000)
        Log.i(tag, "doInBackground [ $identifier ][ END ]")
        return Unit
    }

    override fun onCancelled(result: Unit?) {
        Log.i(tag, "onCancelled [ $identifier ][ END ]")
        super.onCancelled(result)
    }

    override fun onProgressUpdate(vararg values: Int?) {
        val progress = values.first()
        progress?.let {
            Log.i(tag, "onProgressUpdate [ $identifier ][ $progress ]")
        }
        super.onProgressUpdate(*values)
    }

    override fun onPostExecute(result: Unit?) {
```

```
        Log.i(tag, "onPostExecute [ $identifier ]")
        super.onPostExecute(result)
    }
  }
  ...
  private val textWatcher = object : TextWatcher {
    override fun afterTextChanged(p0: Editable?) {
        ...
    }

    override fun beforeTextChanged(p0: CharSequence?, p1: Int, p2:
    Int, p3: Int) {}

    override fun onTextChanged(p0: CharSequence?, p1: Int, p2: Int,
    p3: Int) {
        p0?.let {
            tryAsync(p0.toString())
        }
    }
  }
  ...
  private fun tryAsync(identifier: String) {
    val tryAsync = TryAsync(identifier)
    tryAsync.executeOnExecutor(threadPoolExecutor)
  }
}
```

Since this is not actually something we will keep in the **Journaler** application, do not commit this code. Create it as a separate branch if you wish. We created a new instance of `ThreadPoolExecutor`. The constructor takes several arguments, as shown here:

- `corePoolSize`: This represents a minimal number of threads to keep in the pool.
- `maximumPoolSize`: This represents a maximal number of threads allowed in the pool.
- `keepAliveTime`: If the number of threads is greater than the core, the noncore threads will wait for a new tasks, and if they don't get one within the time defined by this parameter, they will terminate.
- `Unit`: This represents the time unit for `keepAliveTime`.
- `WorkQueue`: This represents the queue instance that will be used to hold the tasks.

- We will run our tasks on this executor. `AsyncTask` concretization will log all events during its life cycle. In the `main` method, we will wait for 5 seconds. Run the application and try to add a new note with `Android` as the title. Observe your Logcat output:

```
08-04 14:56:59.283 21953-21953 ... I/TryAsync: onPreExecute [ A ]
08-04 14:56:59.284 21953-23233 ... I/TryAsync: doInBackground [ A ][ START
]
08-04 14:57:00.202 21953-21953 ... I/TryAsync: onPreExecute [ An ]
08-04 14:57:00.204 21953-23250 ... I/TryAsync: doInBackground [ An ][ START
]
08-04 14:57:00.783 21953-21953 ... I/TryAsync: onPreExecute [ And ]
08-04 14:57:00.784 21953-23281 ... I/TryAsync: doInBackground [ And ][
START ]
08-04 14:57:01.001 21953-21953 ... I/TryAsync: onPreExecute [ Andr ]
08-04 14:57:01.669 21953-21953 ... I/TryAsync: onPreExecute [ Andro ]
08-04 14:57:01.934 21953-21953 ... I/TryAsync: onPreExecute [ Androi ]
08-04 14:57:02.314 21953-2195  ... I/TryAsync: onPreExecute [ Android ]
08-04 14:57:04.285 21953-23233 ... I/TryAsync: doInBackground [ A ][ END ]
08-04 14:57:04.286 21953-23233 ... I/TryAsync: doInBackground [ Andr ][
START ]
08-04 14:57:04.286 21953-21953 ... I/TryAsync: onPostExecute [ A ]
08-04 14:57:05.204 21953-23250 ... I/TryAsync: doInBackground [ An ][ END ]
08-04 14:57:05.204 21953-21953 ... I/TryAsync: onPostExecute [ An ]
08-04 14:57:05.205 21953-23250 ... I/TryAsync: doInBackground [ Andro ][
START ]
08-04 14:57:05.784 21953-23281 ... I/TryAsync: doInBackground [ And ][ END
]
08-04 14:57:05.785 21953-23281 ... I/TryAsync: doInBackground [ Androi ][
START ]
08-04 14:57:05.786 21953-21953 ... I/TryAsync: onPostExecute [ And ]
08-04 14:57:09.286 21953-23233 ... I/TryAsync: doInBackground [ Andr ][ END
]
08-04 14:57:09.287 21953-21953 ... I/TryAsync: onPostExecute [ Andr ]
08-04 14:57:09.287 21953-23233 ... I/TryAsync: doInBackground [ Android ][
START ]
08-04 14:57:10.205 21953-23250 ... I/TryAsync: doInBackground [ Andro ][
END ]
08-04 14:57:10.206 21953-21953 ... I/TryAsync: onPostExecute [ Andro ]
08-04 14:57:10.786 21953-23281 ... I/TryAsync: doInBackground [ Androi ][
END ]
08-04 14:57:10.787 21953-2195  ... I/TryAsync: onPostExecute [ Androi ]
08-04 14:57:14.288 21953-23233 ... I/TryAsync: doInBackground [ Android ][
END ]
08-04 14:57:14.290 21953-2195  ... I/TryAsync: onPostExecute [ Android ]
```

Let's filter logs by the methods we execute in our tasks. Let's look at the filter for the `onPreExecute` method first:

```
08-04 14:56:59.283 21953-21953 ... I/TryAsync: onPreExecute [ A ]
08-04 14:57:00.202 21953-21953 ... I/TryAsync: onPreExecute [ An ]
08-04 14:57:00.783 21953-21953 ... I/TryAsync: onPreExecute [ And ]
08-04 14:57:01.001 21953-21953 ... I/TryAsync: onPreExecute [ Andr ]
08-04 14:57:01.669 21953-21953 ... I/TryAsync: onPreExecute [ Andro ]
08-04 14:57:01.934 21953-21953 ... I/TryAsync: onPreExecute [ Androi ]
08-04 14:57:02.314 21953-21953 ... I/TryAsync: onPreExecute [ Android ]
```

Do the same for each method and focus on the times when the methods were executed. To give more challenge to your code, change the `doInBackground()` method implementation to do some more serious and intensive work. Then, fire more tasks by typing a longer title, for example, the entire sentence. Filter and analyze your log.

Understanding Android Looper

Let's explain the `Looper` class. We used it in previous examples but we did not explain it in details.

`Looper` represents a class that is used to execute `messages` or `runnable` instances in a queue. Ordinary threads do not have any queue like the `Looper` class has.

Where we can use the `Looper` class? For the execution of multiple `messages` or `runnable` instances, `Looper` is needed! One example of use can be adding new tasks to the queue while, at the same time, the operation of task processing is running.

Preparing the Looper

To use the `Looper` class, we must first call the `prepare()` method. When `Looper` is prepared, we can use the `loop()` method. This method is used to create a `message` loop in the current thread. We will give you one short example:

```
class LooperHandler : Handler() {
  override fun handleMessage(message: Message) {
      ...
  }
}

class LooperThread : Thread() {
  var handler: Handler? = null
```

```
    override fun run() {
        Looper.prepare()
        handler = LooperHandler()
        Looper.loop()
    }
}
```

In this example, we demonstrated basic steps to program a `Looper` class. Do not forget to `prepare()` your `Looper` class or you will get an exception and your application can crash!

Delayed execution

There's one more important thing left to show you in this chapter. We will show you some delayed execution in Android. We will give you some examples of delayed operation applied to our UI. Open your `ItemsFragment` and make these changes:

```
class ItemsFragment : BaseFragment() {
  ...
    override fun onResume() {
        super.onResume()
        ...
        val items = view?.findViewById<ListView>(R.id.items)
        items?.let {
            items.postDelayed({
                if (!activity.isFinishing) {
                    items.setBackgroundColor(R.color.grey_text_middle)
                }
            }, 3000)
        }
    }
    ...
}
```

After three seconds, if we don't close this screen, the background color will be changed to a slightly darker grey tone. Run your application and see for yourself. Now, let's do the same thing in a different way:

```
class ItemsFragment : BaseFragment() {
  ...
    override fun onResume() {
        super.onResume()
        ...
        val items = view?.findViewById<ListView>(R.id.items)
        items?.let {
            Handler().postDelayed({
                if (!activity.isFinishing) {
```

```
                    items.setBackgroundColor(R.color.grey_text_middle)
                }
            }, 3000)
        }
      }
     }
     ...
   }
```

This time, we used the `Handler` class to perform delayed modification.

Summary

In this chapter, you were introduced to Android concurrency. We explained and provided you with examples for each of the segments. This is a nice introduction for you before diving into the depths of Android services. Android services are the most powerful concurrency feature Android has to offer, and, as you will see, it can be used as the brain for your application.

10
Android Services

In the previous chapter, we started working with concurrency mechanisms in Android. We made great progress. However, our journey to Android concurrency mechanisms is not over yet. We have to present, perhaps, the most important part of the Android Framework-- Android services. In this chapter, we will explain what are services, and when and how to use them.

In this chapter, we will cover the following topics:

- Service categorization
- Basics of Android services
- Defining the main application service
- Defining the intent service

Service categorization

Before we define the Android service categorization and dive deeper into each type, we must answer the question of what Android service really is. Well, **Android service** is a mechanism provided by the Android Framework by which we can move the execution of long running tasks to the background. Android service provides some nice additional features that can make a developer's work more flexible and easier. To explain how it will make our development easier, we will create a service by extending our **Journaler** application.

Android service is an application component that does not have any UI. It can be started by any Android application component and continue running as long as it's needed, even if we leave our application or kill it.

There are three main types of Android services:

- Foreground
- Background
- Bound

Foreground Android services

A foreground service performs tasks that are noticeable to the end user. These services must display a status bar icon. They continue running even when there is no interaction with the application.

Background Android services

Unlike foreground services, background services perform tasks that aren't noticed by the end user. For example, we will perform synchronization with our backend instance. The user does not need to know about our progress. We decided not to bother the user with that. Everything will be performed silently in the background of our application.

Bound Android services

Our application components can bind to a service and trigger different tasks to be executed. Interacting with a service in Android is very simple. A component binds to a service and, as long there is at least one such component, the service keeps running. When there are no components bound to a service, the service is destroyed.

It is possible to create a background service that is running in the background and have the ability to bind to it.

Android service basics

To define Android service, you have to extend the `Service` class. We must override some of the following methods so the service is functioning:

- `onStartCommand()`: This method is executed when the `startService()` method is triggered by some Android component. After the method is executed, Android service is started and can run in the background indefinitely. To stop this service, you must execute the `stopService()` method that has an opposite functionality to the `startService()` method.

- `onBind()`: To bind to the service from another Android component, use the `bindService()` method. After we bind, the `onBind()` method is executed. In your service implementation of this method, you must provide an interface that clients use to communicate with the service by returning an `Ibinder` class instance. Implementing this method is not optional, but if you don't plan to bind to the service, just return `null`.

- `onCreate()`: This method is executed when the service is created. It is not executed if the service is already running.

- `onDestroy()`: This method is executed when the service is destroyed. Override this method and perform all cleanup tasks for your service here.

- `onUnbind()`: This method is executed when we unbind from the service.

Declaring your service

To declare your service, you need to add its class to the Android Manifest. The following code snippet explains what the service definition in Android Manifest should look like:

```
<manifest xmlns:android=
  "http://schemas.android.com/apk/res/android"
  package="com.journaler">
  ...
  <application ... >
    <service
      android:name=".service.MainService"
      android:exported="false" />
    ...
  </application>
</manifest>
```

As you can see, we defined the `MainService` class that extends the `Service` class and it's located under the `service` package. The exported flag is set to `false`, which means that the `service` will run in the same process as our application. To run your `service` in a separate process, set this flag to `true`.

It's important to note that the `Service` class is not the only one you can extend. The `IntentService` class is also available. So, what do we get when we extend it? `IntentService` represents a class derived from the `Service` class. `IntentService` uses the worker thread to process requests one by one. We must implement the `onHandleIntent()` method for that purpose. This is what it looks like when the `IntentService` class is extended:

```
public class MainIntentService extends IntentService {
  /**
   * A constructor is mandatory!
   */
  public MainIntentService() {
    super("MainIntentService");
  }

  /**
   * All important work is performed here.
   */
  @Override
  protected void onHandleIntent(Intent intent) {
    // Your implementation for handling received intents.
  }
}
```

Let's go back on extending the `Service` class and focus on it. We will override `onStartCommand()` method to look like this:

```
override fun onStartCommand(intent: Intent?, flags: Int, startId:
Int): Int {
  return Service.START_STICKY
}
```

So, what does the `START_STICKY` return result mean? If it happens that our service is killed by the system, or we kill the application to which the service belongs, it will start again. Opposite of this is `START_NOT_STICKY`; in that case, the service will not be recreated and restarted.

Starting the service

To start the service, we need to define the intent that will represent it. This is an example on how the service can be started:

```
val startServiceIntent = Intent(ctx, MainService::class.java)
ctx.startService(startServiceIntent)
```

Here, `ctx` represents any valid instance of the Android `Context` class.

Stopping the service

To stop the service, execute the `stopService()` method from the Android `Context` class like this:

```
val stopServiceIntent = Intent(ctx, MainService::class.java)
ctx.stopService(startServiceIntent)
```

Binding to Android service

A **bound service** is the service that allows Android components to bind to it. To perform binding, we must call the `bindService()` method. When you want to interact with the service from activities or other Android components, service binding is necessary. For bind to work, you must implement the `onBind()` method and return an `IBinder` instance. If there are no interested parties anymore, and all of them are unbound, Android destroys the service. For this type of service, you do not need to perform the stop routine.

Stopping the service

We already mentioned that `stopService` will stop our service. Anyway, we can achieve the same by calling `stopSelf()` within our service implementation.

Service lifecycle

We covered and explained all important methods that are executed during the lifetime of an Android service. Service has its own lifecycle as all other Android components. Everything we mentioned so far is represented in the following screenshot:

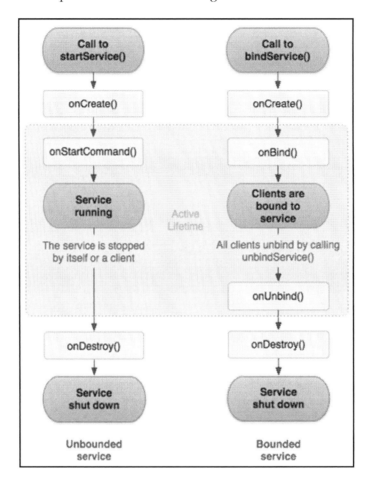

Now, as we have a basic understanding of the Android services, we will create our own service and extend the **Journaler** application. This service will be repeatedly extended later in other chapters with more code. So, pay attention to every line as it can be crucial.

Defining the main application service

As you already know, our application is dealing with **Notes** and **Todos**. The current application implementation keeps our data locally stored in the SQLite database. This data will be synchronized with the backend instance running on some remote server. All operations related to the synchronization will be performed silently in the background of our application. All responsibility will be given to the service, which we will define now. Create a new package called `service` and a new class `MainService` that will extend the Android `service` class. Make sure your implementation looks like this:

```
class MainService : Service(), DataSynchronization {

  private val tag = "Main service"
  private var binder = getServiceBinder()
  private var executor = TaskExecutor.getInstance(1)

  override fun onCreate() {
    super.onCreate()
    Log.v(tag, "[ ON CREATE ]")
  }

  override fun onStartCommand(intent: Intent?, flags: Int, startId:
Int): Int {
    Log.v(tag, "[ ON START COMMAND ]")
    synchronize()
    return Service.START_STICKY
  }

  override fun onBind(p0: Intent?): IBinder {
    Log.v(tag, "[ ON BIND ]")
    return binder
  }

  override fun onUnbind(intent: Intent?): Boolean {
    val result = super.onUnbind(intent)
    Log.v(tag, "[ ON UNBIND ]")
    return result
  }

  override fun onDestroy() {
    synchronize()
    super.onDestroy()
    Log.v(tag, "[ ON DESTROY ]")
  }

  override fun onLowMemory() {
```

```
    super.onLowMemory()
    Log.w(tag, "[ ON LOW MEMORY ]")
}

override fun synchronize() {
  executor.execute {
      Log.i(tag, "Synchronizing data [ START ]")
      // For now we will only simulate this operation!
      Thread.sleep(3000)
      Log.i(tag, "Synchronizing data [ END ]")
  }
}

private fun getServiceBinder(): MainServiceBinder =
MainServiceBinder()

inner class MainServiceBinder : Binder() {
  fun getService(): MainService = this@MainService
}
}
```

Let's explain our main service. As you already know, we will extend Android's `Service` class to get all service functionality. We also implemented the `DataSynchronization` interface that will describe the main functionality of our service, which is synchronization. Please refer to the following code:

```
package com.journaler.service
interface DataSynchronization {
 fun synchronize()
}
```

So, we defined the implementation for the `synchronize()` method that will actually simulate real synchronization. Later, we will update this code to perform real backend communication.

All important lifecycle methods are overridden. Pay attention to the `bind()` method! This method will return an instance of binder that is produced by calling the `getServiceBinder()` method. Thanks to the `MainServiceBinder` class, we will expose our `service` instance to the end user that will be able to trigger the synchronize mechanism whenever it is needed.

Synchronization is not triggered just by the end user, but also automatically by the service itself. We trigger synchronization when a service is started and when it is destroyed.

The next important point for us is the starting and stopping of `MainService`. Open your `Journaler` class that represents your application and apply this update:

```kotlin
class Journaler : Application() {

  companion object {
    val tag = "Journaler"
    var ctx: Context? = null
  }

  override fun onCreate() {
    super.onCreate()
    ctx = applicationContext
    Log.v(tag, "[ ON CREATE ]")
    startService()
  }

  override fun onLowMemory() {
    super.onLowMemory()
    Log.w(tag, "[ ON LOW MEMORY ]")
    // If we get low on memory we will stop service if running.
    stopService()
  }

  override fun onTrimMemory(level: Int) {
    super.onTrimMemory(level)
    Log.d(tag, "[ ON TRIM MEMORY ]: $level")
  }

  private fun startService() {
    val serviceIntent = Intent(this, MainService::class.java)
    startService(serviceIntent)
  }

  private fun stopService() {
    val serviceIntent = Intent(this, MainService::class.java)
    stopService(serviceIntent)
  }

}
```

When the **Journaler** application is created, `MainService` will be started. We will also add one small optimization. If it happens that our application gets low on memory, we will stop our `MainService` class. Since the service is started as sticky, if we explicitly kill our application, the service will restart.

So far, we covered the service starting and stopping and its implementation. As you probably remember our mockup, at the bottom of our application drawer, we planned to put one more item. We planned to have the **synchronize** button. Triggering this button would do synchronization with the backend.

We will add that menu item and connect it with our service. Let's do some preparation first. Open the `NavigationDrawerItem` class and update it as follows:

```
data class NavigationDrawerItem(
  val title: String,
  val onClick: Runnable,
  var enabled: Boolean = true
)
```

We introduced the `enabled` parameter. Like this, some of our application drawer items can be disabled if needed. Our **synchronize** button will be disabled by default and enabled when we bind to the `main` service. These changes must affect `NavigationDrawerAdapter` too. Please refer to the following code:

```
class NavigationDrawerAdapter(
  val ctx: Context,
  val items: List<NavigationDrawerItem>
) : BaseAdapter() {

  private val tag = "Nav. drw. adptr."

  override fun getView(position: Int, v: View?, group:
  ViewGroup?): View {
    ...
    val item = items[position]
    val title = view.findViewById<Button>(R.id.drawer_item)
    ...
    title.setOnClickListener {
      if (item.enabled) {
        item.onClick.run()
      } else {
        Log.w(tag, "Item is disabled: $item")
      }
    }

    return view
  }
  ...
}
```

Finally, we will update our `MainActivity` class as follows, so the synchronization button can trigger synchronization:

```
class MainActivity : BaseActivity() {
  ...
  private var service: MainService? = null
  private val synchronize: NavigationDrawerItem by lazy {
    NavigationDrawerItem(
      getString(R.string.synchronize),
      Runnable { service?.synchronize() },
      false
    )
  }

  private val serviceConnection = object : ServiceConnection {
    override fun onServiceDisconnected(p0: ComponentName?) {
      service = null
      synchronize.enabled = false
    }

    override fun onServiceConnected(p0: ComponentName?, binder:
    IBinder?) {
      if (binder is MainService.MainServiceBinder) {
        service = binder.getService()
        service?.let {
          synchronize.enabled = true
        }
      }
    }
  }

  override fun onCreate(savedInstanceState: Bundle?) {
    super.onCreate(savedInstanceState)
    ...
    val menuItems = mutableListOf<NavigationDrawerItem>()
    ...
    menuItems.add(synchronize)
    ...
  }

  override fun onResume() {
    super.onResume()
    val intent = Intent(this, MainService::class.java)
    bindService(intent, serviceConnection,
    android.content.Context.BIND_AUTO_CREATE)
  }

  override fun onPause() {
```

```
    super.onPause()
    unbindService(serviceConnection)
  }
  ...
}
```

We will bind or unbind the `main` service whether our main activity status is active or not. To perform binding, we need the `ServiceConnection` implementation as it will enable or disable the synchronization button depending on the binding state. Also, we will maintain the `main` service instance depending on the binding state. The synchronization button will have access to the `service` instance and trigger the `synchronize()` method when clicked.

Defining the intent service

We have our `main` service running and responsibility defined. We will now make more improvements to our application by introducing one more service. This time, we will define the `intent` service. The `intent` service will take over the responsibility for the execution of the database CRUD operations. Basically, we will define our `intent` service and perform refactoring of the code we already have.

First, we will create a new class inside the `service` package called `DatabaseService`. Before we put the whole implementation, we will register it in the Android Manifest as follows:

```
<manifest xmlns:android=
  "http://schemas.android.com/apk/res/android"
   package="com.journaler">
   ...
  <application ... >
  <service
    android:name=".service.MainService"
    android:exported="false" />

  <service
    android:name=".service.DatabaseService"
    android:exported="false" />
    ...
  </application>
</manifest>

Define DatabaseService like this:
class DatabaseService :
 IntentService("DatabaseService") {
```

```
companion object {
  val EXTRA_ENTRY = "entry"
  val EXTRA_OPERATION = "operation"
}

private val tag = "Database service"

override fun onCreate() {
  super.onCreate()
  Log.v(tag, "[ ON CREATE ]")
}

override fun onLowMemory() {
  super.onLowMemory()
  Log.w(tag, "[ ON LOW MEMORY ]")
}

override fun onDestroy() {
  super.onDestroy()
  Log.v(tag, "[ ON DESTROY ]")
}

override fun onHandleIntent(p0: Intent?) {
  p0?.let {
    val note = p0.getParcelableExtra<Note>(EXTRA_ENTRY)
    note?.let {
      val operation = p0.getIntExtra(EXTRA_OPERATION, -1)
      when (operation) {
        MODE.CREATE.mode -> {
          val result = Db.insert(note)
          if (result) {
            Log.i(tag, "Note inserted.")
          } else {
            Log.e(tag, "Note not inserted.")
          }
        }
        MODE.EDIT.mode -> {
          val result = Db.update(note)
          if (result) {
            Log.i(tag, "Note updated.")
          } else {
            Log.e(tag, "Note not updated.")
          }
        }
        else -> {
          Log.w(tag, "Unknown mode [ $operation ]")
        }
      }
```

```
                    }
                }
            }
        }

    }
```

The service will receive intents, obtain the operation, and note the instance from it. Depending on the operation, the proper CRUD operation will be triggered. To pass a `Note` instance to `Intent`, we must implement `Parcelable` so that the data is passed efficiently. For example, comparing to `Serializable`, `Parcelable` is much faster. The code, for this purpose, is heavily optimized. We will perform explicit serialization without using reflection. Open your `Note` class and update it as follows:

```
package com.journaler.model
import android.location.Location
import android.os.Parcel
import android.os.Parcelable

class Note(
  title: String,
  message: String,
  location: Location
) : Entry(
  title,
  message,
  location
), Parcelable {

  override var id = 0L

  constructor(parcel: Parcel) : this(
    parcel.readString(),
    parcel.readString(),
    parcel.readParcelable(Location::class.java.classLoader)
  ) {
    id = parcel.readLong()
  }

  override fun writeToParcel(parcel: Parcel, flags: Int) {
    parcel.writeString(title)
    parcel.writeString(message)
    parcel.writeParcelable(location, 0)
    parcel.writeLong(id)
  }

  override fun describeContents(): Int {
    return 0
```

```
            }

        companion object CREATOR : Parcelable.Creator<Note> {
          override fun createFromParcel(parcel: Parcel): Note {
            return Note(parcel)
          }

          override fun newArray(size: Int): Array<Note?> {
            return arrayOfNulls(size)
          }
        }

    }
```

The Note class will be serialized and deserialized efficiently when passed via intent to DatabaseService.

The last piece of puzzle is changing the code, which currently performs CRUD operations. Instead of directly accessing the Db class from our NoteActivity class, we will create intent and fire it so our service handles the rest of the work for us. Open NoteActivity class and update the code like this:

```
class NoteActivity : ItemActivity() {
    ...
    private val locationListener = object : LocationListener {
        override fun onLocationChanged(p0: Location?) {
            p0?.let {
                LocationProvider.unsubscribe(this)
                location = p0
                val title = getNoteTitle()
                val content = getNoteContent()
                note = Note(title, content, p0)

                // Switching to intent service.
                val dbIntent = Intent(this@NoteActivity,
                DatabaseService::class.java)
                dbIntent.putExtra(DatabaseService.EXTRA_ENTRY, note)
                dbIntent.putExtra(DatabaseService.EXTRA_OPERATION,
                MODE.CREATE.mode)
                startService(dbIntent)
                sendMessage(true)
            }
        }

    override fun onStatusChanged(p0: String?, p1: Int, p2: Bundle?) {}
    override fun onProviderEnabled(p0: String?) {}
    override fun onProviderDisabled(p0: String?) {}
```

```
      }
    ...
    private fun updateNote() {
      if (note == null) {
        if (!TextUtils.isEmpty(getNoteTitle()) &&
        !TextUtils.isEmpty(getNoteContent())) {
          LocationProvider.subscribe(locationListener)
        }
      } else {
          note?.title = getNoteTitle()
          note?.message = getNoteContent()

          // Switching to intent service.
          val dbIntent = Intent(this@NoteActivity,
          DatabaseService::class.java)
          dbIntent.putExtra(DatabaseService.EXTRA_ENTRY, note)
          dbIntent.putExtra(DatabaseService.EXTRA_OPERATION,
          MODE.EDIT.mode)
          startService(dbIntent)
          sendMessage(true)
      }
    }
    ...
  }
```

As you can see, the change was really simple. Build your application and run it. As you create or update your `Note` class, you will notice logs about the database operation we perform. Also, you will notice the `DatabaseService` lifecycle methods being logged.

Summary

Congratulations! You mastered Android services and improved the application significantly! In this chapter, we explained what Android services are. We also explained each type of Android service and gave examples of use. Now, when you did these implementations, we encourage you to think about at least one more service that can take over some existing part of the application or to introduce something completely new. Play with the services and try to think about the benefits they can give you.

11
Messaging

In this chapter, we will work with Android broadcasts and use it as a mechanism to receive and send messages. We will comprehend it in several steps. First, we will explain the mechanism that lies beneath and how to use Android broadcast messages. Then, we will listen for some of the most common messages. Since it's not enough just to listen, we will create new ones and broadcast them. Finally, we will meet with boot, shutdown, and network broadcast messages, so our application is aware of this important system event.

In this chapter, we will cover the following topics:

- Android broadcasts
- Listening for broadcasts
- Creating broadcasts
- Listening for network events

Understanding Android broadcasts

Android applications can send or receive messages. Messages can be system-related events or custom ones defined by us. Interested parties are registered for certain messages by defining a proper intent filter and broadcast receiver. When a message is broadcast, all interested parties are notified. It is important to note that once you subscribe for broadcast messages (especially from the `Activity` class), you must unsubscribe at some point. When can we use broadcast messages? We use broadcast messages when we need a messaging system across our application. For example, imagine you started a long running process in the background. At some point, you want to notify multiple contexts about processing results. Broadcast messages are a perfect solution for this.

System broadcasts

System broadcasts are the ones that are sent by the Android system when various system events happen. Every message we send and finally receive is wrapped in the `Intent` class containing information about that particular event. Each `Intent` must have a proper action set. For example--`android.intent.action.ACTION_POWER_CONNECTED`. Information about the event is represented with bundled extra data. For example, we may have bundled an extra string field representing particular data related to the event we are interested in. Let's consider an example of charging and battery information. Each time the battery status changes, interested parties will be notified and receive a broadcast message with information about the battery level:

```
val intentFilter = IntentFilter(Intent.ACTION_BATTERY_CHANGED)
val batteryStatus = registerReceiver(null, intentFilter)
val status = batteryStatus.getIntExtra(BatteryManager.
  EXTRA_STATUS, -1)

val isCharging =
          status == BatteryManager.BATTERY_STATUS_CHARGING ||
          status == BatteryManager.BATTERY_STATUS_FULL

val chargePlug =    batteryStatus.getIntExtra(BatteryManager.
  EXTRA_PLUGGED, -1)
val usbCharge = chargePlug == BatteryManager.
  BATTERY_PLUGGED_USB
val acCharge = chargePlug == BatteryManager.BATTERY_PLUGGED_AC
```

In this example, we registered the intent filter for battery information. However, we did not pass an instance of broadcast receiver. Why? This is because that battery data is sticky. **Sticky intents** are intents that stay around for some time after the broadcast is performed. Registering to this data will immediately return the intent containing the latest data. We could also pass an instance of a broadcast receiver. Let's do it:

```
val receiver = object : BroadcastReceiver() {
  override fun onReceive(p0: Context?, batteryStatus: Intent?) {
  val status = batteryStatus?.getIntExtra
  (BatteryManager.EXTRA_STATUS, -1)
          val isCharging =
              status ==
              BatteryManager.BATTERY_STATUS_CHARGING ||
              status == BatteryManager.BATTERY_STATUS_FULL
              val chargePlug = batteryStatus?.getIntExtra
              (BatteryManager.EXTRA_PLUGGED, -1)
               val usbCharge = chargePlug ==
              BatteryManager.BATTERY_PLUGGED_USB
              val acCharge = chargePlug ==
```

```
                    BatteryManager.BATTERY_PLUGGED_AC
    }
}

val intentFilter = IntentFilter(Intent.ACTION_BATTERY_CHANGED)
registerReceiver(receiver, intentFilter)
```

Every time the battery information changes, the receiver will perform a code we defined in its implementation; we could also define our receiver in the Android Manifest:

```
<receiver android:name=".OurPowerReceiver">
  <intent-filter>
    <action android:name="android.intent.action.
    ACTION_POWER_CONNECTED"/>
    <action android:name="android.intent.action.
    ACTION_POWER_DISCONNECTED"/>
  </intent-filter>
</receiver>
```

Listening for broadcasts

As we displayed in the previous example, we can receive broadcasts in one of the two following ways:

- Registering the broadcast receiver through Android Manifest
- Registering the broadcast using the `registerBroadcast()` method in the contexts

Declaring through Manifest requires the following:

- The `<receiver>` element with `android:name` and `android:exported` parameters.
- The receiver must contain `intent` filters for the actions we subscribe. Take a look at the following example:

```
<receiver android:name=".OurBootReceiver"
  android:exported="true">
  <intent-filter>
    <action android:name=
    "android.intent.action.BOOT_COMPLETED"/>
    ...
    <action android:name="..."/>
    <action android:name="..."/>
    <action android:name="..."/>
```

```
        </intent-filter>

    </receiver>
```

As you can see, the `name` attribute represents a name of our broadcast receiver class. Exported means that the application can or can't receive messages from sources outside the receiver's application.

If you subclass `BroadcastReceiver`, it should look like this example:

```
    val receiver = object : BroadcastReceiver() {
        override fun onReceive(ctx: Context?, intent: Intent?) {
            // Handle your received code.
        }
    }
```

Pay attention that the operations you perform in `onReceive()` method implementation should not take too much time. Otherwise ANR can occur!

Registering from the context

Now we will show you an example of registering a broadcast receiver from the Android Context. To register the receiver you need an instance of it. Let's say that our instance is `myReceiver`:

```
    val myReceiver = object : BroadcastReceiver(){
      ...

    }We need intent filter prepared:
    val filter = IntentFilter(ConnectivityManager.CONNECTIVITY_ACTION)
    registerReceiver(myReceiver, filter)
```

This example will register a receiver that will listen for connectivity information. Since this receiver is registered from the context, it will be valid as long as the context from which we registered is valid. You can also use the `LocalBroadcastManager` class. `LocalBroadcastManager` has a purpose to register for and send broadcasts of intents to local objects within your process. This is the example:

```
    LocalBroadcastManager
      .getInstance(applicationContext)
      .registerReceiver(myReceiver, intentFilter)
```

To unregister, perform the following code snippet:

```
LocalBroadcastManager
    .getInstance(applicationContext)
    .unregisterReceiver(myReceiver)
```

For context subscribed receivers, it's important to pay attention to unregistering. For example, if we register a receiver in the onCreate() method of activity, we must unregister it in the onDestroy() method. If we do not do so, we will have a receiver leaking! Similarly, if we register in onResume() of our activity, we must unregister in onPause(). If we do not do this, we will register multiple times!

Receivers execution

Code we execute in the onReceive() implementation is considered a foreground process. The broadcast receiver is active until we return from the method. The system will always run your code defined in the implementation, except if extreme memory pressure occurs. As we mentioned, you should perform short operations only! Otherwise, ANR can occur! A good example of executing a long running operation when a message is received is by starting AsyncTask and performing all the work there. Next, we will show you an example demonstrating this:

```
class AsyncReceiver : BroadcastReceiver() {
  override fun onReceive(p0: Context?, p1: Intent?) {
    val pending = goAsync()
    val async = object : AsyncTask<Unit, Unit, Unit>() {
      override fun doInBackground(vararg p0: Unit?) {
        // Do some intensive work here...
        pending.finish()
      }
    }
    async.execute()
  }
}
```

In this example, we introduced the use of the goAsync() method. What does it do? The method returns an object of the PendingResult type, which represents a pending result from calling an API method. The Android system considers the receiver alive until we call the finish() method on this instance. Using this mechanism, it's possible to do asynchronous processing in a broadcast receiver. After we finish our intensive work, we call finish() to indicate to the Android system that this component can be recycled.

Sending broadcasts

Android has the following three ways of sending broadcast messages:

- Using the `sendOrderedBroadcast(Intent, String)` method sends messages to one receiver at a time. Since receivers execute in order, it's possible to propagate a result to the next receiver. Also, it's possible to abort the broadcast so that it won't be passed to the rest of the receivers. We can control the order in which receivers are executed. We can use the `android:priority` attribute of the matching intent filter to prioritize.
- Using the `sendBroadcast(Intent)` method sends broadcast messages to all receivers. The sending is not ordered.
- Using the `LocalBroadcastManager.sendBroadcast(Intent)` method sends broadcasts to receivers that are in the same application as the sender.

Let's take a look at an example of sending a broadcast message to all interested parties:

```
val intent = Intent()
intent.action = "com.journaler.broadcast.TODO_CREATED"
intent.putExtra("title", "Go, buy some lunch.")
intent.putExtra("message", "For lunch we have chicken.")
sendBroadcast(intent)
```

We created a broadcast message containing extra data about `note` a we created (title and message). All interested parties will need a proper `IntentFilter` instance for the action:

```
com.journaler.broadcast.TODO_CREATED
```

Don't get confused with starting activities and sending broadcast messages. The `Intent` class is used just as a wrapper for our information. These two operations are completely different! You can achieve the same using the local broadcast mechanism:

```
val ctx = ...
val broadcastManager = LocalBroadcastManager.getInstance(ctx)
val intent = Intent()
intent.action = "com.journaler.broadcast.TODO_CREATED"
intent.putExtra("title", "Go, buy some lunch.")
intent.putExtra("message", "For lunch we have chicken.")
broadcastManager.sendBroadcast(intent)
```

Now, when we showed you the most important aspects of broadcast messaging, we will continue with extending our application. **Journaler** will send and receive our custom broadcast messages containing data and interact with system broadcasts, such as system boot, shutdown, and network.

Creating your own broadcast messages

As you probably remember, we did code refactoring for the `NoteActivity` class. Let's show the last state we had in important parts for our further demonstration:

```kotlin
class NoteActivity : ItemActivity() {
  ...
  private val locationListener = object : LocationListener {
    override fun onLocationChanged(p0: Location?) {
      p0?.let {
            LocationProvider.unsubscribe(this)
            location = p0
            val title = getNoteTitle()
            val content = getNoteContent()
            note = Note(title, content, p0)

            // Switching to intent service.
            val dbIntent = Intent(this@NoteActivity,
            DatabaseService::class.java)
            dbIntent.putExtra(DatabaseService.EXTRA_ENTRY, note)
            dbIntent.putExtra(DatabaseService.EXTRA_OPERATION,
            MODE.CREATE.mode)
            startService(dbIntent)
            sendMessage(true)
      }
    }

    override fun onStatusChanged(p0: String?, p1: Int, p2: Bundle?)
    {}
    override fun onProviderEnabled(p0: String?) {}
    override fun onProviderDisabled(p0: String?) {}
  }
  ...
  private fun updateNote() {
    if (note == null) {
        if (!TextUtils.isEmpty(getNoteTitle()) &&
          !TextUtils.isEmpty(getNoteContent())) {
            LocationProvider.subscribe(locationListener)
        }
    } else {
        note?.title = getNoteTitle()
        note?.message = getNoteContent()

        // Switching to intent service.
        val dbIntent = Intent(this@NoteActivity,
        DatabaseService::class.java)
        dbIntent.putExtra(DatabaseService.EXTRA_ENTRY, note)
```

```
                    dbIntent.putExtra(DatabaseService.EXTRA_OPERATION,
                    MODE.EDIT.mode)
                    startService(dbIntent)
                    sendMessage(true)
                }
            }
            ...
        }
```

If you take a look at this again, you will notice that we sent `intent` to our service on the execution, but since we don't get a return value, we just execute the `sendMessage()` method with Boolean `true` as its parameter. Here, we expected a value that represents the result of a CRUD operation, that is, success or failure. We will connect our service with `NoteActivity` using broadcast messages. Each time we insert or update the `note` broadcast, a message will be fired. Our listener defined in `NoteActivity` will respond to this message and trigger the `sendMessage()` method. Let's update our code! Open the `Crud` interface and extend it with a `companion` object containing constants for an action and a CRUD operation result:

```
interface Crud<T> {
    companion object {
        val BROADCAST_ACTION = "com.journaler.broadcast.crud"
        val BROADCAST_EXTRAS_KEY_CRUD_OPERATION_RESULT = "crud_result"
    }
    ...
}
```

Now, open `DatabaseService` and extend it with a method responsible for sending broadcast messages on CRUD operation execution:

```
class DatabaseService : IntentService("DatabaseService") {
    ...
    override fun onHandleIntent(p0: Intent?) {
        p0?.let {
            val note = p0.getParcelableExtra<Note>(EXTRA_ENTRY)
            note?.let {
                val operation = p0.getIntExtra(EXTRA_OPERATION, -1)
                when (operation) {
                    MODE.CREATE.mode -> {
                        val result = Db.insert(note)
                        if (result) {
                            Log.i(tag, "Note inserted.")
                        } else {
                            Log.e(tag, "Note not inserted.")
                        }
                        broadcastResult(result)
```

```
                }
                MODE.EDIT.mode -> {
                    val result = Db.update(note)
                    if (result) {
                        Log.i(tag, "Note updated.")
                    } else {
                        Log.e(tag, "Note not updated.")
                    }
                    broadcastResult(result)
                }
                else -> {
                    Log.w(tag, "Unknown mode [ $operation ]")
                }
            }
        }
    }
}
...
    private fun broadcastResult(result: Boolean) {
        val intent = Intent()
        intent.putExtra(
            Crud.BROADCAST_EXTRAS_KEY_CRUD_OPERATION_RESULT,
            if (result) {
                1
            } else {
                0
            }
        )
    } }
```

We introduced a new method. Everything else is the same. We take the CRUD operation result and broadcast it as a message. `NoteActivity` will listen for it:

```
class NoteActivity : ItemActivity() {
    ...
    private val crudOperationListener = object : BroadcastReceiver() {
        override fun onReceive(ctx: Context?, intent: Intent?) {
            intent?.let {
                val crudResultValue =
                intent.getIntExtra(MODE.EXTRAS_KEY, 0)
                sendMessage(crudResultValue == 1)
            }
        }
    }
    ...
    override fun onCreate(savedInstanceState: Bundle?) {
        ....
        registerReceiver(crudOperationListener, intentFiler)
```

```
  }

  override fun onDestroy() {
    unregisterReceiver(crudOperationListener)
    super.onDestroy()
  }
  ...
  private fun sendMessage(result: Boolean) {
      Log.v(tag, "Crud operation result [ $result ]")
      val msg = handler?.obtainMessage()
      if (result) {
          msg?.arg1 = 1
      } else {
          msg?.arg1 = 0
      }
      handler?.sendMessage(msg)
  } }
```

This was simple and easy! We reconnected the original `sendMessage()` method with the CRUD operation result. In the next sections, we will consider some significant improvements our application can have by listening to boot, shutdown, and network broadcast messages.

Using on boot and on shutdown broadcasts

Sometimes, it's crucial for services to run as the application starts. Also, sometimes it is important to do some cleanup work before we terminate it. In the following example, we will extend the **Journaler** application to listen for these broadcast messages and do some work. First thing that we will do is create two classes that extend the `BroadcastReceiver` class:

- `BootReceiver`: This is to handle the system boot event
- `ShutdownReceiver`: This is to handle the system shutdown event

Register them in your `manifest` file as follows:

```
<manifest
  ...
>
...
<receiver
    android:name=".receiver.BootReceiver"
    android:enabled="true"
    android:exported="false">
```

```
      <intent-filter>
        <action android:name=
          "android.intent.action.BOOT_COMPLETED" />
      </intent-filter>
      <intent-filter>
        <action android:name=
          "android.intent.action.PACKAGE_REPLACED" />
        data android:scheme="package" />
      </intent-filter>
      <intent-filter>
        <action android:name=
          "android.intent.action.PACKAGE_ADDED" />
        <data android:scheme="package" />
      </intent-filter>
    </receiver>

  <receiver android:name=".receiver.ShutdownReceiver">
    <intent-filter>
      <action android:name=
        "android.intent.action.ACTION_SHUTDOWN" />
      <action android:name=
        "android.intent.action.QUICKBOOT_POWEROFF" />
    </intent-filter>
  </receiver>
  ...
  </manifest>
```

The `BootReceiver` class will be triggered when we boot or replace the application. Shutdown will be triggered when we turn off the device. Let's create proper implementations. Open the `BootReceiver` class and define it like this:

```
package com.journaler.receiver

import android.content.BroadcastReceiver
import android.content.Context
import android.content.Intent
import android.util.Log

class BootReceiver : BroadcastReceiver() {

  val tag = "Boot receiver"

  override fun onReceive(p0: Context?, p1: Intent?) {
    Log.i(tag, "Boot completed.")
    // Perform your on boot stuff here.
  }

}
```

As you can see, we defined the `receiver` package for these two classes. For `ShutdownReceiver`, define the class like this:

```
package com.journaler.receiver

import android.content.BroadcastReceiver
import android.content.Context
import android.content.Intent
import android.util.Log
class ShutdownReceiver : BroadcastReceiver() {

  val tag = "Shutdown receiver"

  override fun onReceive(p0: Context?, p1: Intent?) {
    Log.i(tag, "Shutting down.")
    // Perform your on cleanup stuff here.
  } }
```

To make this work, we need to apply one more change; otherwise, the application will crash. Move by starting the `main` service from the `Application` class into the main activity `onCreate()` method. This is the first update `Journaler` class:

```
class Journaler : Application() {
  ...
  override fun onCreate() { // We removed start service method
    execution.
    super.onCreate()
    ctx = applicationContext
    Log.v(tag, "[ ON CREATE ]")
  }
  // We removed startService() method implementation.
  ...
}
```

Then extend the `MainActivity` class by appending lines at the end of the `onCreate()` method:

```
class MainActivity : BaseActivity() {
  ...
  override fun onCreate(savedInstanceState: Bundle?) {
    ...
    val serviceIntent = Intent(this, MainService::class.java)
    startService(serviceIntent)
  }
  ... } }
```

Build your application and run it. First, shut down your phone and then power it on. Filter your Logcat so it displays only logs for your application. You should have this output:

```
... I/Shutdown receiver: Shutting down.
... I/Boot receiver: Boot completed.
```

Keep in mind that, sometimes, it requires more than two minutes to receive on an boot event!

Listening for network events

The last improvement we want is the ability for our application to execute synchronization when connectivity is established. Create a new class called in the same `NetworkReceiver` package. Make sure you have the implementation like this:

```
class NetworkReceiver : BroadcastReceiver() {
  private val tag = "Network receiver"
  private var service: MainService? = null
  private val serviceConnection = object : ServiceConnection {
    override fun onServiceDisconnected(p0: ComponentName?) {
      service = null
    }

    override fun onServiceConnected(p0: ComponentName?, binder:
    IBinder?) {
        if (binder is MainService.MainServiceBinder) {
            service = binder.getService()
            service?.synchronize()
        }
    }
  }

  override fun onReceive(context: Context?, p1: Intent?) {
  context?.let {

      val cm = context.getSystemService
      (Context.CONNECTIVITY_SERVICE) as ConnectivityManager

      val activeNetwork = cm.activeNetworkInfo
      val isConnected = activeNetwork != null &&
      activeNetwork.isConnectedOrConnecting
      if (isConnected) {
          Log.v(tag, "Connectivity [ AVAILABLE ]")
```

```
                    if (service == null) {
                        val intent = Intent(context,
                        MainService::class.java)
                        context.bindService(
                            intent, serviceConnection,
                            android.content.Context.BIND_AUTO_CREATE
                        )
                    } else {
                        service?.synchronize()
                    }
                } else {
                    Log.w(tag, "Connectivity [ UNAVAILABLE ]")
                    context.unbindService(serviceConnection)
                }
            }
        }
    }
}
```

This receiver will receive messages when a connectivity event occurs. Each time when we have a context and connectivity, we will bind to the service and trigger synchronization. Do not bother with frequent synchronization triggering as, in the next chapters, we will protect ourselves from it in the synchronization method implementation itself. Register your listener by updating the **Journaler** application class as follows:

```
class Journaler : Application() {
    ...
    override fun onCreate() {
        super.onCreate()
        ctx = applicationContext
        Log.v(tag, "[ ON CREATE ]")
        val filter =
        IntentFilter(ConnectivityManager.CONNECTIVITY_ACTION)
        registerReceiver(networkReceiver, filter)
    }
    ...
}
```

Build and run your application. Turn off your connections (Wi-Fi, Mobile) and turn it on again. Observe the following Logcat output:

```
... V/Network receiver: Connectivity [ AVAILABLE ]
... V/Network receiver: Connectivity [ AVAILABLE ]
... V/Network receiver: Connectivity [ AVAILABLE ]
... W/Network receiver: Connectivity [ UNAVAILABLE ]
... V/Network receiver: Connectivity [ AVAILABLE ]
... V/Network receiver: Connectivity [ AVAILABLE ]
... V/Network receiver: Connectivity [ AVAILABLE ]
```

Summary

In this chapter, we learned how to use broadcast messages. We also learned how to listen for the system broadcast messages and the ones we create on our own. The **Journaler** application is significantly improved and has become more flexible. We will not stop there, but we will continue our progress through the Android Framework by learning new stuff and extending our code.

12
Backend and API

In this chapter, we will connect our application to the remote backend instance. All data we create will be synchronized to and from the backend. For the API calls, we will use Retrofit. Retrofit is the most frequently used HTTP client for the Android platform. We will guide you step by step through the common practices so you can easily connect and implement connection to backend in any application you develop in the future.

This chapter is, by far, the longest chapter in this book, and here, we will cover many important things such as the following topics:

- Working with data classes
- Retrofit
- Gson with Kotson library
- Content providers
- Content loaders
- Android adapters
- Data binding
- Using lists and grids

Read this chapter carefully and enjoy playing with your application.

Identifying entities used

Before we synchronize anything, we must identify exactly what we will synchronize. The answer to this question is obvious, but we will recapitulate the list of our entities anyway. We have two main entities we are planning to synchronize:

- `Note` entity
- `Todo` entity

They have the following attributes:

- Common attributes:
    - `title`: `String`
    - `message`: `String`
    - `location`: `Location` (will be serialized)

 Note that, currently, we represent the location with latitude and longitude in our database. We will change this to `Text` type since we will introduce Gson and Kotson for serialization/deserialization purposes!

- Todo specific attributes are as follows:
    - `scheduledFor`: `Long`

Once again, open your classes and take a look at them.

Working with data classes

In Kotlin, it's recommended to use `data` classes as the representation for your entities. In our case, we did not use `data` classes since we extended a common class containing the attributes shared between the `Note` and `Todo` classes.

We recommend the use of `data` classes since it can significantly simplify your work routine, especially if you are using these entities in backend communication.

It's not rare that we have a need for classes that have only one purpose--holding the data. The benefit of using `data` classes is that some functionality that is often used along with its purpose is automatically provided. As you probably already know how to define a `data` class, you have to do something like this:

```
data class Entity(val param1: String, val param2: String)
```

For the `data` class, the compiler automatically provides you with the following:

- The `equals()` and `hashCode()` methods
- The `toString()` method in human readable form,
  `Entity(param1=Something, param2=Something)`
- The `copy()` method for the cloning

All `data` classes must satisfy the following:

- The primary constructor needs to have at least one parameter
- All primary constructor parameters need to be marked as `val` or `var`
- Data classes cannot be `abstract`, `open`, `sealed`, or `inner`

Let's introduce some `data` classes! Since we plan to use a remote backend instance, it will require some authentication. We will create new entities (`data` classes) for the data we pass during the authentication process, and for the result of the authentication. Create a new package called `api`. Then, create a new `data` class called `UserLoginRequest` as follows:

```
package com.journaler.api

data class UserLoginRequest(
    val username: String,
    val password: String
)
```

`UserLoginRequest` class will contain our authentication credentials. The API call will return a JSON that will be deserialized into the `JournalerApiToken` data class as follows:

```
package com.journaler.api
import com.google.gson.annotations.SerializedName

data class JournalerApiToken(
    @SerializedName("id_token") val token: String,
    val expires: Long
)
```

Pay attention that we used the annotation to tell Gson that the token field will be obtained from the `id_token` field in JSON.

 To summarize--Always consider the use of `data` classes! Especially if the data they represent will be used for holding database and backend information.

Connect data models to a database

If you have a scenario like we have with the **Journaler** application to hold the data in the database, and you plan to synchronize it with the remote backend instance, it can be a good idea to first create a persistence layer that will store your data. Keeping data persisted into a local filesystem database prevents data from loss, especially if you have a bigger amount of it!

So, once again, what did we do? We created a persistence mechanism that will store all our data into the SQLite database. Then, in this chapter, we will introduce the backend communication mechanism. Because we don't know if our API calls will fail or whether the backend instance will be available at all, we have the data persisted. If we keep our data in the device memory only, and if the API call for synchronization fails and our application crashes, we can lose this data. Let's say if the API call failed and the application crashed, but we have our data persisted, we can retry the synchronization. The data is still there!

Introduction to Retrofit

As we already mentioned, Retrofit is an open source library. It is the most popular HTTP client for Android used today. Because of that, we will introduce you to Retrofit basics and demonstrate how to use it. The version we will cover is 2.3.0. We will give you step-by-step guidance on how to use it.

First of all, Retrofit depends on some libraries too. We will use it with Okhttp. Okhttp is an HTTP/HTTP2 client developed by the same guys who developed Retrofit. Before we start, we will put dependencies into our `build.gradle` configuration as follows:

```
apply plugin: "com.android.application"
apply plugin: "kotlin-android"
apply plugin: "kotlin-android-extensions"
...
dependencies {
```

```
        ...
        compile 'com.squareup.retrofit2:retrofit:2.3.0'
        compile 'com.squareup.retrofit2:converter-gson:2.0.2'
        compile 'com.squareup.okhttp3:okhttp:3.9.0'
        compile 'com.squareup.okhttp3:logging-interceptor:3.9.0'
    }
```

We updated our Retrofit and Okhttp to the latest version. We added dependencies for the following:

- Retrofit library
- Gson converter that will be used to deserialize the API responses
- Okhttp library
- Logging interceptor for Okhttp so we can log what is going on with our API calls

After we synchronize our Gradle configuration, we are ready to start!

Defining Retrofit service

Retrofit turns your HTTP API into a Kotlin interface. Create an interface called `JournalerBackendService` inside the API package. Let's put some code in it:

```
    package com.journaler.api

    import com.journaler.model.Note
    import com.journaler.model.Todo
    import retrofit2.Call
    import retrofit2.http.*

    interface JournalerBackendService {

      @POST("user/authenticate")
      fun login(
          @HeaderMap headers: Map<String, String>,
          @Body payload: UserLoginRequest
      ): Call<JournalerApiToken>

      @GET("entity/note")
      fun getNotes(
          @HeaderMap headers: Map<String, String>
      ): Call<List<Note>>

      @GET("entity/todo")
      fun getTodos(
          @HeaderMap headers: Map<String, String>
```

```
): Call<List<Todo>>

@PUT("entity/note")
fun publishNotes(
    @HeaderMap headers: Map<String, String>,
    @Body payload: List<Note>
): Call<Unit>

@PUT("entity/todo")
fun publishTodos(
    @HeaderMap headers: Map<String, String>,
    @Body payload: List<Todo>
): Call<Unit>

@DELETE("entity/note")
fun removeNotes(
    @HeaderMap headers: Map<String, String>,
    @Body payload: List<Note>
): Call<Unit>

@DELETE("entity/todo")
fun removeTodos(
    @HeaderMap headers: Map<String, String>,
    @Body payload: List<Todo>
): Call<Unit>

}
```

What do we have in this interface? We defined a list of calls that will be able to execute the following:

- Authentication for the user: This accepts request headers and instances of the `UserLoginRequest` class containing user credentials. It will be used as a payload for our call. Executing the call will return a wrapped `JournalerApiToken` instance. We will need a token for all other calls, and we will put its content into the header of each call.
- `Notes` and `TODOs` obtain: This accepts request headers containing the authentication token as well. As a result of the call, we get a wrapped list of the `Note` or `Todo` class instances.
- `Notes` and `TODOs` putting (when we send new stuff to the server): This accepts request headers containing the authentication token as well. Payload for the call will be a list of the `Note` or `Todo` class instances. We will not return any important data for these calls. It is important that the response code is positive.

- `Notes` and `TODOs` removal--This accepts request headers containing the authentication token as well. Payload for the call will be a list of `Note` or `Todo` class instances to be removed from our remote backend server instance. We will not return any important data for these calls. It is important that the response code is positive.

Each has a proper annotation representing the HTTP method with the path. We also use annotations to mark the payload body and headers map.

Building a Retrofit service instance

Now, after we have described our service, we need a real Retrofit instance that we will use to trigger API calls. First, we will introduce some additional classes. We will hold the latest token instance inside the `TokenManager` object:

```
package com.journaler.api
  object TokenManager {
    var currentToken = JournalerApiToken("", -1)
  }
```

We will also have an object to obtain the API call headers map called `BackendServiceHeaderMap`, as shown here:

```
package com.journaler.api

object BackendServiceHeaderMap {

 fun obtain(authorization: Boolean = false): Map<String, String> {
    val map = mutableMapOf(
            Pair("Accept", "*/*"),
            Pair("Content-Type", "application/json; charset=UTF-8")
    )
    if (authorization) {
        map["Authorization"] = "Bearer
          ${TokenManager.currentToken.token}"
    }
    return map
 }

}
```

Now we can show you how to build a `Retrofit` instance. Create a new object called `BackendServiceRetrofit` and make sure it looks like this:

```
package com.journaler.api

import okhttp3.OkHttpClient
import okhttp3.logging.HttpLoggingInterceptor
import retrofit2.Retrofit
import retrofit2.converter.gson.GsonConverterFactory
import java.util.concurrent.TimeUnit

object BackendServiceRetrofit {

  fun obtain(
        readTimeoutInSeconds: Long = 1,
        connectTimeoutInSeconds: Long = 1
  ): Retrofit {
    val loggingInterceptor = HttpLoggingInterceptor()
    loggingInterceptor.level
  = HttpLoggingInterceptor.Level.BODY
    return Retrofit.Builder()
            .baseUrl("http://127.0.0.1")
            .addConverterFactory(GsonConverterFactory.create())
            .client(
                    OkHttpClient
                            .Builder()
                            .addInterceptor(loggingInterceptor)
                            .readTimeout(readTimeoutInSeconds,
                            TimeUnit.SECONDS)
                              .connectTimeout
                            (connectTimeoutInSeconds,
                            TimeUnit.SECONDS)
                            .build()
            )
            .build()
  }

}
```

Calling the `obtain()` method will return us a `Retrofit` instance ready to fire API calls. We made a `Retrofit` instance with a backend base URL set to local host. We also passed the Gson converter factory to be used as a mechanism for JSON deserialization. Most importantly, we passed an instance of the client that we will use, and we created a new OkHttp client.

Introduction to Gson with Kotson library

JSON serialization and deserialization are very important for every Android application and are frequently used. For that purpose, we will be using the Gson library developed by Google. Also, we will use Kotson and Kotlin bindings for Gson. So, let's start!

First of all, we need to provide dependencies for our `build.gradle` configuration as follows:

```
apply plugin: "com.android.application"
apply plugin: "kotlin-android"
apply plugin: "kotlin-android-extensions"
...
dependencies {
    ...
    compile 'com.google.code.gson:gson:2.8.0'
    compile 'com.github.salomonbrys.kotson:kotson:2.3.0'
    ...
}
```

We will update our code to use Gson with Kotson bindings for location serialization/deserialization in database management. First, we need to apply a small change to the `Db` class:

```
class DbHelper(dbName: String, val version: Int) :
SQLiteOpenHelper(
    Journaler.ctx, dbName, null, version
) {

companion object {
    val ID: String = "_id"
    val TABLE_TODOS = "todos"
    val TABLE_NOTES = "notes"
    val COLUMN_TITLE: String = "title"
    val COLUMN_MESSAGE: String = "message"
    val COLUMN_LOCATION: String = "location"
    val COLUMN_SCHEDULED: String = "scheduled"
}
...
private val createTableNotes =   """
                            CREATE TABLE if not exists
                             $TABLE_NOTES
                            (
                                $ID integer PRIMARY KEY
                                autoincrement,
                                $COLUMN_TITLE text,
                                $COLUMN_MESSAGE text,
```

```
                                        $COLUMN_LOCATION text
                                    )
                                    """

    private val createTableTodos =    """
                                    CREATE TABLE if not exists
                                     $TABLE_TODOS
                                    (
                                        $ID integer PRIMARY KEY
                                         autoincrement,
                                        $COLUMN_TITLE text,
                                        $COLUMN_MESSAGE text,
                                        $COLUMN_SCHEDULED integer,
                                        $COLUMN_LOCATION text
                                    )
                                    """

    ...
}
```

As you can see, we changed the location information handling. Instead of having location latitude and longitude columns, we now have only one database column--`location`. The type is `Text`. We will hold the serialized `Location` class values that will be generated by the Gson library. Also, when we retrieve the serialized values, we will deserialize them using Gson into `Location` class instances.

Now, we have to actually use Gson. Open `Db.kt` and update it to serialize, and deserialize `Location` class instances using Gson, as shown here:

```
package com.journaler.database
...
import com.google.gson.Gson
...
import com.github.salomonbrys.kotson.*

object Db : Crud<DbModel> {
  ...
  private val gson = Gson()
  ...
  override fun insert(what: Collection<DbModel>): Boolean {
    ...
    what.forEach {
        item ->
        when (item) {
            is Entry -> {
                ...
                values.put(DbHelper.COLUMN_LOCATION,
                 gson.toJson(item.location))
```

```
                    ...
            }
        }
        ...
        return success
    }
    ...
    override fun update(what: Collection<DbModel>): Boolean {
        ...
        what.forEach {
            item ->
            when (item) {
                is Entry -> {
                    ...
                    values.put(DbHelper.COLUMN_LOCATION,
                    gson.toJson(item.location))
                }
        ...
        return result
    }
    ...
    override fun select(args: Pair<String, String>, clazz:
KClass<DbModel>): List<DbModel> {
        return select(listOf(args), clazz)
    }

    override fun select(
        args: Collection<Pair<String, String>>, clazz: Kclass<DbModel>
    ): List<DbModel> {
        ...
        if (clazz.simpleName == Note::class.simpleName) {
            val result = mutableListOf<DbModel>()
            val cursor = db.query(
                ...
            )
            while (cursor.moveToNext()) {
                ...
                val locationIdx =
                cursor.getColumnIndexOrThrow(DbHelper.COLUMN_LOCATION)
                val locationJson = cursor.getString(locationIdx)
                val location = gson.fromJson<Location>(locationJson)
                val note = Note(title, message, location)
                note.id = id
                result.add(note)
            }
            cursor.close()
            return result
        }
```

```
        if (clazz.simpleName == Todo::class.simpleName) {
            ...
        )
        while (cursor.moveToNext()) {
            ...
            val locationIdx =
            cursor.getColumnIndexOrThrow(DbHelper.COLUMN_LOCATION)
            val locationJson = cursor.getString(locationIdx)
            val location = gson.fromJson<Location>(locationJson)
            ...
            val todo = Todo(title, message, location, scheduledFor)
            todo.id = id
            result.add(todo)
        }
        cursor.close()
        return result
    }
    db.close()
    throw IllegalArgumentException("Unsupported entry type:
    $clazz")
    }
}
```

As you can see, in the preceding code, to update using Gson is very simple. We rely on the following two Gson library methods accessed from the Gson class instance:

- `fromJson<T>()`
- `toJson()`

Thanks to Kotson and Kotlin bindings, we can use a parameterize type for the data we serialize using the `fromJson<T>()` method.

What else is available?

Now, we will list some alternatives for Retrofit and Gson. Outside, there is a big open source community that makes great things every day. You are not obligated to use any libraries we present. You can choose any of the alternatives, or even create your own implementation!

Retrofit alternative

As its homepage says, Volley is an HTTP library that makes networking for Android apps easier and, most importantly, faster. Some of the key features Volley offers are as follows:

- Automatic scheduling of network requests
- Multiple concurrent network connections
- Transparent disk and memory response caching with standard HTTP cache coherence
- Support for request prioritization.
- Cancellation request API
- Ease of customization
- Strong ordering
- Debugging and tracing tools

Homepage--`https://github.com/google/volley`.

Gson alternative

Jackson is a low-level JSON parser. It's very similar to the Java StAX parser for XML. Some of the key features Jackson offers are as follows:

- Very fast and convenient
- Extensive annotation support
- Streaming reading and writing
- Tree model
- Out-of-box JAX-RS support
- Integrated support for binary content

Homepage--`https://github.com/FasterXML/jackson`.

Executing our first API call

We defined a Retrofit service with all API calls, but we haven't connected anything to it yet. It is time to use it. We will extend our code to use Retrofit. Each API call can be executed synchronously or asynchronously. We will show you both ways. Do you remember that we set our Retrofit service base URL to the localhost? This means that we will need a local backend instance that will respond to our HTTP requests. Since backend implementation is not the subject of this book, we will leave it up to you to create a simple service responding to this request. You can implement it from any programming language you like, such as Kotlin, Java, Python, and PHP.

If you are impatient and don't want to implement your own application for dealing with HTTP requests, you can override the base URL, **Notes**, and **TODOs** paths as shown in the following example and use the backend instance ready for tryout:

- Base URL--`http://static.milosvasic.net/json/journaler`
- Login POST to target:

    ```
    @POST("authenticate")
    // @POST("user/authenticate")
    fun login(
        ...
    ): Call<JournalerApiToken>
    ```

- Notes GET to target:

    ```
    @GET("notes")
    // @GET("entity/note")
    fun getNotes(
        ...
    ): Call<List<Note>>
    ```

- TODOs GET to target:

    ```
    @GET("todos")
    // @GET("entity/todo")
    fun getTodos(
        ...
    ): Call<List<Todo>>
    ```

Like this, we will target the remote backend instance returning us stub `Notes` and `TODOs`. Now open your `JournalerBackendService` interface and extend it as follows:

```
interface JournalerBackendService {
  companion object {
    fun obtain(): JournalerBackendService {
      return BackendServiceRetrofit
              .obtain()
              .create(JournalerBackendService::class.java)
    }
  }
  ...
}
```

The method we just added will give us an instance of `JournalerBackendService` using Retrofit. Through this, we will trigger all our calls. Open the `MainService` class. Find the `synchronize()` method. Remember that we put sleep there to simulate communication with the backend. Now, we will replace it with real backend calls:

```
/**
 * Authenticates user synchronously,
 * then executes async calls for notes and TODOs fetching.
 * Pay attention on synchronously triggered call via execute()
   method.
 * Its asynchronous equivalent is: enqueue().
 */
override fun synchronize() {
    executor.execute {
        Log.i(tag, "Synchronizing data [ START ]")
        var headers = BackendServiceHeaderMap.obtain()
        val service = JournalerBackendService.obtain()
        val credentials = UserLoginRequest("username", "password")
        val tokenResponse = service
                .login(headers, credentials)
                .execute()
        if (tokenResponse.isSuccessful) {
            val token = tokenResponse.body()
            token?.let {
                TokenManager.currentToken = token
                headers = BackendServiceHeaderMap.obtain(true)
                fetchNotes(service, headers)
                fetchTodos(service, headers)
            }
        }
        Log.i(tag, "Synchronizing data [ END ]")
    }
}
```

```kotlin
/**
 * Fetches notes asynchronously.
 * Pay attention on enqueue() method
 */
private fun fetchNotes(
        service: JournalerBackendService, headers: Map<String,
String>
) {
    service
        .getNotes(headers)
        .enqueue(
        object : Callback<List<Note>> {
          verride fun onResponse(
            call: Call<List<Note>>?, response: Response<List<Note>>?
                    ) {
                        response?.let {
                            if (response.isSuccessful) {
                                val notes = response.body()
                                notes?.let {
                                    Db.insert(notes)
                                }
                            }
                        }
                    }

                    override fun onFailure(call:
                    Call<List<Note>>?, t: Throwable?) {
                        Log.e(tag, "We couldn't fetch notes.")
                    }
                }
            )
    }

/**
 * Fetches TODOs asynchronously.
 * Pay attention on enqueue() method
 */
private fun fetchTodos(
        service: JournalerBackendService, headers: Map<String,
 String>
) {
    service
            .getTodos(headers)
            .enqueue(
                object : Callback<List<Todo>> {
                    override fun onResponse(
                            call: Call<List<Todo>>?, response:
      Response<List<Todo>>?
```

```
                        ) {
                            response?.let {
                                if (response.isSuccessful) {
                                    val todos = response.body()
                                    todos?.let {
                                        Db.insert(todos)
                                    }
                                }
                            }
                        }

                        override fun onFailure(call:
                        Call<List<Todo>>?, t: Throwable?) {
                            Log.e(tag, "We couldn't fetch notes.")
                        }
                    }
                )
            }
```

Analyze the code slowly and take your time! There are a lot of things going on! First, we will create instances of headers and the **Journaler** backend service. Then, we performed the authentication synchronously by triggering the `execute()` method. We received `Response<JournalerApiToken>`. The `JournalerApiToken` instance is wrapped in the `Response` class instance. After we check if the response is successful, and that we actually received and deserialized `JournalerApiToken`, we set it to `TokenManager`. Finally, we trigger asynchronous calls for `Notes` and `TODOs` retrieval.

The `enqueue()` method triggers the async operation, and, as a parameter, accepts the Retrofit Callback concretization. We will do the same that we did with the sync call. We will check if it is successful and if there is data. If everything is ok, we will pass all instances to our database manager for saving.

We only implemented the `Notes` and `TODOs` retrieval. For the rest of the API calls, we leave it up to you to do the implementation. It is a great way to learn Retrofit!

Let's build you an application and run it. As an application and its main service starts, the API calls are executed. Filter the Logcat output by OkHttp. Observe the following.

Authentication log lines:

- Request:

```
D/OkHttp: --> POST
http://static.milosvasic.net/jsons/journaler/authenticate
D/OkHttp: Content-Type: application/json; charset=UTF-8
D/OkHttp: Content-Length: 45
D/OkHttp: Accept: */*
D/OkHttp: {"password":"password","username":"username"}
D/OkHttp: --> END POST (45-byte body)
```

- Response:

```
D/OkHttp: <-- 200 OK
http://static.milosvasic.net/jsons/journaler/
authenticate/ (302ms)
D/OkHttp: Date: Sat, 23 Sep 2017 15:46:27 GMT
D/OkHttp: Server: Apache
D/OkHttp: Keep-Alive: timeout=5, max=99
D/OkHttp: Connection: Keep-Alive
D/OkHttp: Transfer-Encoding: chunked
D/OkHttp: Content-Type: text/html
D/OkHttp: {
D/OkHttp:    "id_token": "stub_token_1234567",
D/OkHttp:    "expires": 10000
D/OkHttp: }
D/OkHttp: <-- END HTTP (58-byte body)
```

Notes log lines:

- Request:

```
D/OkHttp: --> GET
http://static.milosvasic.net/jsons/journaler/notes
D/OkHttp: Accept: */*
D/OkHttp: Authorization: Bearer stub_token_1234567
D/OkHttp: --> END GET
```

- Response:

```
D/OkHttp: <-- 200 OK
http://static.milosvasic.net/jsons/journaler/notes/ (95ms)
D/OkHttp: Date: Sat, 23 Sep 2017 15:46:28 GMT
D/OkHttp: Server: Apache
D/OkHttp: Keep-Alive: timeout=5, max=97
D/OkHttp: Connection: Keep-Alive
D/OkHttp: Transfer-Encoding: chunked
```

```
D/OkHttp: Content-Type: text/html
D/OkHttp: [
D/OkHttp:    {
D/OkHttp:       "title": "Test note 1",
D/OkHttp:       "message": "Test message 1",
D/OkHttp:       "location": {
D/OkHttp:          "latitude": 10000,
D/OkHttp:          "longitude": 10000
D/OkHttp:       }
D/OkHttp:    },
D/OkHttp:    {
D/OkHttp:       "title": "Test note 2",
D/OkHttp:       "message": "Test message 2",
D/OkHttp:       "location": {
D/OkHttp:          "latitude": 10000,
D/OkHttp:          "longitude": 10000
D/OkHttp:       }
D/OkHttp:    },
D/OkHttp:    {
D/OkHttp:       "title": "Test note 3",
D/OkHttp:       "message": "Test message 3",
D/OkHttp:       "location": {
D/OkHttp:          "latitude": 10000,
D/OkHttp:          "longitude": 10000
D/OkHttp:       }
D/OkHttp:    }
D/OkHttp: ]
D/OkHttp: <-- END HTTP (434-byte body)
```

TODOs log lines:

- Request: This is an example of the request part we do:

```
D/OkHttp: --> GET
http://static.milosvasic.net/jsons/journaler/todos
D/OkHttp: Accept: */*
D/OkHttp: Authorization: Bearer stub_token_1234567
D/OkHttp: --> END GET
```

- Response: This is an example of the response we receive:

```
D/OkHttp: <-- 200 OK
 http://static.milosvasic.net/jsons/journaler/todos/ (140ms)
D/OkHttp: Date: Sat, 23 Sep 2017 15:46:28 GMT
D/OkHttp: Server: Apache
D/OkHttp: Keep-Alive: timeout=5, max=99
D/OkHttp: Connection: Keep-Alive
D/OkHttp: Transfer-Encoding: chunked
```

```
D/OkHttp: Content-Type: text/html
D/OkHttp: [
D/OkHttp:    {
D/OkHttp:       "title": "Test todo 1",
D/OkHttp:       "message": "Test message 1",
D/OkHttp:       "location": {
D/OkHttp:          "latitude": 10000,
D/OkHttp:          "longitude": 10000
D/OkHttp:       },
D/OkHttp:       "scheduledFor": 10000
D/OkHttp:    },
D/OkHttp:    {
D/OkHttp:       "title": "Test todo 2",
D/OkHttp:       "message": "Test message 2",
D/OkHttp:       "location": {
D/OkHttp:          "latitude": 10000,
D/OkHttp:          "longitude": 10000
D/OkHttp:       },
D/OkHttp:       "scheduledFor": 10000
D/OkHttp:    },
D/OkHttp:    {
D/OkHttp:       "title": "Test todo 3",
D/OkHttp:       "message": "Test message 3",
D/OkHttp:       "location": {
D/OkHttp:          "latitude": 10000,
D/OkHttp:          "longitude": 10000
D/OkHttp:       },
D/OkHttp:       "scheduledFor": 10000
D/OkHttp:    }
D/OkHttp: ]
D/OkHttp: <-- END HTTP (515-byte body)
```

Congratulations! You have implemented your first Retrofit service! Now it is time to implement the rest of the calls. Also, do some code refactoring! This is a small homework task for you. Update your service so it can accept login credentials. In our current code, we hardcoded the username and password. Your mission will be to refactor the code and pass the parameterized credential.

Optionally, improve the code so it's no longer possible to execute the same call multiple times at the same moment. We left this as the legacy from our previous work.

Content providers

It's time to further improve our application and introduce you to Android content providers. Content providers are one of the top power features Android Framework has to offer. What is the purpose of content providers? As its name suggests, content providers have the purpose of managing access to data stored by our application or stored by other applications. They provide a mechanism for sharing the data with other applications and provide a security mechanism for data access, that may or may not be from the same process.

Take a look at the following illustration displaying how content provider can manage access to shared storage:

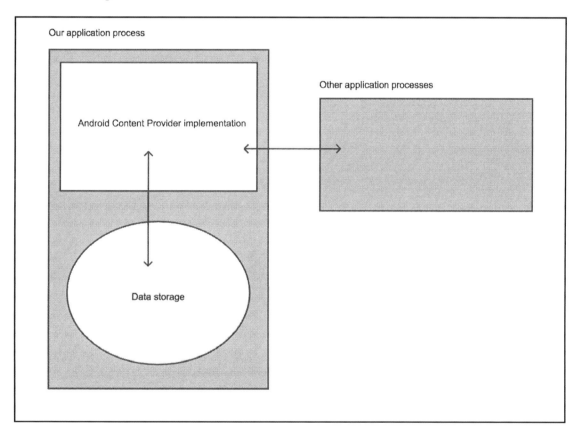

We have a plan to share `Notes` and the `TODOs` data with other applications. Thanks to the abstraction layer content providers offers, it's easy to make the changes in the storage implementation layer without affecting the upper layers. Because of this, you can use content providers even if you do not plan to share any data with other applications. We can, for example, completely replace the persistence mechanism from SQLite to something completely different. Take a look at the following illustration showing this:

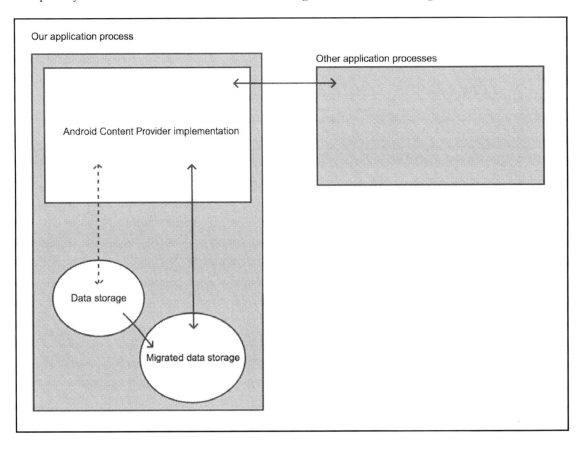

If you are not sure whether you need content provider or not, here is when you should implement it:

- If you are planning to share your application's data with other applications
- If you are planning to copy and paste complex data or files from your application to other applications
- If you are planning to support custom search suggestions

The Android Framework comes with an already defined content provider that you can use; for example, to manage contacts, audio, video, or other files. Content providers are not limited to SQLite access only, but you can use it for other structured data.

Let's once again highlight the main benefits:

- Permissions over accessing the data
- Abstracting the data layer

So, as we already said, we are planning to support data exposure from the **Journaler** application. Before we create our content provider, we must note that this will require refactoring of the current code. Don't worry, we will present content provider, explain it to you and all the refactoring we do. After we do this--finish our implementation and refactoring--we will create an example client application that will use our content provider and trigger all the CRUD operations.

Let's create a ContentProvider class. Create a new package called provider with the JournalerProvider class extending the ContentProvider class.

Class beginning:

```
package com.journaler.provider

import android.content.*
import android.database.Cursor
import android.net.Uri
import com.journaler.database.DbHelper
import android.content.ContentUris
import android.database.SQLException
import android.database.sqlite.SQLiteDatabase
import android.database.sqlite.SQLiteQueryBuilder
import android.text.TextUtils

class JournalerProvider : ContentProvider() {

  private val version = 1
  private val name = "journaler"
  private val db: SQLiteDatabase by lazy {
    DbHelper(name, version).writableDatabase
  }
}
```

Defining a `companion` object:

```
companion object {
    private val dataTypeNote = "note"
    private val dataTypeNotes = "notes"
    private val dataTypeTodo = "todo"
    private val dataTypeTodos = "todos"
    val AUTHORITY = "com.journaler.provider"
    val URL_NOTE = "content://$AUTHORITY/$dataTypeNote"
    val URL_TODO = "content://$AUTHORITY/$dataTypeTodo"
    val URL_NOTES = "content://$AUTHORITY/$dataTypeNotes"
    val URL_TODOS = "content://$AUTHORITY/$dataTypeTodos"
    private val matcher = UriMatcher(UriMatcher.NO_MATCH)
    private val NOTE_ALL = 1
    private val NOTE_ITEM = 2
    private val TODO_ALL = 3
    private val TODO_ITEM = 4
}
```

Class initialization:

```
/**
 * We register uri paths in the following format:
 *
 * <prefix>://<authority>/<data_type>/<id>
 * <prefix> - This is always set to content://
 * <authority> - Name for the content provider
 * <data_type> - The type of data we provide in this Uri
 * <id> - Record ID.
 */
init {
    /**
     * The calls to addURI() go here,
     * for all of the content URI patterns that the provider should
       recognize.
     *
     * First:
     *
     * Sets the integer value for multiple rows in notes (TODOs) to
     1.
     * Notice that no wildcard is used in the path.
     *
     * Second:
     *
     * Sets the code for a single row to 2. In this case, the "#"
     wildcard is
     * used. "content://com.journaler.provider/note/3" matches, but
     * "content://com.journaler.provider/note doesn't.
```

```
 *
 * The same applies for TODOs.
 *
 * addUri() params:
 *
 * authority    - String: the authority to match
 *
 * path         - String: the path to match.
 *                * may be used as a wild card for any text,
 *                and # may be used as a wild card for numbers.
 *
 * code              - int: the code that is returned when a
URI
 *                is matched against the given components.
 */
matcher.addURI(AUTHORITY, dataTypeNote, NOTE_ALL)
matcher.addURI(AUTHORITY, "$dataTypeNotes/#", NOTE_ITEM)
matcher.addURI(AUTHORITY, dataTypeTodo, TODO_ALL)
matcher.addURI(AUTHORITY, "$dataTypeTodos/#", TODO_ITEM)
}
```

Overriding the `onCreate()` method:

```
/**
 * True - if the provider was successfully loaded
 */
override fun onCreate() = true
```

Insert the operation as follows:

```
override fun insert(uri: Uri?, values: ContentValues?): Uri {
    uri?.let {
        values?.let {
            db.beginTransaction()
            val (url, table) = getParameters(uri)
            if (!TextUtils.isEmpty(table)) {
                val inserted = db.insert(table, null, values)
                val success = inserted > 0
                if (success) {
                    db.setTransactionSuccessful()
                }
                db.endTransaction()
                if (success) {
                    val resultUrl = ContentUris.withAppendedId
                    (Uri.parse(url), inserted)
                    context.contentResolver.notifyChange(resultUrl,
                    null)
                    return resultUrl
```

```
                }
            } else {
                throw SQLException("Insert failed, no table for
                uri: " + uri)
            }
        }
    }
    throw SQLException("Insert failed: " + uri)
}
```

Update the operation as follows:

```
override fun update(
        uri: Uri?,
        values: ContentValues?,
        where: String?,
        whereArgs: Array<out String>?
): Int {
    uri?.let {
        values?.let {
            db.beginTransaction()
            val (_, table) = getParameters(uri)
            if (!TextUtils.isEmpty(table)) {
                val updated = db.update(table, values, where,
                 whereArgs)
                val success = updated > 0
                if (success) {
                    db.setTransactionSuccessful()
                }
                db.endTransaction()
                if (success) {
                    context.contentResolver.notifyChange(uri, null)
                    return updated
                }
            } else {
                throw SQLException("Update failed, no table for
                 uri: " + uri)
            }
        }
    }
    throw SQLException("Update failed: " + uri)
}
```

Delete the operation as follows:

```kotlin
override fun delete(
        uri: Uri?,
        selection: String?,
        selectionArgs: Array<out String>?
): Int {
    uri?.let {
        db.beginTransaction()
        val (_, table) = getParameters(uri)
        if (!TextUtils.isEmpty(table)) {
            val count = db.delete(table, selection, selectionArgs)
            val success = count > 0
            if (success) {
                db.setTransactionSuccessful()
            }
            db.endTransaction()
            if (success) {
                context.contentResolver.notifyChange(uri, null)
                return count
            }
        } else {
            throw SQLException("Delete failed, no table for uri: "
             + uri)
        }
    }
    throw SQLException("Delete failed: " + uri)
}
```

Performing query:

```kotlin
override fun query(
        uri: Uri?,
        projection: Array<out String>?,
        selection: String?,
        selectionArgs: Array<out String>?,
        sortOrder: String?
): Cursor {
    uri?.let {
        val stb = SQLiteQueryBuilder()
        val (_, table) = getParameters(uri)
        stb.tables = table
        stb.setProjectionMap(mutableMapOf<String, String>())
        val cursor = stb.query(db, projection, selection,
         selectionArgs, null, null, null)
        // register to watch a content URI for changes
        cursor.setNotificationUri(context.contentResolver, uri)
        return cursor
```

```
        }
        throw SQLException("Query failed: " + uri)
    }

    /**
     * Return the MIME type corresponding to a content URI.
     */
    override fun getType(p0: Uri?): String = when (matcher.match(p0)) {
        NOTE_ALL -> {
            "${ContentResolver.
            CURSOR_DIR_BASE_TYPE}/vnd.com.journaler.note.items"
        }
        NOTE_ITEM -> {
            "${ContentResolver.
             CURSOR_ITEM_BASE_TYPE}/vnd.com.journaler.note.item"
        }
        TODO_ALL -> {
            "${ContentResolver.
             CURSOR_DIR_BASE_TYPE}/vnd.com.journaler.todo.items"
        }
        TODO_ITEM -> {
            "${ContentResolver.
             CURSOR_ITEM_BASE_TYPE}/vnd.com.journaler.todo.item"
        }
        else -> throw IllegalArgumentException
        ("Unsupported Uri [ $p0 ]")
    }
```

Class ending:

```
    private fun getParameters(uri: Uri): Pair<String, String> {
        if (uri.toString().startsWith(URL_NOTE)) {
            return Pair(URL_NOTE, DbHelper.TABLE_NOTES)
        }
        if (uri.toString().startsWith(URL_NOTES)) {
            return Pair(URL_NOTES, DbHelper.TABLE_NOTES)
        }
        if (uri.toString().startsWith(URL_TODO)) {
            return Pair(URL_TODO, DbHelper.TABLE_TODOS)
        }
        if (uri.toString().startsWith(URL_TODOS)) {
            return Pair(URL_TODOS, DbHelper.TABLE_TODOS)
        }
        return Pair("", "")
    }

}
```

Going from top to bottom, we did the following:

- Defined the database name and version
- Defined the database instance lazy initialization
- Defined the URI(s) we will use to access the data
- Implemented all the CRUD operations
- Defined the MIME type for the data

Now, when you have a content provider implementation, it is required to register it in your `manifest` as follows:

```
<manifest xmlns:android=
"http://schemas.android.com/apk/res/android"
package="com.journaler">
...
  <application
    ...
  >
    ...
    <provider
        android:exported="true"
        android:name="com.journaler.provider.JournalerProvider"
        android:authorities="com.journaler.provider" />
    ...
  </application>
...
</manifest>
```

Observe. We set the exported attribute to `True`. What does this mean? It means that, if `True`, the **Journaler** provider is available to other applications. Any application can use the provider's content URI to access the data. One more important attribute is `multiprocess`. If the app runs in multiple processes, this attribute determines whether multiple instances of the **Journaler** provider are created. If `True`, each of the applications' processes has its own content provider instance.

Let's continue. In the `Crud` interface, add this to the `companion` object if you do not have it already:

```
companion object {
    val BROADCAST_ACTION = "com.journaler.broadcast.crud"
    val BROADCAST_EXTRAS_KEY_CRUD_OPERATION_RESULT = "crud_result"
}
```

We will rename our `Db` class into Content. Update the `Content` implementation, as follows, to use `JournalerProvider`:

```
package com.journaler.database

import android.content.ContentValues
import android.location.Location
import android.net.Uri
import android.util.Log
import com.github.salomonbrys.kotson.fromJson
import com.google.gson.Gson
import com.journaler.Journaler
import com.journaler.model.*
import com.journaler.provider.JournalerProvider

object Content {

  private val gson = Gson()
  private val tag = "Content"

  val NOTE = object : Crud<Note> { ...
```

`Note` insert operation:

```
    ...
    override fun insert(what: Note): Long {
      val inserted = insert(listOf(what))
      if (!inserted.isEmpty()) return inserted[0]
        return 0
    }

    override fun insert(what: Collection<Note>): List<Long> {
        val ids = mutableListOf<Long>()
        what.forEach { item ->
          val values = ContentValues()
          values.put(DbHelper.COLUMN_TITLE, item.title)
          values.put(DbHelper.COLUMN_MESSAGE, item.message)
          values.put(DbHelper.COLUMN_LOCATION,
          gson.toJson(item.location))
          val uri = Uri.parse(JournalerProvider.URL_NOTE)
          val ctx = Journaler.ctx
          ctx?.let {
            val result = ctx.contentResolver.insert(uri, values)
            result?.let {
                try {
                    ids.add(result.lastPathSegment.toLong())
                  } catch (e: Exception) {
```

```
                    Log.e(tag, "Error: $e")
                }
            }
        }
    }
    return ids
} ...
```

Note update operation:

```
    ..
    override fun update(what: Note) = update(listOf(what))

    override fun update(what: Collection<Note>): Int {
      var count = 0
      what.forEach { item ->
          val values = ContentValues()
          values.put(DbHelper.COLUMN_TITLE, item.title)
          values.put(DbHelper.COLUMN_MESSAGE, item.message)
          values.put(DbHelper.COLUMN_LOCATION,
          gson.toJson(item.location))
          val uri = Uri.parse(JournalerProvider.URL_NOTE)
          val ctx = Journaler.ctx
          ctx?.let {
            count += ctx.contentResolver.update(
              uri, values, "_id = ?", arrayOf(item.id.toString())
            )
          }
        }
        return count
    } ...
```

Note delete operation:

```
    ...
    override fun delete(what: Note): Int = delete(listOf(what))

    override fun delete(what: Collection<Note>): Int {
      var count = 0
      what.forEach { item ->
        val uri = Uri.parse(JournalerProvider.URL_NOTE)
        val ctx = Journaler.ctx
        ctx?.let {
          count += ctx.contentResolver.delete(
          uri, "_id = ?", arrayOf(item.id.toString())
        )
      }
    }
  }
```

```
   return count
} ...
```

Note **select operation:**

```
    ...
    override fun select(args: Pair<String, String>
     ): List<Note> = select(listOf(args))

    override fun select(args: Collection<Pair<String, String>>):
    List<Note> {
        val items = mutableListOf<Note>()
        val selection = StringBuilder()
        val selectionArgs = mutableListOf<String>()
        args.forEach { arg ->
            selection.append("${arg.first} == ?")
            selectionArgs.add(arg.second)
        }
        val ctx = Journaler.ctx
        ctx?.let {
            val uri = Uri.parse(JournalerProvider.URL_NOTES)
            val cursor = ctx.contentResolver.query(
                    uri, null, selection.toString(),
              selectionArgs.toTypedArray(), null
            )
            while (cursor.moveToNext()) {
               val id = cursor.getLong
               (cursor.getColumnIndexOrThrow(DbHelper.ID))
               val titleIdx = cursor.getColumnIndexOrThrow
               (DbHelper.COLUMN_TITLE)
               val title = cursor.getString(titleIdx)
               val messageIdx = cursor.getColumnIndexOrThrow
              (DbHelper.COLUMN_MESSAGE)
               val message = cursor.getString(messageIdx)
               val locationIdx = cursor.getColumnIndexOrThrow
              (DbHelper.COLUMN_LOCATION)
               val locationJson = cursor.getString(locationIdx)
               val location = gson.fromJson<Location>
               (locationJson)
               val note = Note(title, message, location)
               note.id = id
               items.add(note)
            }
            cursor.close()
            return items
        }
        return items
    }
```

```
override fun selectAll(): List<Note> {
    val items = mutableListOf<Note>()
    val ctx = Journaler.ctx
    ctx?.let {
        val uri = Uri.parse(JournalerProvider.URL_NOTES)
        val cursor = ctx.contentResolver.query(
                uri, null, null, null, null
        )
        while (cursor.moveToNext()) {
            val id = cursor.getLong
            (cursor.getColumnIndexOrThrow(DbHelper.ID))
            val titleIdx = cursor.getColumnIndexOrThrow
            (DbHelper.COLUMN_TITLE)
            val title = cursor.getString(titleIdx)
            val messageIdx = cursor.getColumnIndexOrThrow
            (DbHelper.COLUMN_MESSAGE)
            val message = cursor.getString(messageIdx)
            val locationIdx = cursor.getColumnIndexOrThrow
            (DbHelper.COLUMN_LOCATION)
            val locationJson = cursor.getString(locationIdx)
            val location = gson.fromJson<Location>
            (locationJson)
            val note = Note(title, message, location)
            note.id = id
            items.add(note)
        }
        cursor.close()
    }
    return items
}
}
```

Todo object definition and its insert operation:

```
...
val TODO = object : Crud<Todo> {
    override fun insert(what: Todo): Long {
        val inserted = insert(listOf(what))
        if (!inserted.isEmpty()) return inserted[0]
        return 0
    }

    override fun insert(what: Collection<Todo>): List<Long> {
        val ids = mutableListOf<Long>()
        what.forEach { item ->
            val values = ContentValues()
            values.put(DbHelper.COLUMN_TITLE, item.title)
            values.put(DbHelper.COLUMN_MESSAGE, item.message)
```

```
                    values.put(DbHelper.COLUMN_LOCATION,
                    gson.toJson(item.location))
                    val uri = Uri.parse(JournalerProvider.URL_TODO)
                    values.put(DbHelper.COLUMN_SCHEDULED,
                    item.scheduledFor)
                    val ctx = Journaler.ctx
                    ctx?.let {
                        val result = ctx.contentResolver.insert(uri,
                        values)
                        result?.let {
                            try {
                                ids.add(result.lastPathSegment.toLong())
                            } catch (e: Exception) {
                                Log.e(tag, "Error: $e")
                            }
                        }
                    }
                }
                return ids
        } ...
```

Todo **update operation:**

```
        ...
        override fun update(what: Todo) = update(listOf(what))

        override fun update(what: Collection<Todo>): Int {
            var count = 0
            what.forEach { item ->
                    val values = ContentValues()
                    values.put(DbHelper.COLUMN_TITLE, item.title)
                    values.put(DbHelper.COLUMN_MESSAGE, item.message)
                    values.put(DbHelper.COLUMN_LOCATION,
                    gson.toJson(item.location))
                    val uri = Uri.parse(JournalerProvider.URL_TODO)
                    values.put(DbHelper.COLUMN_SCHEDULED,
                    item.scheduledFor)
                    val ctx = Journaler.ctx
                    ctx?.let {
                        count += ctx.contentResolver.update(
                                uri, values, "_id = ?",
                            arrayOf(item.id.toString())
                        )
                    }
                }
                return count
        } ...
```

Todo **delete operation:**

```
    ...
    override fun delete(what: Todo): Int = delete(listOf(what))

    override fun delete(what: Collection<Todo>): Int {
        var count = 0
        what.forEach { item ->
            val uri = Uri.parse(JournalerProvider.URL_TODO)
            val ctx = Journaler.ctx
            ctx?.let {
                count += ctx.contentResolver.delete(
                    uri, "_id = ?", arrayOf(item.id.toString())
                )
            }
        }
        return count
    }
```

Todo **select operation:**

```
      ...
      override fun select(args: Pair<String, String>): List<Todo> =
      select(listOf(args))

      override fun select(args: Collection<Pair<String, String>>):
       List<Todo> {
          val items = mutableListOf<Todo>()
          val selection = StringBuilder()
          val selectionArgs = mutableListOf<String>()
          args.forEach { arg ->
              selection.append("${arg.first} == ?")
              selectionArgs.add(arg.second)
          }
          val ctx = Journaler.ctx
          ctx?.let {
              val uri = Uri.parse(JournalerProvider.URL_TODOS)
              val cursor = ctx.contentResolver.query(
                  uri, null, selection.toString(),
                  selectionArgs.toTypedArray(), null
              )
              while (cursor.moveToNext()) {
                  val id = cursor.getLong
                 (cursor.getColumnIndexOrThrow(DbHelper.ID))
                  val titleIdx = cursor.getColumnIndexOrThrow
                 (DbHelper.COLUMN_TITLE)
                  val
                  title =
```

```
                    cursor.getString(titleIdx)
                    val messageIdx = cursor.getColumnIndexOrThrow
                    (DbHelper.COLUMN_MESSAGE)
                    val message = cursor.getString(messageIdx)
                    val locationIdx = cursor.getColumnIndexOrThrow
                    (DbHelper.COLUMN_LOCATION)
                    val locationJson = cursor.getString(locationIdx)
                    val location = gson.fromJson<Location>
                    (locationJson)
                    val scheduledForIdx = cursor.getColumnIndexOrThrow(
                        DbHelper.COLUMN_SCHEDULED
                    )
                    val scheduledFor = cursor.getLong(scheduledForIdx)
                    val todo = Todo(title, message, location,
                    scheduledFor)
                    todo.id = id
                    items.add(todo)
                }
            cursor.close()
        }
        return items
    }

    override fun selectAll(): List<Todo> {
        val items = mutableListOf<Todo>()
        val ctx = Journaler.ctx
        ctx?.let {
            val uri = Uri.parse(JournalerProvider.URL_TODOS)
            val cursor = ctx.contentResolver.query(
                    uri, null, null, null, null
            )
            while (cursor.moveToNext()) {
                val id = cursor.getLong
                (cursor.getColumnIndexOrThrow(DbHelper.ID))
                val titleIdx = cursor.getColumnIndexOrThrow
                (DbHelper.COLUMN_TITLE)
                val title = cursor.getString(titleIdx)
                val messageIdx = cursor.getColumnIndexOrThrow
                (DbHelper.COLUMN_MESSAGE)
                val message = cursor.getString(messageIdx)
                val locationIdx = cursor.getColumnIndexOrThrow
                (DbHelper.COLUMN_LOCATION)
                val locationJson = cursor.getString(locationIdx)
                val location = gson.fromJson<Location>
                (locationJson)
                val scheduledForIdx = cursor.getColumnIndexOrThrow(
                    DbHelper.COLUMN_SCHEDULED
                )
```

```
                    val scheduledFor = cursor.getLong(scheduledForIdx)
                    val todo = Todo
                    (title, message, location, scheduledFor)
                    todo.id = id
                    items.add(todo)
                }
                cursor.close()
            }
            return items
        }
    }
}
```

Read the code carefully. We replaced the direct database access with content provider. Update your UI classes to use the new refactored code. If you have trouble doing this, you can take a look at the GitHub branch containing these changes:

```
https://github.com/PacktPublishing/-Mastering-Android-Development-with-Kotlin/
tree/examples/chapter_12.
```

The branch also contains an example of the Journaler content provider client application. We will highlight an example of use on the client application's main screen containing four buttons. Each button triggers an example of the CRUD operation, as shown here:

```
package com.journaler.content_provider_client

import android.content.ContentValues
import android.location.Location
import android.net.Uri
import android.os.AsyncTask
import android.os.Bundle
import android.support.v7.app.AppCompatActivity
import android.util.Log
import com.github.salomonbrys.kotson.fromJson
import com.google.gson.Gson
import kotlinx.android.synthetic.main.activity_main.*

class MainActivity : AppCompatActivity() {

    private val gson = Gson()
    private val tag = "Main activity"

    override fun onCreate(savedInstanceState: Bundle?) {
        super.onCreate(savedInstanceState)
        setContentView(R.layout.activity_main)

        select.setOnClickListener {
```

```
val task = object : AsyncTask<Unit, Unit, Unit>() {
    override fun doInBackground(vararg p0: Unit?) {
        val selection = StringBuilder()
        val selectionArgs = mutableListOf<String>()
        val uri = Uri.parse
        ("content://com.journaler.provider/notes")
        val cursor = contentResolver.query(
                uri, null, selection.toString(),
                selectionArgs.toTypedArray(), null
        )
        while (cursor.moveToNext()) {
            val id = cursor.getLong
            (cursor.getColumnIndexOrThrow("_id"))
            val titleIdx =  cursor.
            getColumnIndexOrThrow("title")
            val title = cursor.getString(titleIdx)
            val messageIdx = cursor.
            getColumnIndexOrThrow("message")
            val message = cursor.getString(messageIdx)
            val locationIdx = cursor.
            getColumnIndexOrThrow("location")
            val locationJson = cursor.
            getString(locationIdx)
            val location =
            gson.fromJson<Location>(locationJson)
            Log.v(
                    tag,
                    "Note retrieved via content provider [
                    $id, $title, $message, $location ]"
            )
        }
        cursor.close()
    }
}
task.execute()
}

insert.setOnClickListener {
    val task = object : AsyncTask<Unit, Unit, Unit>() {
        override fun doInBackground(vararg p0: Unit?) {
            for (x in 0..5) {
                val uri = Uri.parse
                ("content://com.journaler.provider/note")
                val values = ContentValues()
                values.put("title", "Title $x")
                values.put("message", "Message $x")
                val location = Location("stub location $x")
                location.latitude = x.toDouble()
```

```
                    location.longitude = x.toDouble()
                    values.put("location", gson.toJson(location))
                    if (contentResolver.insert(uri, values) !=
                    null) {
                        Log.v(
                                tag,
                                "Note inserted [ $x ]"
                        )
                    } else {
                        Log.e(
                                tag,
                                "Note not inserted [ $x ]"
                        )
                    }
                }
            }
        }
        task.execute()
    }

    update.setOnClickListener {
        val task = object : AsyncTask<Unit, Unit, Unit>() {
            override fun doInBackground(vararg p0: Unit?) {
                val selection = StringBuilder()
                val selectionArgs = mutableListOf<String>()
                val uri =
                Uri.parse("content://com.journaler.provider/notes")
                val cursor = contentResolver.query(
                        uri, null, selection.toString(),
                        selectionArgs.toTypedArray(), null
                )
                while (cursor.moveToNext()) {
                    val values = ContentValues()
                    val id = cursor.getLong
                    (cursor.getColumnIndexOrThrow("_id"))
                    val titleIdx =
                    cursor.getColumnIndexOrThrow("title")
                    val title = "${cursor.getString(titleIdx)} upd:
                    ${System.currentTimeMillis()}"
                    val messageIdx =
                    cursor.getColumnIndexOrThrow("message")
                    val message =
                    "${cursor.getString(messageIdx)} upd:
                    ${System.currentTimeMillis()}"
                    val locationIdx =
                    cursor.getColumnIndexOrThrow("location")
                    val locationJson =
                    cursor.getString(locationIdx)
```

```kotlin
                    values.put("_id", id)
                    values.put("title", title)
                    values.put("message", message)
                    values.put("location", locationJson)

                    val updated = contentResolver.update(
                            uri, values, "_id = ?",
                            arrayOf(id.toString())
                    )
                    if (updated > 0) {
                        Log.v(
                                tag,
                                "Notes updated [ $updated ]"
                        )
                    } else {
                        Log.e(
                                tag,
                                "Notes not updated"
                        )
                    }
                }
                cursor.close()
            }
        }
        task.execute()
    }


    delete.setOnClickListener {
        val task = object : AsyncTask<Unit, Unit, Unit>() {
            override fun doInBackground(vararg p0: Unit?) {
                val selection = StringBuilder()
                val selectionArgs = mutableListOf<String>()
                val uri = Uri.parse
            ("content://com.journaler.provider/notes")
                val cursor = contentResolver.query(
                        uri, null, selection.toString(),
                        selectionArgs.toTypedArray(), null
                )
                while (cursor.moveToNext()) {
                    val id = cursor.getLong
                    (cursor.getColumnIndexOrThrow("_id"))
                    val deleted = contentResolver.delete(
                            uri, "_id = ?", arrayOf(id.toString())
                    )
                    if (deleted > 0) {
                        Log.v(
                                tag,
                                "Notes deleted [ $deleted ]"
```

```
                              )
                         } else {
                             Log.e(
                                      tag,
                                      "Notes not deleted"
                             )
                         }
                    }
                    cursor.close()
              }
         }
         task.execute()
       }
     }
   }
```

This example demonstrates how to trigger CRUD operations from other applications using content provider.

Android adapters

To present content on our main screen, we will use the Android Adapter class. The Android Framework offers adapters as a mechanism to provide items to view groups as lists or grids. To show an example of Adapter usage, we will define our own adapter implementation. Create a new package called `adapter` and an `EntryAdapter` member class extending the `BaseAdapter` class:

```
package com.journaler.adapter

import android.annotation.SuppressLint
import android.content.Context
import android.view.LayoutInflater
import android.view.View
import android.view.ViewGroup
import android.widget.BaseAdapter
import android.widget.TextView
import com.journaler.R
import com.journaler.model.Entry

class EntryAdapter(
    private val ctx: Context,
    private val items: List<Entry>
) : BaseAdapter() {

@SuppressLint("InflateParams", "ViewHolder")
```

```
override fun getView(p0: Int, p1: View?, p2: ViewGroup?): View {
    p1?.let {
        return p1
    }
    val inflater = LayoutInflater.from(ctx)
    val view = inflater.inflate(R.layout.adapter_entry, null)
    val label = view.findViewById<TextView>(R.id.title)
    label.text = items[p0].title
    return view
}

override fun getItem(p0: Int): Entry = items[p0]
override fun getItemId(p0: Int): Long = items[p0].id
override fun getCount(): Int = items.size
}
```

We overrode the following methods:

- getView(): This returns the instance of the populated view based on the current position in the container
- getItem(): This returns the instance of the item we use to create the view; in our case, this is the Entry class instance (Note or Todo)
- getItemId(): This returns the ID for the current item instance
- getCount(): This returns the total number of items

We will connect the adapter and our UI. Open ItemsFragment and updated its onResume() method to instantiate the adapter and assign it to a ListView, as follows:

```
override fun onResume() {
    super.onResume()
    ...
    executor.execute {
        val notes = Content.NOTE.selectAll()
        val adapter = EntryAdapter(activity, notes)
        activity.runOnUiThread {
            view?.findViewById<ListView>(R.id.items)?.adapter =
             adapter
        }
    }
}
```

When you build and run your application, you should see every page of `ViewPager` populated with the loaded items, as shown in the following screenshot:

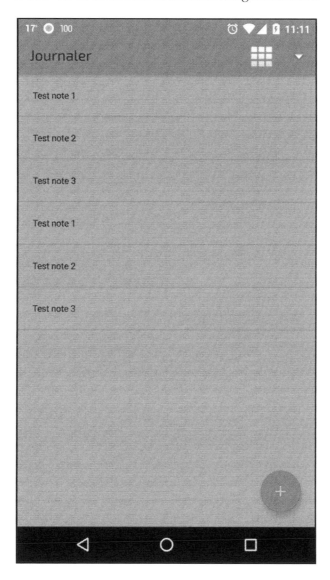

Content loaders

Content loaders provide you with a mechanism to load data from a content provider or other data source for display in a UI component, such as Activity or Fragment. These are the benefits that loaders provide:

- Running on a separate thread
- Simplifying thread management by providing callback methods
- Loaders persist and cache results across configuration changes, which prevents duplicated queries
- We can implement and be observers to monitor changes in the data

We will create our content loader implementation. First, we need to update the Adapter class. Since we will deal with cursors, we will use a CursorAdapter instead of BaseAdapter. CursorAdapter accepts a Cursor instance as a parameter in the primary constructor. The CursorAdapter implementation is much simpler than the one we have right now. Open EntryAdapter and update it as follows:

```
class EntryAdapter(ctx: Context, crsr: Cursor) : CursorAdapter(ctx,
crsr) {

override fun newView(p0: Context?, p1: Cursor?, p2: ViewGroup?):
View {
    val inflater = LayoutInflater.from(p0)
    return inflater.inflate(R.layout.adapter_entry, null)
}

override fun bindView(p0: View?, p1: Context?, p2: Cursor?) {
    p0?.let {
        val label = p0.findViewById<TextView>(R.id.title)
        label.text = cursor.getString(
            cursor.getColumnIndexOrThrow(DbHelper.COLUMN_TITLE)
        )
    }
}

}
```

We have the following two methods to override:

- newView(): This returns the instance of the view to populate with data
- bindView(): This populates data from the Cursor instance

Finally, let's update our `ItemsFragment` class, so it uses the content loader implementation:

```
class ItemsFragment : BaseFragment() {
  ...
  private var adapter: EntryAdapter? = null
  ...
  private val loaderCallback = object :
  LoaderManager.LoaderCallbacks<Cursor> {
    override fun onLoadFinished(loader: Loader<Cursor>?, cursor:
    Cursor?) {
        cursor?.let {
            if (adapter == null) {
                adapter = EntryAdapter(activity, cursor)
                items.adapter = adapter
            } else {
                adapter?.swapCursor(cursor)
            }
        }
    }

    override fun onLoaderReset(loader: Loader<Cursor>?) {
        adapter?.swapCursor(null)
    }

    override fun onCreateLoader(id: Int, args: Bundle?):
    Loader<Cursor> {
        return CursorLoader(
                activity,
                Uri.parse(JournalerProvider.URL_NOTES),
                null,
                null,
                null,
                null
        )
    }
}

override fun onCreate(savedInstanceState: Bundle?) {
    super.onCreate(savedInstanceState)
    loaderManager.initLoader(
            0, null, loaderCallback
    )
}

override fun onResume() {
    super.onResume()
    loaderManager.restartLoader(0, null, loaderCallback)
```

```
    val btn = view?.findViewById
    <FloatingActionButton>(R.id.new_item)
    btn?.let {
        animate(btn, false)
    }
  }
}
```

We initialize `LoaderManager` by calling the `LoaderManager` member of our Fragment. The two crucial methods we execute are as follows:

- `initLoader()`: This ensures a loader is initialized and active
- `restartLoader()`: This starts a new or restarts an existing `loader` instance

Both methods accept the loader ID and bundle data as arguments and the `LoaderCallbacks<Cursor>` implementation, which provides the following three methods to override:

- `onCreateLoader()`: This instantiates and returns a new loader instance for the ID we provided
- `onLoadFinished()`: This is called when a previously created loader has finished loading
- `onLoaderReset()`: This is called when a previously created loader is being reset, and, because of that, making its data unavailable

Data binding

Android supports a mechanism for data binding so that data is bound with views and the glue code is minimized. Enable data binding by updating your build Gradle configuration as follows:

```
android {
  ....
  dataBinding {
   enabled = true
  }
}
...
dependencies {
  ...
  kapt 'com.android.databinding:compiler:2.3.1'
}
...
```

Now, you can define your binding expressions. Take a look at the following example:

```xml
<?xml version="1.0" encoding="utf-8"?>
<layout xmlns:android="http://schemas.android.com/apk/res/android">

<data>
    <variable
        name="note"
        type="com.journaler.model.Note" />
</data>

<LinearLayout
    android:layout_width="match_parent"
    android:layout_height="match_parent"
    android:orientation="vertical">

    <TextView
        android:layout_width="wrap_content"
        android:layout_height="wrap_content"
        android:text="@{note.title}" />

</LinearLayout>
</layout>
```

Let's bind the data as follows:

```kotlin
package com.journaler.activity

import android.databinding.DataBindingUtil
import android.location.Location
import android.os.Bundle
import com.journaler.R
import com.journaler.databinding.ActivityBindingBinding
import com.journaler.model.Note

abstract class BindingActivity : BaseActivity() {

override fun onCreate(savedInstanceState: Bundle?) {
    super.onCreate(savedInstanceState)
    /**
     * ActivityBindingBinding is auto generated class
     * which name is derived from activity_binding.xml filename.
     */
    val binding : ActivityBindingBinding =
    DataBindingUtil.setContentView(
        this, R.layout.activity_binding
    )
    val location = Location("dummy")
```

```
        val note = Note("my note", "bla", location)
        binding.note = note
    }


}
```

That's it! See how simple it is to bind data to layout views! We strongly recommend that you play with data binding as much as you can. Create your own examples! Feel free to experiment!

Using lists

We showed you how to work with data. As you noticed, in the main view data container, we used ListView. Why did we choose it? First of all, it's the most commonly used container to hold your data. In most cases, you will use ListView to hold the data from your adapters. Never put a large number of views in a scrollable container like LinearLayout! Whenever possible, use ListView. It will recycle views when they are not needed anymore and reinstantiate them when needed.

Using lists can affect your application performance since it's a well-optimized container for displaying your data. Displaying a list is an essential functionality of almost any application! Any application that produces a set of data as a result of some operation needs a list. It's almost impossible that you will not use it in your application.

Using grids

We noted how lists are important. However, what if we plan to present our data as a grid? Lucky for us!! The Android Framework provides us with a GridView that works very similar to ListView. You define your GridView in layout and assign the adapter instance to GridView's adapter property. GridView will recycle all views for you and perform instantiation when needed. The main difference between the list and the grid is that you have to define the number of columns for your GridView. The following example will present you with an example of GridView's use:

```xml
<?xml version="1.0" encoding="utf-8"?>
<GridView xmlns:android="http://schemas.android.com/apk/res/android"
    android:id="@+id/my_grid"
    android:layout_width="match_parent"
    android:layout_height="match_parent"
    android:columnWidth="100dp"
    android:numColumns="3"
```

```
        android:verticalSpacing="20dp"
        android:horizontalSpacing="20dp"

        android:stretchMode="columnWidth"
        android:gravity="center"
    />
```

We will highlight the important attributes we used in this example:

- `columnWidth`: This specifies the width for each column
- `numColumns`: This specifies the number of columns
- `verticalSpacing`: This specifies the vertical spacing between the rows
- `horizontalSpacing`: This specifies the horizontal spacing between the items in the grid

Try updating the current application's main `ListView` to present the data as `GridView`. Adjust it so it looks pleasant for the end user. Once again, feel free to experiment!

Implementing drag and drop

Here, in the last section of this chapter, we will show you how to implement the drag and drop feature. It's a feature that you will probably need in most applications containing data in lists. Using lists is not mandatory for performing drag and drop, because you can drag anything (view) and release it anywhere where a proper listener is defined. For a better understanding of what we are talking about, we will show you an example of how to implement it.

Let's define a view. On that view, we will set a long press listener that will trigger the drag and drop operation:

```
    view.setOnLongClickListener {
        val data = ClipData.newPlainText("", "")
        val shadowBuilder = View.DragShadowBuilder(view)
        view.startDrag(data, shadowBuilder, view, 0)
        true
    }
```

We used the `ClipData` class to pass the data to drop a target. We defined `dragListener` like this and assigned it to a view where we expect it to drop:

```
private val dragListener = View.OnDragListener {
    view, event ->
    val tag = "Drag and drop"
    event?.let {
        when (event.action) {
            DragEvent.ACTION_DRAG_STARTED -> {
                Log.d(tag, "ACTION_DRAG_STARTED")
            }
            DragEvent.ACTION_DRAG_ENDED -> {
                Log.d(tag, "ACTION_DRAG_ENDED")
            }
            DragEvent.ACTION_DRAG_ENTERED -> {
                Log.d(tag, "ACTION_DRAG_ENDED")
            }
            DragEvent.ACTION_DRAG_EXITED -> {
                Log.d(tag, "ACTION_DRAG_ENDED")
            }
            else -> {
                Log.d(tag, "ACTION_DRAG_ ELSE ...")
            }
        }
    }
    true
}

target?.setOnDragListener(dragListener)
```

Drag listener will fire up the code when we start dragging a view and finally release it on the `target` view that has the listener assigned.

Summary

In this chapter, we covered a lot of topics. We learned about backend communication, how to establish communication with the backend remote instance using Retrofit, and how to handle the data we obtain. The aim of this chapter was to work with content providers and content loaders. We hope you realized their importance and what their benefits are. Finally, we demonstrated data binding; noted the importance of our data view containers, such as `ListView` and `GridView`; and showed you how to carry out the drag and drop operation. In the next chapter, we will start testing our code. Be ready for the performance optimization since that is what we will do in the next chapter!

13
Tuning Up for High Performance

We just finished mastering work with backend and API. We are approaching the end of our journey, but it's not over yet! We have to cover some very important points! One such is performance optimization. We will guide you through some good practices in achieving this. Think about the code we have developed so far and how can we apply these advices on it.

In this chapter, we will cover the following topics:

- Layout optimization
- Optimization to preserve battery life
- Optimizing to get maximal responsiveness

Optimizing layouts

To achieve maximal UI performance, follow these points:

- **Optimize your layout hierarchies**: Avoid nested layouts since it can be a performance killer! For example, you can have multiple `LinearLayout` views nested. Instead of this, switch to `RelativeLayout`. This can save your performance significantly! Nested layouts require more processing power to be used on calculations and drawing.
- **Reuse layouts if possible**: Android provides `<include />` to allow this.

Take a look at the following example:

```
to_be_included.xml:
<RelativeLayout xmlns:android=
"http://schemas.android.com/apk/res/android"
  xmlns:tools="http://schemas.android.com/tools"
  android:layout_width="match_parent"
  android:layout_height="wrap_content"
  android:background="@color/main_bg"
  tools:showIn="@layout/includes" >

  <TextView
    android:id="@+id/title"
    android:layout_width="wrap_content"
    android:layout_height="wrap_content"
  />

</RelativeLayout>

includes.xml
  <LinearLayout xmlns:android=
  "http://schemas.android.com/apk/res/android"
   android:orientation="vertical"
   android:layout_width="match_parent"
   android:layout_height="match_parent"
   android:background="@color/main_bg"
  >
   ...
   <include layout="@layout/to_be_included"/>
   ...
</LinearLayout>
```

• Beside this, you can use <merge>. Merge eliminates redundant view groups in your view hierarchy when you include one layout within another. Let's take a look at the following example:

```
to_merge.xml
<merge xmlns:android="http://schemas.android.com/apk/res/android">

  <ImageView
    android:id="@+id/first"
    android:layout_width="fill_parent"
    android:layout_height="wrap_content"
    android:src="@drawable/first"/>

  <ImageView
    android:id="@+id/second"
    android:layout_width="fill_parent"
```

```
        android:layout_height="wrap_content"
        android:src="@drawable/second"/>

    </merge>
```

When we include `to_merge.xml` in another layout using include, like we did in the previous example, Android will ignore the `<merge>` element and add our views directly to the container in which `<include />` is placed:

- Include layouts into your screens only when they are needed--If you don't need view at the moment, set its visibility to `Gone` instead of `Invisible`. `Invisible` will still create an instance of view. When using `Gone`, Android will instantiate view only when visibility is changed to `Visible`.
- Use containers like `ListView` or `GridView` to hold your groups of data. We already explained why you should use them in the previous chapter.

Optimizing battery life

There are many ways to drain your battery. Just one of the examples is doing too much work in your application. Too much processing can affect your battery. However, we will point out ways you can save your battery and what you must avoid. Follow these points and keep them in mind every time you develop an application.

To keep your battery in the best condition, apply these advices:

- Reduce network communication as much as possible. Frequent network calls can affect your battery. Because of this, try to make this optimal.
- Determine if your phone is charging. That can be a good time to fire up intensive and performance demanding actions your application may need to do.
- Monitor connectivity status and perform connectivity related operations only when the connectivity status is proper.
- Make use of broadcast messages rationally. Frequent and unnecessary sending of broadcast messages can cost you your performance. Think how frequent you need them and also unregister your receivers when you don't need to receive messages anymore and when there is no benefit to receiving them.
- Pay attention to the intensity of GPS use. Frequent location requests can affect your battery significantly.

Keeping your application responsive

How many times has it happened to you that you use some Android application and get the message saying that the application is not responding? Why does this happen? We will explain! Pay attention to these points so you don't have the same thing happening with your application:

- Make sure nothing blocks your input (any intensive operation, especially network traffic).
- Don't perform long tasks on the main application thread.
- Don't perform long running operations in the `onReceive()` method for your broadcast receivers.
- Make use of the `AsyncTask` class as much as you can. Consider the use of `ThreadPoolExecutor`.
- Try using content loaders whenever it's possible.
- Avoid executing too many threads at the same time.
- If writing to filesystem, do it from a separate thread.

If it still happens that you have ANRs, or your application behaves sluggishly, use tools such as systrace and Traceview to track the roots of your problems.

Summary

In this short but important chapter, we highlighted important points about maintaining and achieving good application performance and responsiveness. These advices are crucial in application optimization. So, if your application doesn't follow these rules, you must optimize it accordingly. By finishing this chapter, we covered all you need to develop Android applications. In the next chapter, we will test it. Be ready to write some unit and instrumentation tests!

14
Testing

We have developed an application with a significant code base. We tried it and we think that our application has no bugs. However, we can be wrong! Sometimes, even if we are sure that there are no bugs in our application, it can happen that a dangerous issue is waiting. How to prevent this? Simple! We will write tests that will check our code for us. In this chapter, we will introduce you to testing and give examples on how to set up, write, and run your tests.

In this chapter, we will cover the following topics:

- How to write your first test
- Using test suites
- How to test UI
- Running tests
- Unit and instrumentation tests

Adding dependencies

To run tests, we must satisfy some dependencies. We will update our application configuration by extending `build.gradle` to support testing and to provide the classes we need. Open `build.gradle` and extend it as follows:

```
apply plugin: "com.android.application"
apply plugin: "kotlin-android"
apply plugin: "kotlin-android-extensions"

repositories {
  maven { url "https://maven.google.com" }
}
```

```
android {
  ...
  sourceSets {
    main.java.srcDirs += [
            'src/main/kotlin',
            'src/common/kotlin',
            'src/debug/kotlin',
            'src/release/kotlin',
            'src/staging/kotlin',
            'src/preproduction/kotlin',
            'src/debug/java',
            'src/release/java',
            'src/staging/java',
            'src/preproduction/java',
            'src/testDebug/java',
            'src/testDebug/kotlin',
            'src/androidTestDebug/java',
            'src/androidTestDebug/kotlin'
    ]
  }
  ...
  testOptions {
    unitTests.returnDefaultValues = true
  }
}
...
dependencies {
  ...
  compile "junit:junit:4.12"
  testCompile "junit:junit:4.12"

  testCompile "org.jetbrains.kotlin:kotlin-reflect:1.1.51"
  testCompile "org.jetbrains.kotlin:kotlin-stdlib:1.1.51"

  compile "org.jetbrains.kotlin:kotlin-test:1.1.51"
  testCompile "org.jetbrains.kotlin:kotlin-test:1.1.51"

  compile "org.jetbrains.kotlin:kotlin-test-junit:1.1.51"
  testCompile "org.jetbrains.kotlin:kotlin-test-junit:1.1.51"

  compile 'com.android.support:support-annotations:26.0.1'
  androidTestCompile 'com.android.support:support
-annotations:26.0.1'

  compile 'com.android.support.test:runner:0.5'
  androidTestCompile 'com.android.support.test:runner:0.5'

  compile 'com.android.support.test:rules:0.5'
```

```
    androidTestCompile 'com.android.support.test:rules:0.5'
  }

It is important to highlight use of:
testOptions {
    unitTests.returnDefaultValues = true
}
```

This will enable us to test content providers and use all related classes in our tests. If we do not enable this, we will get this error:

```
Error: "Method ... not mocked"!
```

Updating folder structure

The folder structure and code in it must follow the convention about build variants. For our tests, we will use the following part of the structure:

- For unit tests:

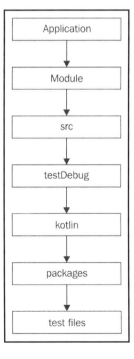

- For instrumentation tests:

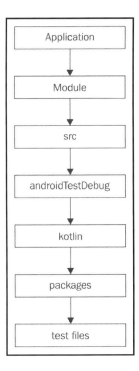

Now we are ready to start writing our tests!

Writing your first test

Locate the `root` package of your unit tests and create a new class called `NoteTest` as follows:

```
package com.journaler

import android.location.Location
import com.journaler.database.Content
import com.journaler.model.Note
import org.junit.Test

class NoteTest {

  @Test
  fun noteTest() {
```

```
val note = Note(
        "stub ${System.currentTimeMillis()}",
        "stub ${System.currentTimeMillis()}",
        Location("Stub")
)

val id = Content.NOTE.insert(note)
note.id = id

assert(note.id > 0)
    }
}
```

The test is very simple. It creates a new instance of Note, triggers the CRUD operation in our content provider to store it, and verifies the ID received. To run the test, right-click on **class** from the **Project** pane and choose **Run 'NoteTest'**:

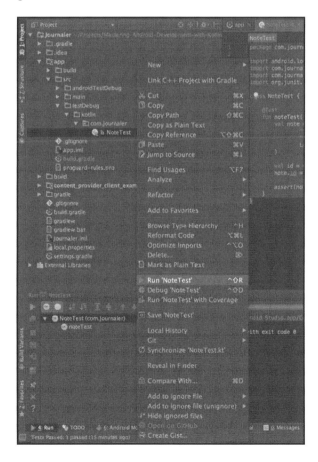

The unit test is executed like this:

As you can see, we successfully inserted our `Note` into the database. Now, after we created our first unit test, we will create our first instrumentation test. However, before we do that, let's explain the difference between unit and instrumentation tests. Instrumentation tests run on a device or an emulator. They can be used when you need to test the code that has dependency on the Android Context. Let's test our main service. Create a new class inside the instrumentation tests `root` package called `MainServiceTest`, as shown here:

```
package com.journaler

import android.content.ComponentName
import android.content.Context
import android.content.Intent
import android.content.ServiceConnection
import android.os.IBinder
import android.support.test.InstrumentationRegistry
import android.util.Log
import com.journaler.service.MainService
import org.junit.After
import org.junit.Before
import org.junit.Test
import kotlin.test.assertNotNull

class MainServiceTest {

    private var ctx: Context? = null
    private val tag = "Main service test"

    private val serviceConnection = object : ServiceConnection {
        override fun onServiceConnected(p0: ComponentName?, binder:
        IBinder?) {
```

```
      Log.v(tag, "Service connected")
    }

    override fun onServiceDisconnected(p0: ComponentName?) {
      Log.v(tag, "Service disconnected")
    }
  }

  @Before
  fun beforeMainServiceTest() {
    Log.v(tag, "Starting")
    ctx = InstrumentationRegistry.getInstrumentation().context
  }

  @Test
  fun testMainService() {
    Log.v(tag, "Running")
    assertNotNull(ctx)
    val serviceIntent = Intent(ctx, MainService::class.java)
    ctx?.startService(serviceIntent)
    val result = ctx?.bindService(
      serviceIntent,
      serviceConnection,
      android.content.Context.BIND_AUTO_CREATE
    )
    assert(result != null && result)
  }

  @After
  fun afterMainServiceTest() {
    Log.v(tag, "Finishing")
    ctx?.unbindService(serviceConnection)
    val serviceIntent = Intent(ctx, MainService::class.java)
    ctx?.stopService(serviceIntent)
  }

}
```

To run it, create a new configuration as it's illustrated in the following screenshot:

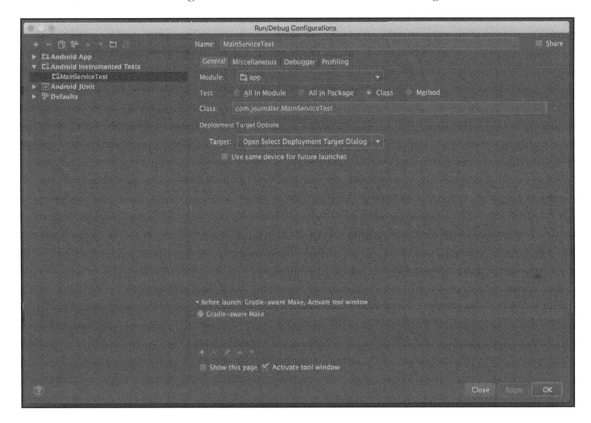

Run the newly created configuration. You will be asked to choose the Android device or the emulator instance on which you will run the test:

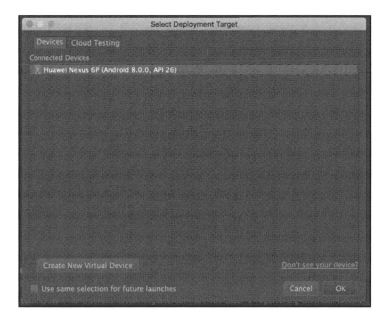

Wait until the test is executed. Congratulations! You have successfully created and run the instrumentation test. Now, for your exercise, define as many tests as you can to cover all the code your application has. Pay attention if the test should be a unit or an instrumentation test.

Using test suites

A **test suite** is a collection of tests. We will show you how to create a test collection. Create a test to represent the container for collection. Let's call it `MainSuite`:

```
package com.journaler

import org.junit.runner.RunWith
import org.junit.runners.Suite

@RunWith(Suite::class)
@Suite.SuiteClasses(
    DummyTest::class,
    MainServiceTest::class
)
class MainSuite
```

Repeat the procedure we did for the instrumentation test from our example to run your test suite.

How to test UI

Testing the UI can help us prevent the user from discovering unexpected situations, crashing the application, or getting poor performance. We strongly recommend you to write UI tests so you are sure your UI performs as expected. For this purpose, we will introduce the Espresso Framework.

First of all, we will add the dependency for it as follows:

```
...
compile 'com.android.support.test.espresso:espresso-core:2.2.2'
androidTestCompile 'com.android.support.test.espresso:espresso-core:2.2.2'
...
```

Before you write and run Espresso tests, disable animations on your testing device because this will affect tests, expected timings, and behaviors. We strongly recommend you to do that! On your device, go to **Settings** | **Developer options** | and turn off the following:

- **Window animation scale**
- **Transition animation scale**
- **Animator duration scale**

Now you are ready to write Espresso tests. Learning the Espresso Framework can take some effort. It can be time consuming for you, but its benefit will be huge! Let's take a look at the example of one Espresso test:

```
@RunWith(AndroidJUnit4::class)
class MainScreenTest {
    @Rule
    val mainActivityRule =
    ActivityTestRule(MainActivity::class.java)

    @Test
    fun testMainActivity(){
     onView((withId(R.id.toolbar))).perform(click())
     onView(withText("My dialog")).check(matches(isDisplayed()))
    }

}
```

We defined that we will test the `MainActivity` class. After the test triggers the toolbar button click, we check if the dialog is present. We do that by checking the label availability-- `"My dialog"`. Learning the entire Espresso Framework is beyond this book, but at least we gave you a hint of possibilities. Invest some time in learning it because it will definitely help you!

Running tests

We already executed our tests through the Android Studio. However, once you write them all, you will want to run them all at once. You can run all the unit tests for all build variants, but only for a certain flavor or build type. The same applies for instrumentation tests. We will show you several examples to do so using existing build variants for the **Journaler** application.

Running unit tests

Open the terminal and navigate to the `root` package of the project. To run all unit tests, execute the following command line:

```
$ ./gtradlew test
```

This will run all the unit tests we wrote. The testing will fail since `NoteTest` uses content provider. For this, it's required to be executed with the proper `Runner` class. Android Studio, by default, does that. However, since this is a unit test, and we execute it from the terminal, testing will fail. You will agree that this test is actually something that has to be considered as instrumentation since it uses the Android Framework components. Common practice is that if your class relies on the Android Framework components, it has to be executed as instrumentation. Because of this, we will move `NoteTest` into an instrumentation tests directory. Now we don't have any unit test. Create at least one that does not depend on the Android Framework components. You can move the existing `DummyTest` for that purpose in the unit tests folder. Drag and drop it from your IDE and rerun the tests with the same command.

To run all tests for the build variant, execute the following command line:

```
$ ./gradlew testCompleteDebug
```

We execute tests for the `Complete` flavor and the `Debug` build type.

Running instrumentation tests

To run all instrumentation tests, use the following command line:

```
$ ./gradlew connectedAndroidTest
```

Its precondition is to have a device connected or emulator running. If you have more than one device or emulator present, all of them will run tests.

To run the instrumentation test for the build variant, use the following command line:

```
$ ./gradlew connectedCompleteDebugAndroidTest
```

This will trigger all instrumentation tests for the Connected flavor with the Debug build type.

Summary

In this chapter, we learned how to write and run tests for our application. This is one more step toward production. We established a well-written and bug-free product. Soon, we will actually publish it. Be patient because that moment is coming!

15
Migration to Kotlin

If you have a legacy project or an existing Java module that you want to migrate to Kotlin, migration should be easy. People who made it, thought about this. As you remember, Kotlin is interoperable. Because of that, some modules don't need full migration; instead, they can be included into a Kotlin project. It's up to you to decide. So, let's prepare our migration!

In this chapter, we will cover the following topics:

- Preparing the migration
- Converting classes
- Refactoring and cleanup

Preparing the migration

As we said, we need to make a decision whether we will completely rewrite our modules into Kotlin or continue writing our code in Kotlin but keep its legacy in pure Java. What will we do? In this chapter, we will demonstrate a little bit of each.

Our current project, at this point, doesn't have anything to migrate. So, we will create some code. If you don't have the Java sources directory with the packages structure, create it. Now, add the following packages:

- `activity`
- `model`

These packages are equivalent to the packages we already have in our Kotlin source code. In the `activity` package, add the following classes:

- The `MigrationActivity.java` code is as follows:

```java
package com.journaler.activity;

import android.os.Bundle;
import android.support.annotation.Nullable;
import android.support.v7.app.AppCompatActivity;

import com.journaler.R;

public class MigrationActivity extends AppCompatActivity {

  @Override
  protected void onCreate(@Nullable Bundle savedInstanceState) {
    super.onCreate(savedInstanceState);
    setContentView(R.layout.activity_main);
  }

  @Override
  protected void onResume() {
    super.onResume();
  }
}
```

- `MigrationActivity2.java`: Make sure it has exactly the same implementation as `MigrationActivity.java`. We just need some code base to present and migrate.
  Register both activities in the Android `manifest` file as follows:

```xml
<manifest xmlns:android=
"http://schemas.android.com/apk/res/android"
package="com.journaler">
...
<application
 ...
>
...
 <activity
    android:name=".activity.MainActivity"
    android:configChanges="orientation"
    android:screenOrientation="portrait">
    <intent-filter>
      <action android:name="android.intent.action.MAIN" />
      <category android:name=
```

```
            "android.intent.category.LAUNCHER" />
        </intent-filter>
    </activity>

    <activity
        android:name=".activity.NoteActivity"
        android:configChanges="orientation"
        android:screenOrientation="portrait" />

    <activity
        android:name=".activity.TodoActivity"
        android:configChanges="orientation"
        android:screenOrientation="portrait" />

    <activity
        android:name=".activity.MigrationActivity"
        android:configChanges="orientation"
        android:screenOrientation="portrait" />

    <activity
        android:name=".activity.MigrationActivity2"
        android:configChanges="orientation"
        android:screenOrientation="portrait" />
    </application>
</manifest>
```

As you can see, the Java code stands together with the Kotlin code without any issue. Your Android project can use both! Now, think, do you really need to do any conversion at all or are you fine to keep the existing Java stuff? Let's add classes in the `model` package:

- The `Dummy.java` code is as follows:

```
package com.journaler.model;

public class Dummy {

  private String title;
  private String content;

  public Dummy(String title) {
    this.title = title;
  }

  public Dummy(String title, String content) {
    this.title = title;
    this.content = content;
```

```
      }

      public String getTitle() {
        return title;
      }

      public void setTitle(String title) {
        this.title = title;
      }

      public String getContent() {
        return content;
      }

     public void setContent(String content) {
        this.content = content;
      }

    }
```

- The Dummy2.java code is as follows:

```
    package com.journaler.model;

    import android.os.Parcel;
    import android.os.Parcelable;

    public class Dummy2 implements Parcelable {

      private int count;
      private float result;

      public Dummy2(int count) {
        this.count = count;
        this.result = count * 100;
      }

      public Dummy2(Parcel in) {
        count = in.readInt();
        result = in.readFloat();
      }

      public static final Creator<Dummy2>
      CREATOR = new Creator<Dummy2>() {
        @Override
        public Dummy2 createFromParcel(Parcel in) {
          return new Dummy2(in);
        }
```

```
          @Override
          public Dummy2[] newArray(int size) {
            return new Dummy2[size];
          }
        };

        @Override
        public void writeToParcel(Parcel parcel, int i) {
          parcel.writeInt(count);
          parcel.writeFloat(result);
        }

        @Override
        public int describeContents() {
          return 0;
        }

        public int getCount() {
          return count;
        }

        public float getResult() {
          return result;
        }
    }
```

Let's check again if the Kotlin part of the project sees these classes. Create a new `.kt` file in the root of your Kotlin sources directory. Let's call it `kotlin_calls_java.kt`:

```
package com.journaler

import android.content.Context
import android.content.Intent
import com.journaler.activity.MigrationActivity
import com.journaler.model.Dummy2

fun kotlinCallsJava(ctx: Context) {

  /**
   * We access Java class and instantiate it.
   */
  val dummy = Dummy2(10)

  /**
   * We use Android related Java code with no problems as well.
   */
   val intent = Intent(ctx, MigrationActivity::class.java)
   intent.putExtra("dummy", dummy)
```

```
            ctx.startActivity(intent)

    }
```

As you can see, Kotlin doesn't have any problems using the Java code. So, if you still want to proceed with the migration, you can do it. No problem. We will do so in the following sections.

Danger signs

Converting huge and complex Java classes into Kotlin is still an option to do. Anyway, provide proper unit or instrumentation tests so the functionality of these classes is retested after conversion. If any of your tests fails, double-check the causes of that failure.

The classes you want to migrate can migrate in the following two ways:

- Automatic conversion
- Rewriting by hand

In case of huge and complex classes, both approaches can give us certain drawbacks. Fully automatic conversion can sometimes give you the code that is not the prettiest code to look at. So, after you do it, you should recheck and reformat something. The second option can take you a lot of time.

Conclusion--you can always use the original Java code. From the moment you switch to Kotlin as your primary language, you can write all new stuff in Kotlin.

Updating dependencies

If you switch 100% pure Java code of the Android project into Kotlin, you have to start from the bottom up. This means that your first migration effort will be to update your dependencies. You must change your `build.gradle` configuration so Kotlin is recognized and source code paths are available. We already explained how to do this in Chapter 1, *Starting with Android*, in the Setting up Gradle section; so, if your project does not have Kotlin-related configuration in it, you have to provide it.

Let's recapitulate our Gradle configuration:

- The `build.gradle` root project represents the main `build.gradle` file, as shown here:

```
buildscript {
  repositories {
    jcenter()
    mavenCentral()
  }
  dependencies {
    classpath 'com.android.tools.build:gradle:2.3.3'
    classpath 'org.jetbrains.kotlin:kotlin-gradle-
    plugin:1.1.51'
  }
}

repositories {
 jcenter()
 mavenCentral()
}
```

- The main application `build.gradle` resolves all the dependencies of the application, as shown here:

```
apply plugin: "com.android.application"
apply plugin: "kotlin-android"
apply plugin: "kotlin-android-extensions"

repositories {
  maven { url "https://maven.google.com" }
}

android {
 ...
 sourceSets {
  main.java.srcDirs += [
        'src/main/kotlin',
        'src/common/kotlin',
        'src/debug/kotlin',
        'src/release/kotlin',
        'src/staging/kotlin',
        'src/preproduction/kotlin',
        'src/debug/java',
        'src/release/java',
        'src/staging/java',
        'src/preproduction/java',
```

```
            'src/testDebug/java',
            'src/testDebug/kotlin',
            'src/androidTestDebug/java',
            'src/androidTestDebug/kotlin'
        ]
      }
      ...
      }
    ...
}

  repositories {
    jcenter()
    mavenCentral()
  }

  dependencies {
    compile "org.jetbrains.kotlin:kotlin-reflect:1.1.51"
    compile "org.jetbrains.kotlin:kotlin-stdlib:1.1.51"
      ...
    compile "com.github.salomonbrys.kotson:kotson:2.3.0"
      ...

    compile "junit:junit:4.12"
    testCompile "junit:junit:4.12"

    testCompile "org.jetbrains.kotlin:kotlin-reflect:1.1.51"
    testCompile "org.jetbrains.kotlin:kotlin-stdlib:1.1.51"

    compile "org.jetbrains.kotlin:kotlin-test:1.1.51"
    testCompile "org.jetbrains.kotlin:kotlin-test:1.1.51"

    compile "org.jetbrains.kotlin:kotlin-test-junit:1.1.51"
    testCompile "org.jetbrains.kotlin:kotlin-test-junit:1.1.51"
      ...
  }
```

These are all the Kotlin-related dependencies you should fulfil. One of them is Kotson, providing Kotlin bindings for the Gson library.

Converting classes

Finally, we will migrate our classes. We have two automatic options available. We will use both. Locate `MigrationActivity.java` and open it. Choose the **Code | Convert Java** file to the `Kotlin` file. It takes a couple of seconds to convert. Now, drag and drop the file from the `Java` package into the `Kotlin` sources package. Observe the following source code:

```
package com.journaler.activity

import android.os.Bundle
import android.support.v7.app.AppCompatActivity

import com.journaler.R

class MigrationActivity : AppCompatActivity() {

  override fun onCreate(savedInstanceState: Bundle?) {
    super.onCreate(savedInstanceState)
    setContentView(R.layout.activity_main)
  }

  override fun onResume() {
    super.onResume()
  }

}
```

As we have mentioned, fully automatic conversion doesn't give the perfect code. In the next section, we will do a refactoring and clean up. The second way to do the same thing is by copying and pasting Java code into a `Kotlin` file. Copy all source code from `MigrationActivity2`. Create a new Kotlin class with the same name and paste the code. If asked, confirm that you wish to perform automatic conversion. After the code appears, remove the Java version of the class. Observe that the source code is the same as it is for the migrated `MigrationActivity` class.

Repeat both approaches for `Dummy` and `Dummy2` classes. The classes you get will look like this:

- `Dummy`, first `Dummy` class example:

```
package com.journaler.model

class Dummy {

  var title: String? = null
```

```
      var content: String? = null

      constructor(title: String) {
        this.title = title
      }

      constructor(title: String, content: String) {
        this.title = title
        this.content = content
      }

  }
```

- Dummy2, the second Dummy class example:

```
package com.journaler.model

import android.os.Parcel
import android.os.Parcelable

class Dummy2 : Parcelable {

  var count: Int = 0
  private set
  var result: Float = 0.toFloat()
  private set
  constructor(count: Int) {
    this.count = count
    this.result = (count * 100).toFloat()
  }

  constructor(`in`: Parcel) {
    count = `in`.readInt()
    result = `in`.readFloat()
  }

  override fun writeToParcel(parcel: Parcel, i: Int) {
    parcel.writeInt(count)
    parcel.writeFloat(result)
  }

  override fun describeContents(): Int {
    return 0
  }

  companion object {

    val CREATOR: Parcelable.Creator<Dummy2>
```

```
      = object : Parcelable.Creator<Dummy2> {
        override fun createFromParcel(`in`: Parcel): Dummy2 {
          return Dummy2(`in`)
      }

      override fun newArray(size: Int): Array<Dummy2> {
        return arrayOfNulls(size)
      }
    }
  }
}
```

The `Dummy2` class has issues with conversion. In this situation, you must fix it by yourself. Fix the source code. The problem happened in the following line:

```
override fun newArray(size: Int): Array<Dummy2> { ...
```

Fix it by switching type from `Array<Dummy2> int Array<Dummy2?>` as follows:

```
override fun newArsray(size: Int): Array<Dummy2?> { ...
```

Simple!

This is exactly the challenge you may face when doing the migration! It's noticeable that in both `Dummy` and `Dummy2` classes, we significantly reduced the code base by switching to Kotlin. Since there are no Java implementations anymore, we can do refactoring and cleanup.

Refactoring and cleanup

To have the best possible code after conversion, we must perform refactoring and cleanup. We will adapt our code base to conform Kotlin standards and idioms. For that purpose, you must read it whole. Only when this is done, we can consider our migration done!

Open your classes and read the code. There is a lot of space for improvements! After you do some work, you should get something like this:

The `MigrationActivity` code is as follows:

```
...
override fun onResume() = super.onResume()
...
```

As you can see, there is not too much work for `MigrationActivity` (and `MigrationActivity2`). Both classes are really small. A bigger effort is expected for classes such as Dummy and Dummy2:

- The Dummy class code is as follows:

```
package com.journaler.model

class Dummy(
  var title: String,
  var content: String
  ) {

    constructor(title: String) : this(title, "") {
    this.title = title
    }

}
```

- The Dummy2 class code is as follows:

```
package com.journaler.model

import android.os.Parcel
import android.os.Parcelable

class Dummy2(
  private var count: Int
) : Parcelable {

  companion object {
    val CREATOR: Parcelable.Creator<Dummy2>
    = object : Parcelable.Creator<Dummy2> {
      override fun createFromParcel(`in`: Parcel):
      Dummy2 = Dummy2(`in`)
      override fun newArray(size: Int): Array<Dummy2?> =
      arrayOfNulls(size)
    }
  }

  private var result: Float = (count * 100).toFloat()

  constructor(`in`: Parcel) : this(`in`.readInt())

  override fun writeToParcel(parcel: Parcel, i: Int) {
    parcel.writeInt(count)
  }
```

```
        override fun describeContents() = 0

    }
```

These two class versions are now drastically improved after refactoring compared to their first Kotlin versions after the conversion. Try to compare the current versions with the original Java code we had. What do you think?

Summary

In this chapter, we discovered the secrets of migration to the Kotlin programming language. We demonstrated techniques and gave advice on how to do the migration and when. Luckily, for us, it appears that this is not something difficult after all! The next chapter will be our last, so, as you already know, it's time to publish our application to the world!

16
Deploying Your Application

It's time for the world to see your work. There are a few things left to do before we release it. We will do some preparation and then finally release our application to the Google Play store.

In this chapter, we will get familiar with the following topics:

- Preparing for deployment
- Code obfuscation
- Signing your application
- Publishing to Google Play

Preparing for deployment

Before we release your application, it's required to do some preparation work. First of all, remove any unused resources or classes. Then, mute your logging! It's good practice to use some of the mainstream logging library. You can a create a wrapper around the `Log` class and, for each log output to have a condition, check that it must not be the `release` build type.

If you haven't yet set your release configuration as debuggable, do so as follows:

```
...
buildTypes {
  ...
  release {
    debuggable false
  }
}
...
```

Once you have completed this, check your manifest once again and clean it up. Remove any permission you don't need anymore. In our case, we will remove this:

```
<uses-permission android:name="android.permission.VIBRATE" />
```

We added it, but never used it. The last thing we will do is check about application compatibility. Check that the minimum and maximum SDK versions are in accordance to your device targeting plans.

Code obfuscation

The next step in the release process is to enable code obfuscation. Open your `build.gradle` configuration and update it as follows:

```
...
buildTypes {
  ...
  release {
    debuggable false
    minifyEnabled true
    proguardFiles getDefaultProguardFile('proguard-android.txt'),
      'proguard-rules.pro'
  }
}
...
```

The configuration we just added will shrink resources and perform obfuscation. For the obfuscation, we will use ProGuard. ProGuard is a free Java class file shrinker, optimizer, obfuscator, and preverifier. It performs detection of unused classes, fields, methods, and attributes. It optimizes bytecode as well!

In most cases, the default ProGuard configuration (the one we use) is enough to remove all the unused code. However, it can happen for ProGuard to remove the code your app actually needs! For that purpose, you must define the ProGuard configuration to keep those classes. Open your project's ProGuard configuration file and append the following:

```
-keep public class MyClass
```

Here is the list of ProGuard directives you will need to add if using some libraries:

- Retorfit:

```
-dontwarn retrofit.**
-keep class retrofit.** { *; }
-keepattributes Signature
-keepattributes Exceptions
```

- Okhttp3:

```
-keepattributes Signature
-keepattributes *Annotation*
-keep class okhttp3.** { *; }
-keep interface okhttp3.** { *; }
-dontwarn okhttp3.**
-dontnote okhttp3.**

# Okio
-keep class sun.misc.Unsafe { *; }
-dontwarn java.nio.file.*
-dontwarn org.codehaus.mojo.animal_sniffer.IgnoreJRERequirement
```

- Gson:

```
-keep class sun.misc.Unsafe { *; }
-keep class com.google.gson.stream.** { *; }
```

Update your `proguard-rules.pro` file with these lines.

Signing your application

The last step before we upload the release to the Google Play store is to generate a signed APK. Open your project and choose **Build** | **Generate Signed APK**:

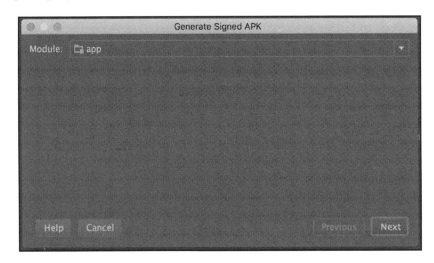

Choose the main application module and continue by clicking on **Next**:

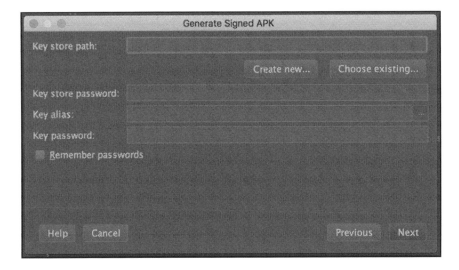

Since we don't have the key store yet, we will create a new one. Click on **Create new...** as follows:

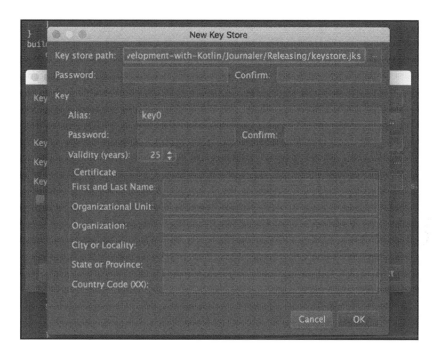

Populate the data and click on **OK**. Click on **Next** and enter your master password if asked. Check both signatures and choose the **complete** flavor to build. Click on **Finish**:

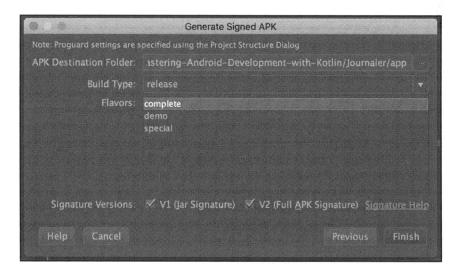

Wait until the build is ready. We will also update our `build.gradle` so the build is signed each time we build a release:

```
...
android {
  signingConfigs {
    release {
      storeFile file("Releasing/keystore.jks")
      storePassword "1234567"
      keyAlias "key0"
      keyPassword "1234567"
    }
  }
  release {
    debuggable false
    minifyEnabled false
    signingConfig signingConfigs.release
    proguardFiles getDefaultProguardFile('proguard-android.txt'),
    'proguard-rules.pro'
  }
}
...
```

If it's easier for you, you can run the build process from the terminal as follows:

```
$ ./gradlew clean
$ ./gradlew assembleCompleteRelease
```

In this example, we assembled the release build for the **Complete** application flavor.

Publishing to Google Play

The last step in deployment will be publishing the signed release APK. Beside the APK, we need to provide a few more things:

- Screenshots--Prepare screenshots from your application. You can do this by doing the following: From Android Studio Logcat, click on the Screen Capture icon (a little camera icon). From the **Preview** window, click on **Save**. You will be asked to save your image:

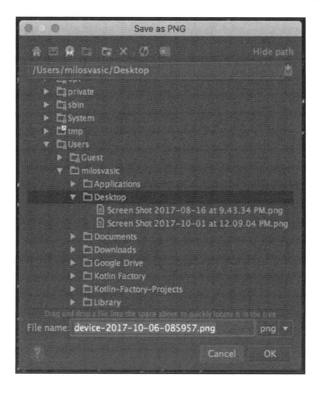

- High resolution icon with the following specification:

    PNG image of 32-bit (with alpha)

    512 px by 512 px in dimensions

    1024 K maximal file size

- Feature graphics (main banner for your application):

    JPEG image or PNG of 24-bit (without alpha!)

    1024 px by 500 px in dimensions

- If you publish the application as a TV application or a TV banner:

    JPEG image or PNG of 24-bit (without alpha!)

    1280p x by 720 px in dimensions

- Promo video--YouTube video (not playlist)

- Textual description of your application

Log in to the developer's console (`https://play.google.com/apps/publish`).

If you haven't registered yet, do so. It will enable you to publish your applications. The main console page is displayed like this:

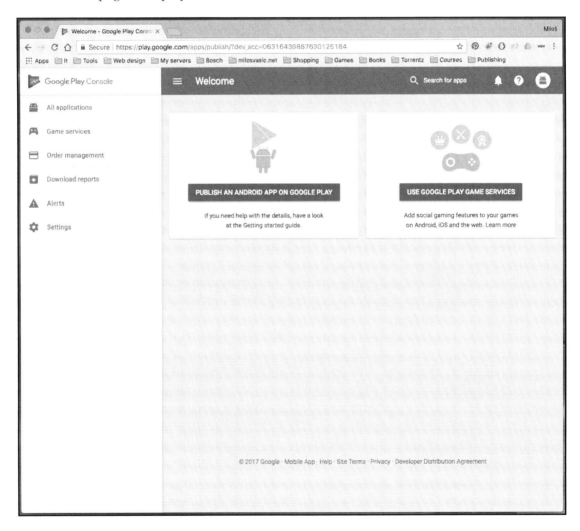

We don't have any application published yet. Click on **PUBLISH AN ANDROID APP ON GOOGLE PLAY**. A **Create application** dialog appears. Fill in the data and click on the **Create** button:

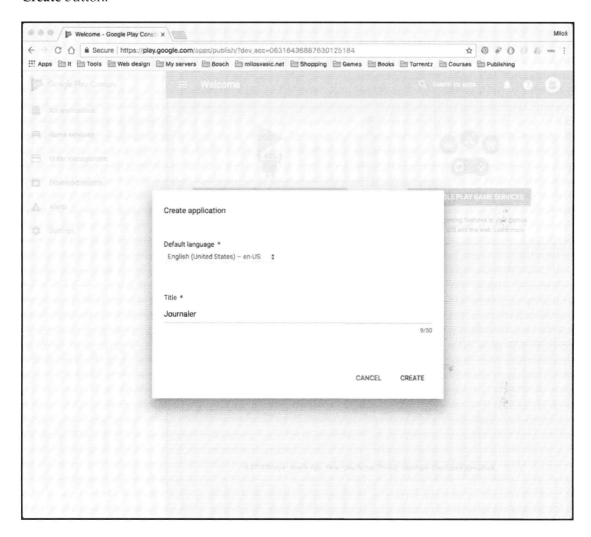

Fill in the form data as follows:

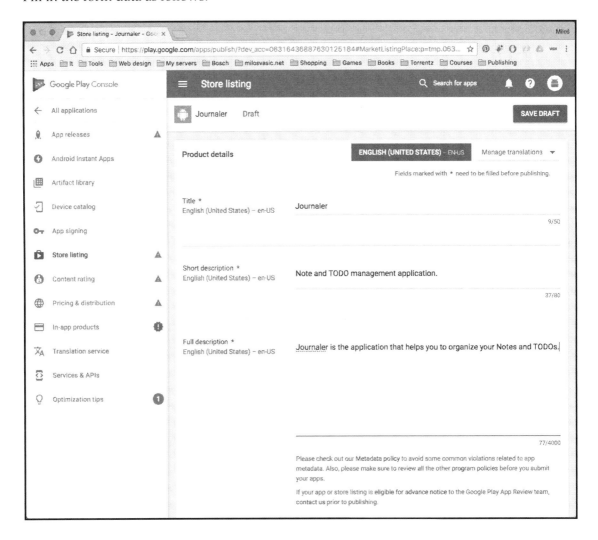

Upload your graphical assets as follows:

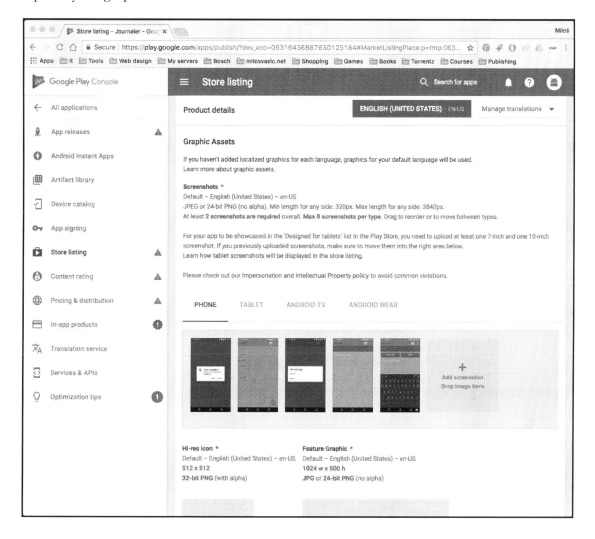

Please see the following screenshot:

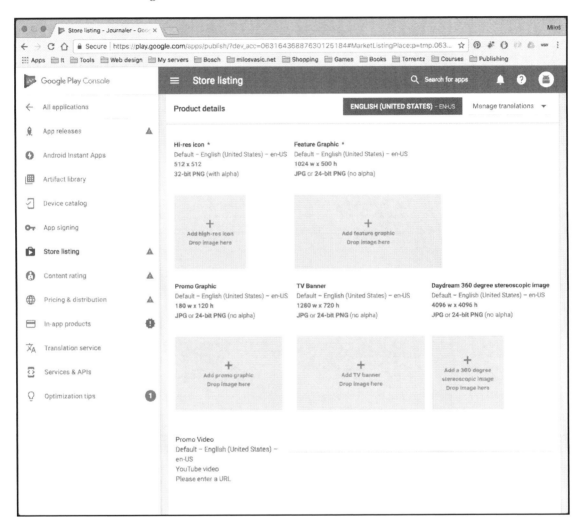

Continue towards application categorization:

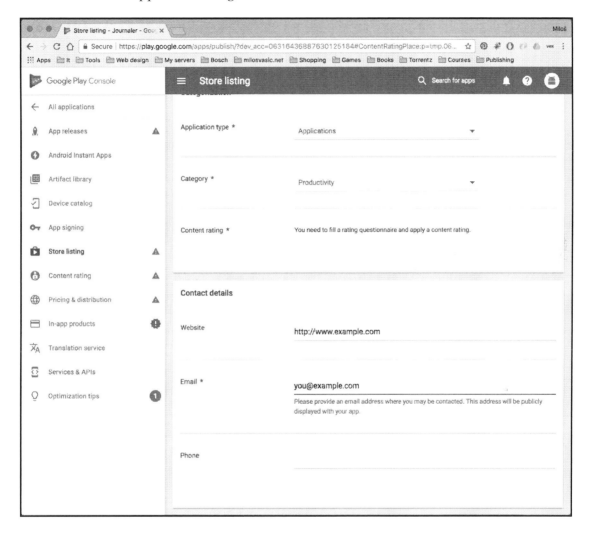

Finish with contact information and **Privacy policy**:

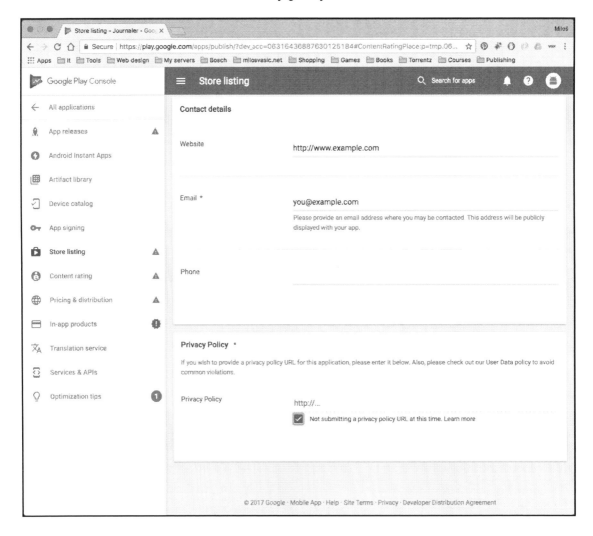

When you have completed all mandatory data, scroll back to the top and click on the **SAVE DRAFT** button. From the left side, now choose **App Releases**. You will be taken to the **App Releases** screen, as shown in this screenshot:

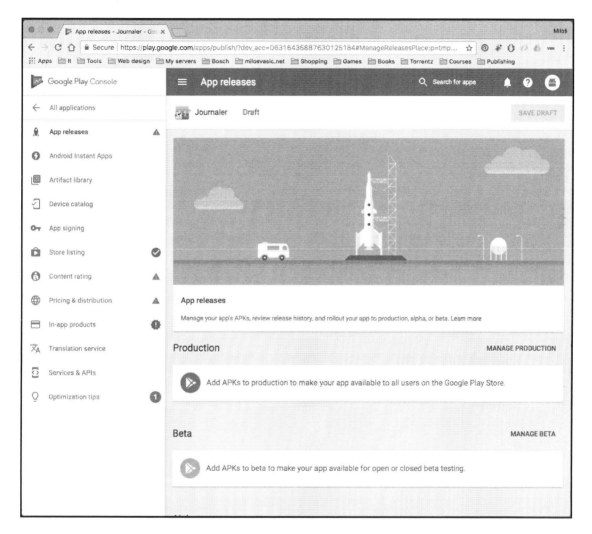

Here, you have the following three options:

- Manage production
- Manage beta
- Manage alpha

Depending on the version you plan to release, choose the option that suits you most. We will choose **MANAGE PRODUCTION** and click on the **CREATE RELEASE** button, as shown here:

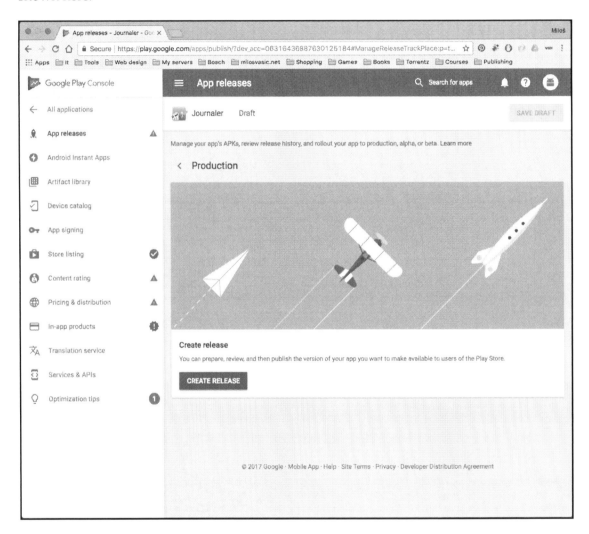

Start filling in the data about your release:

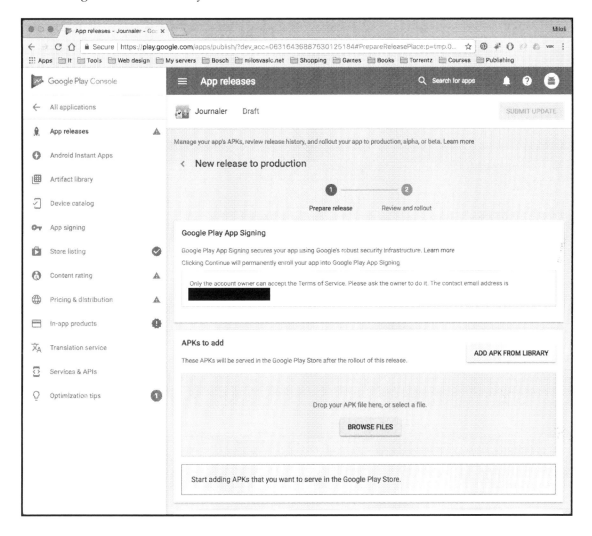

First of all, add the APK you recently generated. Then continue to the bottom of the page and fill in the rest of the form. When you are done, click on the **Review** button to review your application release:

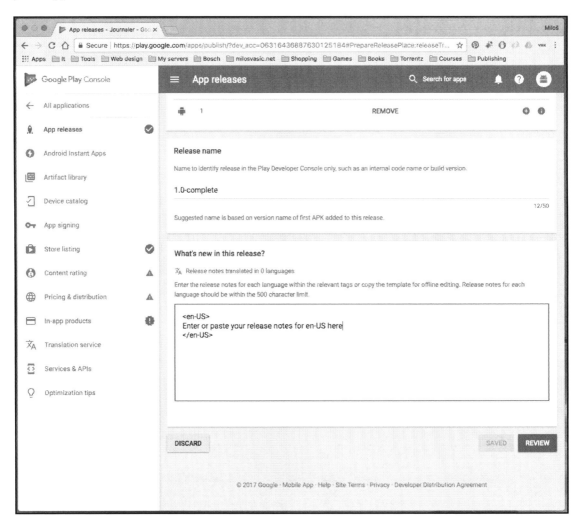

Before we roll our release to production, click on the **Content rating** link on the left side and then on **CONTINUE**, as shown in the following screenshot:

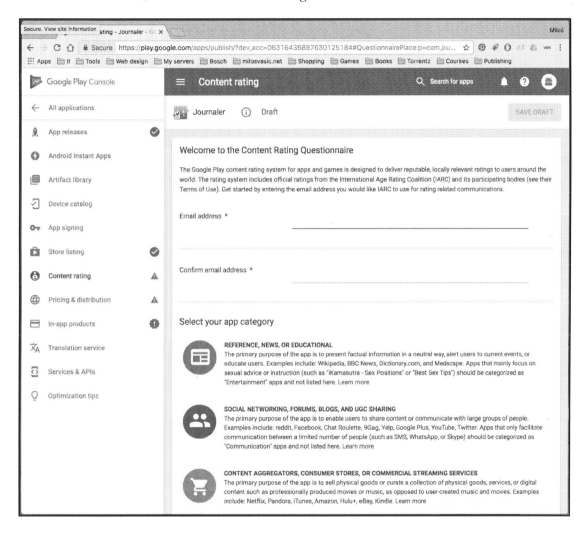

Fill in your **Email address** and scroll to the lower part of the page. Choose your category:

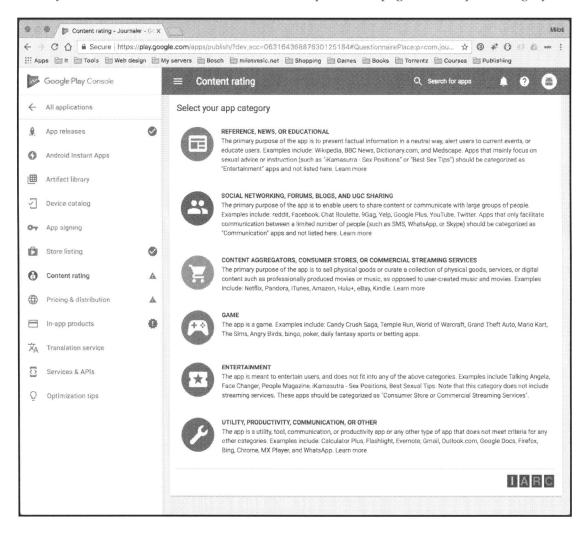

We choose **UTILITY, PRODUCTIVITY, COMMUNICATION, OR OTHER**; on the next screen, fill in the information you are asked about, as shown here:

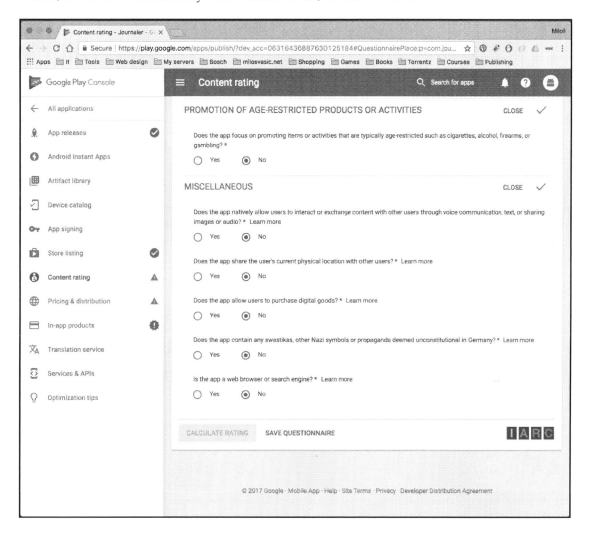

Save your questionnaire and click on **APPLY RATING**:

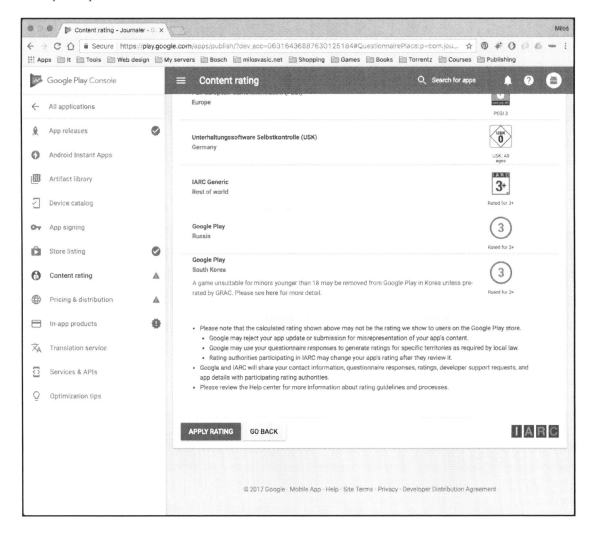

Now switch to the **Pricing & distribution** section:

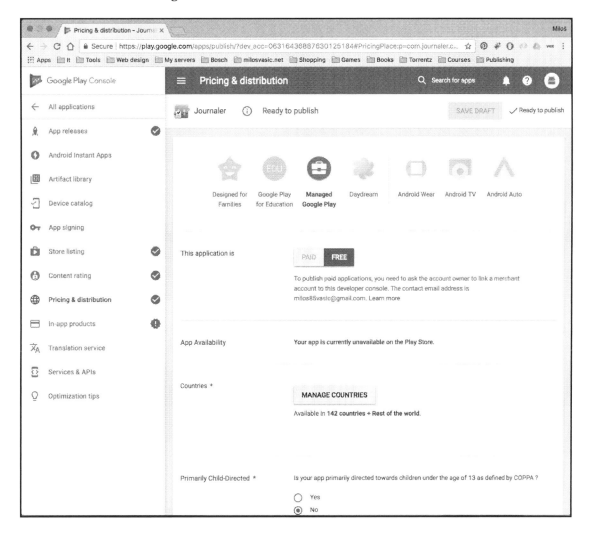

The form is easy to populate. Follow the form and set the data you are asked about. When you are done, click on the **Save Draft** button at the top of the screen. You will see that the **Ready to Publish** link has appeared. Click on it:

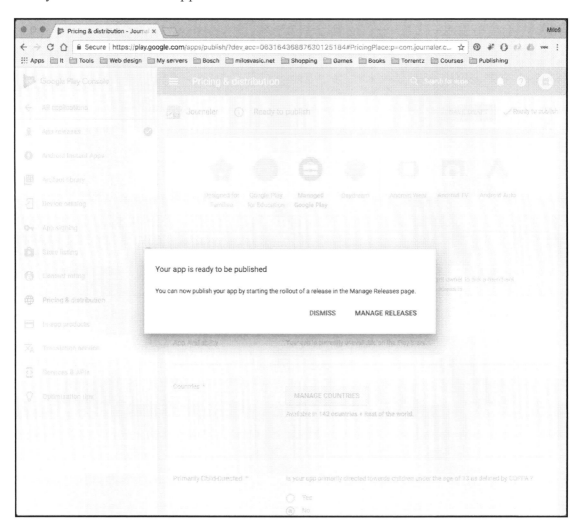

Click on **MANAGE RELEASES**, as shown in earlier screenshot. Follow the screens until you reach the last screen from the **App Releases** section. Now you can clearly see the **START ROLLOUT TO PRODUCTION** button enabled. Click on it and, when asked, click **CONFIRM**:

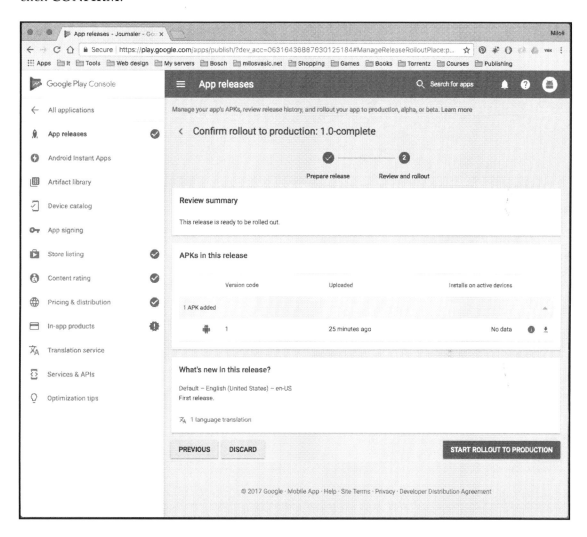

Continued:

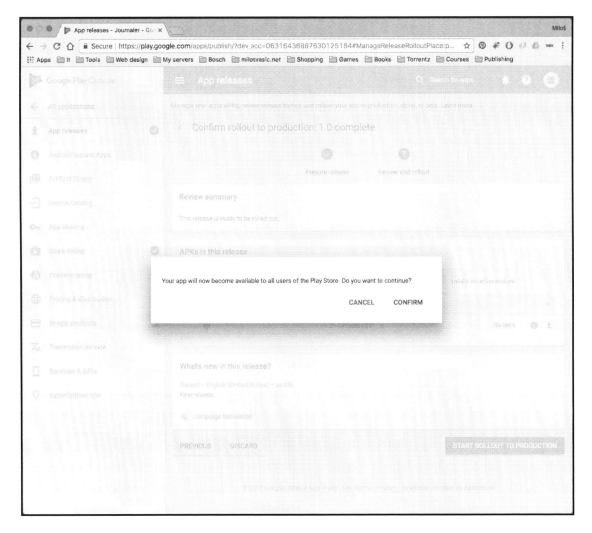

That is it! You have successfully published your application to the Google Play store!

Summary

I hope you have enjoyed this book! This was a great journey! We began from nothing and started with learning the basics. Then, we continued toward the medium, difficult, and advanced topics about Android. This chapter allowed us the final word on the story about Android we wanted to tell you. We did a huge amount of work! We developed the application and went through the whole process of deployment, step by step.

What is next? Well, the next thing you should do is think about an application you want to build and start making it from scratch. Take your time. Don't rush yourself! During the development, you will discover many things we did not mention. Android is tremendously big! It can take years to know the entire framework. Many developers don't know every part of it. You will not be the only one. Continue your progress and do as much code as you can. It will improve your skills and make all that you learned routine to you. Do not hesitate! Get into the action! Good luck!

Index

L

layout hierarchies
optimizing 301
layouts
optimizing 301
reusing 301
libraries
about 44
Gson 44
retrofit 44
linear layout 82
list view layout 82
lists
using 298
Logcat
about 54, 57
cases 62, 64
Logger 37

M

margins attribute 93
migration
classes, converting 325
cleanup 327
dependencies, updating 322
failure causes 322
preparing 317
refactoring 327
mockup plan
analyzing 75
application activities, defining 78, 82

N

navigation drawer
using 115, 117
network events
listening for 247, 248
notifications 105

O

onClick attribute 94

P

padding attribute 93
pencil 75
preferences manager
defining 201

R

relative layout 82
Retrofit 44, 254
Retrofit alternatives
Volley 263
Retrofit service
defining 255, 257
instance, building 257, 258

S

screens
Add/Edit note screen 78
Add/Edit TODO screen 78
scroll view layout 82
service categorization
about 219
background Android services 220
bound Android services 220
foreground Android services 220
shared preferences
about 199
removing 201
storing preferences 200
using 200
shutdown broadcast
using 244
sp (Scale-independent Pixels) 85
SQLite
about 173
benefits 173
src attribute 94
sticky intents 236
styles
assets, working with 141
custom fonts, using 141
in Android 135
SurfaceView 107
system broadcasts 236

Made in the
USA
Middletown, DE